A Part, Yet Apart

South Asians in Asian America

A Part,

In the series

ASIAN AMERICAN HISTORY AND CULTURE

edited by Sucheng Chan, David Palumbo-Liu, and Michael Omi

A list of books in this series appears at the back of this volume

Yet Apart

*South Asians
in Asian America*

Edited by

LAVINA DHINGRA SHANKAR
AND RAJINI SRIKANTH

TEMPLE UNIVERSITY PRESS
Philadelphia

Temple University Press, Philadelphia 19122
Copyright © 1998 by Temple University
All rights reserved
Published 1998
Printed in the United States of America

Library of Congress Cataloging-in-Publication Data

A part, yet apart : South Asians in Asian America / edited by
  Lavina Dhingra Shankar and Rajini Srikanth,
        p.   cm. — (Asian American history and culture)
    Includes bibliographical references.
    ISBN 1-56639-577-1 (alk. paper). — ISBN 1-56639-578-X (pbk. :
  alk. paper)
    1. South Asian Americans.   I. Shankar, Lavina Dhingra, 1965–   .
  II. Srikanth, Rajini.   III. Series.
  E184.S69P37   1998
  973'.04914—dc21   97-38354
                                                                  CIP

Contents

Acknowledgments

WE WOULD like to thank our contributors for their cooperation, patience, and meticulous revisions; Sucheta Mazumdar for believing in the importance of this book; Roshni Rustomji-Kerns for her trust and continuous concern; Sau-ling Wong, Amy Ling, and Elizabeth Ammons for their encouragement and reviews; David Palumbo-Liu for his commitment to the project and his comprehensive critiques; our students, who continuously reminded us of the need for this volume; and Janet Francendese for her resilience in bringing it all together.

Lavina Shankar is grateful to Bates College for the Roger Schmutz Research Award, to her colleagues in the English Department for a supportive environment, and to Rajiv for coining the book's title, for his inspiration and advice, and for his professional and personal collaboration.

Rajini Srikanth thanks Sri for his good humor, patience, and companionship.

Rajiv Shankar

Foreword

South Asian Identity in Asian America

ASIANS ARE a distinct minority group in the United States, and in the past few decades they have contributed significantly to its overall population growth. In fact, in the half-century ahead, after Hispanics (which is a linguistic and not a geographic classification, anyway), Asians, with attendant economic, social, and cultural shifts, will affect the country's demographic makeup more than any other single group.[1] With this in mind, government and academic institutions are increasingly focusing attention on Asians—for instance, by developing a fully detailed census category,[2] or by adding Asian American Studies to the standard college curriculum.

Although Asians *in Asia* have been molded by similar historic currents and perhaps share some distinctive traits that set them apart from people from other continents,[3] Asians *in America* are quite differentiated from one another, largely as a result of differing relationships between their home countries and the United States. Specifically, the two broad and rather separate groups that are well represented in the United States (and are the principal subjects of this book) are those who originate from East/Southeast Asia[4]—which includes China, Taiwan, the Koreas, Japan, Vietnam, Laos, Cambodia, and Philippines—and South Asia, which includes India, Pakistan, Nepal, Bhutan, Bangladesh, Sri Lanka, and Maldives.

Aside from geography, why is this categorization relevant? East/Southeast Asians dominate the Asian American platform, in terms of their sheer number in this country,[5] because of their shared sense of trauma with America, and their (by now) highly developed and motivated social and political structures within the American establishment. This is true to the extent that, to the average non–Asian American mind, they are nearly synonymous with (all of) Asian America. South Asians, on the other hand, are a significant and fast-growing branch within the Asian family, and are by themselves highly successful and self-conscious participants in the American idiom. They want their unique attributes to be recognized and their particular issues discussed; and some of them want this to occur, initially at least, within the Asian American paradigm, for they think that they must surely belong there. Yet, they find themselves so unnoticed as an entity that they feel as if they are merely a crypto-group,[6] often included but easily marginalized within the house of Asian America. They often believe that their voices are not being heard or that their unique perspective and potential for leadership roles are being overlooked. Ultimately, South Asians ask why are they a part, yet apart, admitted, but not acknowledged?

The complex, yet rational, answer is that the nomenclature of "Asian American" seems perfectly appropriate for all Asian immigrants, but in this century East/Southeast Asia has played a much more central, even critical, role in the American identity and consciousness than South Asia. Let us not underestimate what East/Southeast Asia has meant to the American psyche, and what America has meant to East/Southeast Asia. In past centuries America has had comparable contacts with East/Southeast and South Asia alike (as with the Oriental trade of the Boston merchants[7]), which combined, however, were insignificant in comparison with its ties to Europe. But in this century, East/Southeast Asia has played a much more central role in the American identity than South Asia and has, at times, been as critical to it as any other region on the globe. Americans have in the past defined themselves mostly in relation and reaction to the "frontier" to the east, that is, Europe—not only in terms of where they came from or what they left behind, but also in terms of what to be or not to be, and who to beat and where to seek recognition. In the past half-century, however, they have often been forced to define themselves in response and relation to the "frontier" of the East, that is, East/Southeast Asia—not only to defend their sovereignty or increase their geopolitical influence, but also, as the pupils have learnt the master's art too well, to "protect" themselves and the "American way" economically, as the Europeans in the previous era had had to do against them.

It was the United States that first recognized "the meteor to the east" that became the other jaw of the Axis vise, and led to one of history's greatest catastrophes; the time from Pearl Harbor to Hiroshima-Nagasaki cost millions in casualties but marked the beginning of American world hegemony, created the unforgettable image of the mushroom clouds that catalyzed the self-annihilating arms race and defined our ultimate fear,[8] and created in its wake the modern Japanese state. The popular television series *M.A.S.H.* offered the next portrait of America in Asia, the "police action" in Korea to support the neo-ideal of *pax Americana* that would kill another 54,000 Americans;[9] the show introduced us to the "Red Menace" in combat, leaving as its legacy Hawkeye's antiwar aphorisms and Hyundai's ubiquitous cars. The Vietnam War altered America's cultural, social, and political landscape like the napalm-bombed "Killing Fields," and left Americans still suffering from psychological scars like some victim of Agent Orange. The heinous acts of the Khmer Rouge in Cambodia are part of the aftermath, as is the continuing instability of that region.

But America's East/Southeast Asian odyssey did not begin only in the middle of this century. Chinese laborers were "imported" and indentured to build the railroads that would bind together and industrialize America; they were then ghettoized into Chinatowns, from which they have grown and prospered into the significant players of today; Taiwan, China's eternal ulcer, has survived and developed only because of explicit American support, while with the demise of the Soviet Union, China has emerged as the only other world superpower. The United States has had a more symbiotic relationship with the Philippines, its only major (one-time) colony, than with any other Asian country; it is the only large land area under the American flag ever to be occupied by foreign (Japanese) forces; and American involvement in its internal politics has been extensive.

From the perspective of the countries of East/Southeast Asia and their people, many of whom came (whether or not as refugees) to live in the United States, the United States in this century has often been the yin and yang of their own narratives, either nemesis or savior, the flood that has either ravaged its existence or left a bountiful harvest as it ebbed, and often both. Few countries have been able to disregard the massive presence of the United States. If chess was the game of choice in Europe between the forces of "communism" and "capitalism," then domino tumbling was played in East/Southeast Asia, and in an effort to resist and reverse the "Domino Effect," America and East/Southeast Asia have been militarily and economically deeply enmeshed.

In contrast, South Asia and America have been far more distant associates. While the Japanese, Korean, and Vietnam conflicts have convoluted life in America in the twentieth century, affecting every individual and institution and inscribing indelible chapters in modern American history, there has been no remotely comparable direct military action associated with South Asia. Arming India against China, and Pakistan against the Soviet Union (via India or Afghanistan), or positioning an aircraft carrier in high seas during the India-Pakistan war hardly compares with completely exhausting U.S. manpower and drafting its common citizenry during the Vietnam War.

South Asia, with its legacy of British imperialism and all its internal strife and poverty, has offered to America (and the world) considerable wealth in terms of spirituality, peace, and civilization. Buddhism (which grew out of Hinduism), Gandhi, Mother Teresa, the Taj Mahal, and the sitar have all influenced this country's culture. South Asia also has had much less economic interaction with America. Japan, Korea, and the Philippines, for example, have been heavily aided by, and "reared" in the image of, America (even aside from the military bases, which have at times contributed to their economies, too). Recent U.S. imports from East/ Southeast Asia are more than thirty times that from South Asia, with Japan and China as two of its largest worldwide trading partners.[10]

South Asian migration to America has had a different sense of pathos or urgency or conflict associated with it. South Asians weren't recruited in large numbers as laborers, colonial subjects, or refugees of war; although they were subject to racism, they weren't permanently separated from their families by male-only immigration policies that welcomed their labor but not their descendants,* and they weren't put into internment camps. In the last fifty years, South Asians have come largely of their own volition, bringing with them a high level of skill or education that has often allowed them to become affluent in the first generation,† and they are seen more as competing with "the brain or business trust" of America than with ordinary labor. All in all, it is difficult to support the statement that the lot of the South Asians has been very comparable to, let alone worse than, that of East/Southeast Asians.

Yet, as the population of South Asians in America rapidly increases, both in absolute and relative terms, the question of South Asian inclusion in Asian America becomes increasingly complex: should South Asian America be part of Asian America, or should it be a separate paradigm altogether? Strictly in terms of nomenclature, that is the *genus* Asian American, it is perhaps inevitable that all persons who have migrated from that continent to this, and their descendants, whether from East/Southeast or South Asia (or for that matter, from West or Central Asia), will belong to it. Dull science and simple geography deem it so, universal (i.e., worldwide) acceptance endorses it, and it is ratified by formal usage in American officialdom, such as by the U.S. Bureau of Census and the U.S. Department of Justice (including the Immigration and Naturalization Service), even if only recently.

The consciousness that is at present associated with the term "Asian American," however, is another matter entirely. South Asians may now be "a part" of the new Asian American banner, but too many differences and

---

* Turn-of-the-century Indian farmers in California were subject to racism and victimized by male-only immigration policies and discriminatory land ownership laws.

† See Manju Sheth 177–78. But even as this volume goes to press, the demographics of South Asian American communities are undergoing rapid changes. Increasing numbers of recent South Asian immigrants now come with only the most basic education skills and are, therefore, employed in low-paying jobs in the United States.

divergences keep them "apart" from the established Asian American (i.e., East/Southeast Asian American) identity. They may be readily "admitted" to the Asian American category, but their issues need not be "acknowledged" as belonging to the East/Southeast Asian American discourse. Thus, under the *genus* Asian American we may have the *species* of East/Southeast Asian American and South Asian American, the former more numerous and more deeply etched into the prevailing American epic, but the latter fast unfolding its own unique drama to claim an equally special place in the standard American repertoire.

NOTES

1. Some interesting statistics on U.S. minority groups: in terms of demographic changes—i.e., the fastest-changing or -growing population segments—Asians are clearly in the lead, with a 108 percent increase during the 1980s, and they are expected to continue to grow the fastest (about 4 percent per year); the number of Hispanics grew by 53 percent, and African Americans by 13 percent.

The Census Bureau projects that by 2050 Hispanics will comprise 23 percent of the population (from 10 percent in mid-1995); African Americans, 16 percent (12 percent in mid-1995); and Asian Americans, 10 percent (3 percent in mid-1995). Thus, as a percentage of the total population of the country, Hispanics will grow the most (13 percent), followed by Asian-Americans (7 percent), and then African Americans (4 percent) (from *Information Please Almanac 1996*, 830, 834; *The Universal Almanac 1996*, 290; *Statistical Abstract of the United States 1994*, 18).

Note: Since the 1980 census, geographic roots have gained predominance over race in the classification scheme, though both are still used, along with ethno-linguistic sets. Also, "it is important to note that the Census Bureau's classification of the population by race, in its own words, 'reflects common usage, not an attempt to define biological stock'" (*The Universal Almanac 1996*, 294). There are about 8.7 million people of Asian origin living in the United States today, or about 3.3 percent of the general resident population (mid-1995 data, *Information Please Almanac 1996*, 830).

Of the total population growth in the 1980s, about a third was due to immigration, of which over 40 percent, or 2.4 million persons, came from Asia. That is, a third of the Asian population arrived in just one decade.

In each of the last two decades, the total Asian American population—including not only immigrants, but domestic growth as well—has more than doubled in size, from 1.5 million to 3.5 million (133 percent increase) in the 1970s, and again from 3.5 million to 7.3 million (108 percent increase) in the 1980s, making it, in each period, the fastest-growing immigrant group.

All these figures exclude, of course, illegal immigrants and nonresident aliens (i.e., "green card" holders), who would obviously increase the relative proportions and absolute numbers considerably.

Of the Asians in America today, those who originated from East/Southeast Asia compose about three-quarters of the total, while those from South Asia compose just over a tenth.

Historically, in the period 1820–1990, the number of immigrants from East Asia has been more than seven times that from South Asia, though since the 1980s, with the increasing percentage of South Asians entering, this ratio is reducing somewhat. (And, as a general point of reference it is worth noting that the total population of these East/Southeast and South Asian countries alone is about 55 percent of the world's total population.) (From *The Universal Almanac 1996*, 290, 294, 298, 313.) Note: In some instances, "Pacific Islanders" are grouped together with Asians.

2. The U.S. Bureau of Census classification scheme has undergone numerous shifts in emphasis and nomenclature over a century: "Chinese" and "Japanese" were the only two Asian categories in 1890; "Hindu" appeared in 1930, then disappeared in 1950; "Asian Indian" (re)appeared in 1980. In 1990 "Asian or Pacific Islander" (API) become a main category, with nine "national" subcategories and one "Other" subcategory. This is quite significant because (a) the few national groups of the past (now included under API) put together counted less people than the new API supergroup, because those who did not belong to the few national categories fell under the general "Other" group, while now they fall under the API "Other" group, and thus literally the whole is greater than the sum, and (b) being now banded together and acknowledged as a much larger supergroup, their gain in prominence is huge, and so figuratively too the whole is relevantly greater than the sum (Lee 78).

3. For instance, the vast majority of Asians are adherents of Hinduism, Buddhism, or Islam, whereas the vast majority of the rest of the world's population are not.

4. Clearly, there are important differences between the cultures of East Asia and Southeast Asia: much has been written about these differences, and discussing these two regions together in this Foreword is not intended to minimize them. However, the similarities between them are greater than the similarities between either of them and South Asia. For instance, both East and Southeast Asian are studied under the traditional Asian American curriculum, while South Asian culture and literature are usually not. This book is about the issue of the place of South Asians within the Asian American category, and so it is useful to group East and Southeast Asians together for the purpose of comparing them to the South Asians.

5. See note 1.

6. "It is in danger of becoming a crypto-class, a group of people whose significance in any larger scheme of things, whose very existence, is known only to themselves" (Aldrich xvi).

7. For a good discussion of this, see Adams, *The Boston Money Tree*.

8. From the infamous anti–Barry Goldwater campaign ad to the current *Terminator* films.

9. *Information Please Almanac 1996*, 384.

10. *The World Almanac 1995*, 201

Works Cited

Adams, Russell B., Jr. *The Boston Money Tree*. New York: Crowell, 1977.

Aldrich, Nelson W., Jr. *Old Money: The Mythology of America's Upper Class*. New York: Knopf, 1988.

Information Please Almanac 1996. Otto Johnson, ed. Boston: Houghton Mifflin, 1995.

Lee, Sharon M. "Racial Classification in the U.S. Census: 1890–1990." *Ethnic and Racial Studies* 16.1 (Jan. 1993): 74–94.

Sheth, Manju. "Asian Indian Americans." In *Asian Americans: Contemporary Trends and Issues*, edited by Pyong Gap Min. Thousand Oaks, Calif.: Sage, 1995, 169–98.

Statistical Abstract of the United States 1994. Washington D.C.: U.S. Dept. of Commerce, Bureau of the Census, 1994.

The Universal Almanac 1996, John W. Wright, ed. Kansas City: Andrews and McMeel, 1991.

The World Almanac 1995, Robert Famighetti, ed. Mahwah, N.J.: Funk & Wagnalls, 1994.

Lavina Dhingra Shankar and Rajini Srikanth

Introduction

Closing the Gap? South Asians Challenge Asian American Studies

As the "Asian American" label broadens to accommodate new immigrant groups, the term is coming under critical scrutiny. It is now used to refer to any person originating from the vast continent of Asia (with over 60 percent of the world's population)[1] who immigrates to the United States; this is a radical change from the narrower East Asian view of the concept that prevailed a few decades ago.[2] The more recent perception of Asian American identity encompasses people of many different races, linguistic groups, religions, cultures, and nations; people with different preimmigration histories and dissimilar immigration patterns; and people whose educational, economic, and social positions within this country vary greatly as well.

Before 1965, the number of South Asians in the United States was considerably fewer than the number of East Asians. Following the relaxation of immigration laws in 1965, there has been a dramatic increase in South Asian immigration. Since the 1980s, South Asians have constituted one of the fastest-growing Asian American communities, and this disparity has decreased.[3] Thus South Asians make up about 14 percent of the Asian American population, a percentage larger than that of either the Japanese Americans or Korean Americans. As they struggle with attempts at self-definition, South Asian Americans are beginning to examine the ways in which they can participate in the social, economic, and political life of the United States.[4]

When we use the phrase "Asian American," we do so with the understanding that it refers to an identity, a census label, and a political and social consciousness. The gaps among the various Asian American subgroups are both wide and narrow, often deeply entrenched but sometimes easy to bridge. This collection of essays explores the ways in which Americans who come from one particular region of Asia—South Asia—do or do not "fit" into traditional Asian America. The essays debate what constitutes the gaps between South Asian Americans and the rest of Asian America. Who perceives the existence of gaps? And who is willing or able to close the gaps? And, finally, can they be closed at all?

1

IN SEARCH OF A SOUTH ASIAN IDENTITY

Geographically, South Asia is relatively clearly delineated: it consists of the seven countries of Bangladesh, Bhutan, India, Maldives, Nepal, Pakistan, and Sri Lanka.[5] The classification "South Asian," while denoting the people who live in and originate from these seven countries, is a strained construct.[6] It implies a common identity among these peoples and brings together diverse populations on the basis of shared history and culture and political and economic interdependency. But the idea of a South Asian union, even in the best of times, translates into only a tenuous reality. India, the hegemonic center with three-quarters of the population, three-quarters of the land area, and four-fifths of the annual production of this region, easily dominates South Asia, while marginalizing the other states. Over 730 million adherents of Hinduism live in South Asia, mostly in India, while over 290 million followers of Islam make up most of Bangladesh and Pakistan. Geographically, South Asia has been the scene of conflict for nearly a millennium.[7] In just the last half-century since the British left, full-scale war has broken out three times between India, Pakistan, and Bangladesh (and once against a "foreign" force, China).

Even within India, the concept of "Unity in Diversity" has often faced severe challenges: the country itself was politically unified only in the face of foreign invaders, the Muslims and the British. The Muslim influence affected northern India much more than the South, with the result that attempts to impose Hindi, a northern language, on a national level failed in the South, leaving English as India's lingua franca. Numerous states have tried to secede from the union, notably Punjab, Kashmir, and Assam. Civil violence is not unique to India; similar religious and separatist strife is also tearing apart Sri Lanka and Pakistan.

South Asians, whether they live in their homelands or abroad, therefore usually see themselves in national, linguistic, or religious terms.[8] They do not naturally think of themselves as South Asians, and feel that the term "South Asia" is a purely politicized construct. Thus, we wish to emphasize that while we address the issue of the gap between South Asian America and Asian America, we fully recognize that the fissures among South Asian American subgroups are themselves far from being closed.

The term "South Asian," often viewed with suspicion by first-generation immigrants, is more readily accepted by later generations in America. For these Americans of South Asian ancestry, the similarities among those who have originated from anywhere on the "South Asian" subcontinent seem to overcome the national and cultural walls that their parents knew "back home,"[9] and they are thus able to envision forging coalitions among themselves. In addition, having grown up with an awareness of the history of racial discrimination in the United States (or having experienced it themselves), they are attempting to move outward, to associate with other minority groups. As the essays by Gupta and Sinha in this volume reveal, second-generation South Asian immigrants who (usually unlike their parents) view themselves as American, may feel that being part of Asian America involves crossing the fewest psychological and cultural chasms.

Not only generation, but class, too, is a factor in the readiness of South Asians to associate with other minority groups. In her incisive and scathing attack in the essay "Race and Racism," Mazumdar castigates South Asians for their racism, attributing this attitude not only to a colonized consciousness but also to the "class fear of upper caste Hindus who have long sought to use notions of 'purity of blood' and Caucasian features to exercise hegemony over the majority of the population whom they dubbed the 'non-Aryan' Untouchables" (1989, 31). As Srikanth's and Sinha's essays in this volume point out, South Asian Americans who see themselves as socioeconomically disenfranchised and hence more "ethnicized," often find it easier to form coalitions with other minorities than do their upper-class counterparts who do not face similar marginalization.

THE NARROW PREMISE OF "ASIAN AMERICA"

As discussed in the Foreword, the term "Asian American" means different things to different people today. In the context of census data collection, the term has an extremely broad usage as a category based on geography ("Asian and Pacific Islander"), encompassing all people who originate from Asia and live in this country. A narrower definition of "Asian America" focuses on "consciousness"—or what we call *felt* identity—and commonly includes only people from East and Southeast Asia.

The development of an Asian American consciousness and identity has evolved from much soul-searching and painful activism on the part of a determined minority in this country, as described by Yen Le Espiritu, Glenn Omatsu, and William Wei. In a sense, the activists of the late 1960s were pioneers who began the process of reversing gross errors of terminology and belief by establishing the term "Asian American" and bequeathing to it a specific legacy.

To seize the essentializing terminology of the majority culture as applied to one's minority group, and to transform it into a label of power involves at least two stages: first, replacing the pejorative or incorrect label with a self-chosen name (as happened when "Negro" and worse names were replaced by "black," and then by "African American"), and second, assuming that self-articulated label as a badge of pride, describing the group's historical and cultural foundations and asserting its unique identity. The Asian American movement born in the late 1960s experienced both these stages of empowerment.

Glenn Omatsu, in his essay "The 'Four Prisons' and the Movements of Liberation," stresses the antiauthoritarian stance of the Asian American student activists at San Francisco State University in 1968 and their connection with the civil rights and Third World movements. He observes that "strike leaders drew inspiration—as well as new ideology—from international Third World leaders and revolutions occurring in Asia, Africa, Latin America, and the Middle East" (26). The grassroots Asian minority activists, who imbibed the philosophies of Marx, Lenin, Stalin, Frantz Fanon, Malcolm X, Che Guevara, Amilcar Cabral, W.E.B. Du Bois, Frederick Douglass, Paulo Freire, and the women's liberation movement, designated themselves as "Asian American" (31) and demanded the establishment of Asian American Studies programs in universities. The San Francisco State student uprising was, as Omatsu points out, the longest student strike in the United States. Asian American students, along with African American, Native American, and Latino students, demanded "ethnic studies, open admissions, and a redefinition of the education system" (25). The students' protests resulted in the establishment of the country's first School of Ethnic Studies.

Whereas Omatsu celebrates the international, revolutionary, and proletarian nature of the Asian American movement, Yen Le Espiritu focuses on racial identity politics *within* the United States. In her book *Asian American Panethnicity: Bridging Institutions and Identities* (1992), Espiritu points out that student and community activists in the late sixties began the self-naming process for the Asian community in America, transforming the label "Oriental" (associated with "slant eyes," "yellow peril," or "yellow skin") to "Asian American," as a defiant response to the majority culture's perceptions of peoples from Asia (31–33). Thus, "Asian American" came to be a term of political empowerment, meant to bring together those peoples of Asian descent to whom the racist and discriminatory terms of "Oriental" had been applied.

In practice, however, this construction of identity excluded everyone outside East Asia; in fact, even within the "included" groups, membership was limited to the Chinese, Japanese, and Filipinos, with the Koreans and the Vietnamese being "added" later. The racial dimension implicit in the term "Asian American," automatically excluded all non-Mongoloids from membership, including, of course, South Asians. At that time, the omission of South Asians was not that obvious or relevant an issue, perhaps, as there were relatively few South Asians in America.[10] However, Michael Omi points out that ironically "the term came into vogue at precisely the historical moment when new Asian groups [especially, South and Southeast Asians] were entering the U.S. who would render the term problematic" (205). The discrepancies between the names assigned to (or chosen by) the newcomers and the "native" Asian Americans' self-chosen label have persisted into the present, but not without challenge and opposition from both sides.

Thus, the original notion of who should be characterized as Asian American has expanded slowly. By contrast, the official category of "Asian and Pacific Islander" has grown in the last two decades to include persons who identify themselves as Chinese, Filipino, Japanese, Asian Indian, Korean, Vietnamese, Cambodian, Hmong, Laotian, Thai, or Other Asian (into which category fall the South Asian groups of Bangladeshi, Pakistani, Sri Lankan, Bhutanese, Nepalese, and Maldivians).

Anthropologist Karen Leonard and historians, such as Sucheng Chan, S. Chandrasekhar, Joan Jensen, Howard Brett Melendy, Gary Okihiro, Jane Singh, and Ronald Takaki, have recorded the early presence and experience of South Asians in turn-of-the-century America, as well as their increasing numbers since 1965.[11] They seem to accept the geographical basis for categorization of immigrants from Asia, and point out the similarities between the immigration and naturalization discriminations endured by early South Asian immigrants and those from China and Japan.[12] Manju Sheth, however, has a less sanguine view of the treatment of "Asian Indians" by historians. In her recent essay "Asian Indian Americans" (1995), she reminds us that "neither American nor ethnic Indian scholars have given this group [Indian immigrants in the United States] sufficient attention" (169). She acknowledges Gary Hess's "The Forgotten Asian Americans: The East Indian Community in the United States" (1976) and P. K. Nandi's "The World of an Invisible Minority: Pakistanis in America" (1980) as bringing attention to the invisibility of South Asians within Asian American studies.

Our issue, therfore, is not with the official title itself. In fact, one might argue that the label "Asian American" is too broad to refer to a coherent identity at all, and that smaller and more compact platforms must be used for making focused deliberations.[13] In any case, there is a need to educate the American public about parts of Asia other than East Asia. We are challenging the state of "Asian American" studies in the universities and "Asian American" minority opportunities in the society at large, where the traditionally narrow definition of Asian American excludes all but bona fide East Asians.

"THE HOME AND THE WORLD"[14]

As early as 1989, Shirley Hune, in "Expanding the International Dimension of Asian American Studies," viewed Asian American Studies as "an integral part of American Studies and global studies" (xx), and announced the "need to develop a theoretical explanation of the contemporary Asian diaspora in the post colonial period" (xii). Recent immigrants from Southeast Asia and Hong Kong exhibit, like South Asians and Filipinos, diasporic and postcolonial sensibilities. Lisa Lowe's essay "Heterogeneity, Hybridity, Multiplicity: Marking Asian American Differences" (1991) reaffirms the changing face of Asian America. Lowe calls for a recognition of transnational imperatives and the hybrid identities of new Asian immigrants within Asian American studies. An immigrant group like the South Asians contributes heavily to this rethinking because many individuals come "twice, thrice, and quadruple migrant" (Bhachu 224) from Africa, West Indies, and Britain, carrying with them memories and affiliations from many countries. An important question that emerges from Lowe's argument is whether transnational South Asians, with their hybridized identities and multiple homelands can become able navigators in charting Asian America through the unexplored waters of late-twentieth-century demographics.

Sau-ling C. Wong, however, sounds a cautionary note against the too-ready acceptance of the "denationalized" or diasporic consciousness as an advanced stage of Asian American studies. In a complex and well-reasoned examination of the globalizing trend within Asian American studies, in her essay "Denationalization Reconsidered: Asian American Cultural Criticism at a Theoretical Crossroads" (1995), she reminds us of the hard-fought battles and the struggles endured by Asian American activists to claim space and voice for peoples of Asian descent not globally, but specifically *inside* America.

BACK TO THE FUTURE

Without question, every Asian American group must acknowledge the immense contributions of the 1968 activists. However, a continued emphasis on that moment as the point of origin of Asian American group identity obliterates common histories among Asian subgroups in the United States before 1968 and centuries-old links in Asia before immigration. It excludes groups that were not directly a part of the movement and postpones their legitimate claim to America and Asian America. Additionally, the emphasis on 1968 promotes an overemphasis on California and Hawaii, what we term "Pacificophilia."[15] For example, the theme for the

1997 conference of the Association for Asian American Studies, "Defining the Pacific Century," celebrates Pacific Rim American immigrants but implicitly excludes Asians who do not originate from the Pacific.

Scholarship and teaching in the field of Asian American studies have only recently begun to include South Asian perspectives—even though the first wave of South Asian immigrants to this country dates back to the early part of the twentieth century. In a provocative article "What to Do with All These New Immigrants or Refiguring Asian American History" (1992), Sucheta Mazumdar calls for a rethinking of Asian American studies. Dissatisfied with the West Coast orientation and the Chinese and Japanese American emphasis of Asian American studies courses, she reminds readers that those who are called the "new immigrants," including the Korean, Filipino, and South Asian, have actually been here for at least a hundred years; highlighting the "problem with this division and terminology of 'old' versus 'new,'" she asks, "Do 'old' immigrants and their histories have greater legitimacy than the histories of 'newer' Americans? Are we all engaged in some kind of nativist telling of history, 'we were here before you, therefore we are more American than you, therefore our history is more important than yours'?" (65)

Further, she cautions against ignoring Asian immigrants who come to the United States in multiple stages (including among others, British African Asians, Korean Argentinians, Sri Lankan Tamil Canadians, Latino Asian Americans):

> Shall we claim only those who come directly from Asia as Asian Americans, following some notion of "purity" and "pollution" . . . or do we anoint the immigrants 'Asian American' and ask that they submerge their Caribbean/ Fijian/Cuban/etc. histories? Is it not ironic that Asian American Studies, should become the vehicle for a process of homogenization of immigrants which strips away multiple layers of ethnic identity in favor of a single census category? (67)

Mazumdar's compelling challenge is timely. As we write this introduction, at least three new Asian American Studies programs are being developed in prominent East coast academic institutions—the University of Pennsylvania, New York University, and the University of Connecticut. New intellectual frameworks are required to challenge sacred truths and to construct new pedagogical models based on today's political-sociocultural realities. Models that take the present moment as their focus would benefit from seeing the 1968 strike as *one* of several charged points in the trajectory of Asian American history, without assuming it as the *only* point of origin.

South Asian American (In)Visibility
in Literary Studies

As both the editors of this collection are trained in the field of literary studies, we have chosen to focus on the gaps around South Asian American (in)visibility in this discipline. Asian American literature has come a long way from the days of Frank Chin's 1974 declaration that Asian American means "Filipino-, Chinese-, and Japanese-Americans, American born and raised, who got their China and Japan from the radio, off the silver screen, from television, out of comic books" (*Aiiieeeee!* vii).[16]

Almost a decade after Chin et al.'s first venture, Elaine H. Kim's groundbreaking *Asian American Literature: An Introduction to Writings and Their Social Context* (1982) added the Korean American viewpoints, but still excluded Southeast Asians and South Asians. In spite of this omission, and the conflicted use of the term "Asian American," Kim's introductory essay reveals a considerably more sophisticated understanding of the problems of nomenclature and identity than Chin's. However, like Chin et al., Kim too is only interested in what "Asians *in America* share . . . within the context of their *American* experiences" (1982, xiii, emphasis added). While Kim's approach is understandable, the social context of American demographics was itself changing rapidly in the 1970s and 1980s to include diasporic South Asian immigrants.

Not surprisingly then, several feminist-edited anthologies that began appearing since 1989 blurred the early exclusionary boundaries of Asian American literature and included a wide range of Asian American (including some South Asian American) voices: Shirley Geok-lin Lim, Mayumi Tsutakawa, and Margarita Donnelly's *The Forbidden Stitch: An Asian American Women's Anthology* (1989); the Asian Women United of California's anthology *Making Waves: An Anthology of Writings By and About Asian American Women* (1989); and Sylvia Watanabe and Carol Bruchac's *Home to Stay* (1990). In her essay "Feminist and Ethnic Literary Theories in Asian American Literature," Shirley Lim suggests that these feminist editors resisted the exclusive definition of Asian America proposed by Frank Chin et al., and brought to their collections an approach that was "nonauthoritative, decentered, nondogmatic, unprogrammatic, uncategorizing, inclusive, qualities that some feminist theoreticians . . . argue characterize female sensibilities" (579). By 1993, even Elaine Kim, in her preface to Jessica Hagedorn's *Charlie Chan Is Dead: An Anthology of Contemporary Asian American Fiction*, continues this inclusionary trend. She states emphatically that since the experiences of contemporary Asian American communities "are being shaped by the internationalization of the world's political economies and cultures" (x), Asian American literature today is "*both* Asian American literature *and* world literature" (xiii; Kim's emphasis).

As this volume goes to press, the Asian American literary milieu is informed by Garrett Hongo's 1994 flexible vision that includes individuals born to a "politically shifting and postcolonial world" whose writings have the range of "feeling and flavor of Hawaiian pidgin, a creole English, and . . . the smoothness of Mallarmé's French or mirror the *bric-a-brac* of Frank O'Hara's pop art lunch poems" ("Asian American Literature: Questions of Identity," 3). These writers include immigrants, sojourners, diasporics, multiple migrants, "postnationals" (Appadurai, "Heart of Whiteness"), refugees, and postcolonials who acknowledge multiple homelands, return to multifarious sites of knowledge, and deploy varied modes of knowing.

This rapid globalization of contemporary Asian America is not, however, an unequivocal matter of celebration for all, and can be confusing and even frustrating to those attempting to understand what constitutes "authentic" Asian American literature. Although anthologies such as Hagedorn's may inhibit an easy reading of Asian America, their inclusiveness and enlargement of the markers of Asian American identity can be anxiety-producing for some. For instance, Sven Birkerts, in his review of Hagedorn's book in the *New York Times Book Review*, sarcastically objects that in this collection "Asian America . . . has become a term so hospitable that half the world's population can squeeze in under its banner. Generous and catholic, yes, but the mix is also jarring and too eclectic" (17). Birkerts's objection is a simplistic rejection of the increasing heterogeneity of Asian America and a not entirely unexpected response from a member of the "majority" European American culture attempting reductive definitions of a minority group. Yet, Birkerts raises questions that may also exist both among the "majority" East Asians and the "minority" South Asians within Asian America. The inclusion of the newer Asian groups might seem "too jarring and eclectic," both for those who are being included and for those who have to relinquish their territory to make space for newcomers.

And South Asian writers have indeed arrived with a bang in America, especially in the 1990s. Even a cursory glance at some recently published works by South Asians in the United States reveals the abundance of literary activity: Meena Alexander's *Fault Lines* (1993) and *Manhattan Music* (1997), Agha Shahid Ali's *A Nostalgist's Map of America* (1991), Indran Amirthanayagam's *The Elephants of Reckoning* (1993), Chitra Divakaruni's *Black Candle* (1991), *Arranged Marriage* (1995) and *Mistress of Spices* (1997), Ginu Kamani's *Junglee Girl* (1995), Ameena Meer's *Bombay Talkie* (1994), Bharati Mukherjee's *The Holder of the World*

(1993), Kirin Narayan's *Love, Stars, and All That* (1994), Bapsi Sidhwa's *An American Brat* (1993), Abraham Verghese's *My Own Country* (1994), and various stories by Tahira Naqvi. A spate of South Asian American anthologies further underscores the voicing of literary energy by post-1965 South Asian Americans and their offspring: *Our Feet Walk the Sky: Women of the South Asian Diaspora* (1993), *A Lotus of Another Color: An Unfolding of the South Asian Gay and Lesbian Experience* (1993), *Her Mother's Ashes* (1994), *Living in America: Poetry and Fiction by South Asian American Writers* (1995), and *Contours of the Heart: South Asians Map North America* (1996). Madhulika Khandelwal's praise for the pioneering efforts of the undergraduate students who edited *Our Feet Walk the Sky* (1993)—for [taking] "up the challenge of dealing with the lack of documentation on South Asians . . . [and for making] Asian American studies programs pause and think carefully about inclusion and development strategies for Asian communities such as those of South Asians (100)"—is also applicable to the others who have followed the initiative of the young editors. Ironically enough, these South Asian women replicated a form of literary self-representation that another well-known group of Asian American student activists had performed two decades earlier.

Thus, it is not possible to ignore South Asian writers in a course on Asian American literature today because of the voluminous available material. The fact that so few of them are taught, however, suggests that quantity is not the obstacle to the inclusion of these works in Asian American literature courses. In fact, the acceptance of Bharati Mukherjee's *Jasmine* (1989), one of the few works by a South Asian American that is included in Asian American literature curricula, points to two central criteria that still appear to be operative in the definition of Asian American literature—adoption of America as home and the experience of persecution/oppression/lack of privilege. Jasmine, like her creator, rejects her life and history in India and enthusiastically embraces the United States as her new home. While South Asian American scholars such as Samir Dayal, Inderpal Grewal, and Lavina Shankar have denounced *Jasmine* as presenting a too-simplistic opposition of stagnant and oppressive India and an ever-changing, ever-renewing, and progressive America, what makes *Jasmine* easily a part of Asian American literature is the neatness with which it enacts the conventional Asian immigrant's story—determined survival against all odds and an ultimate claiming of America. While Mukherjee herself enjoys all the privilege of mainstream recognition, the persecution her characters endure permits her entry into an ethnic canon that Hongo denounces as "chained by traits of bitterness and anger in a kind of political activist model" ("Asian American Literature: Questions of Identity," 4).

The issue of privilege is significant and explains why an Indian American writer such as Ved Mehta was rendered invisible to the Asian American literary community. Years before Mukherjee arrived on the American literary landscape, Mehta was publishing actively in this country. His stories and articles had appeared since 1961 in publications such as the *Atlantic Monthly, Harper's,* and the *New Yorker.* Mehta, blind since the age of four, left India at age fifteen to attend a school for the blind in Little Rock, Arkansas. Following his graduation, he attended Pomona College in California and became a successful novelist, short story writer, and journalist who has published twenty-one books. Mehta's visibility to the editors of prestigious publications such as the *New Yorker* probably had much to do with his being ignored by scholars of Asian American literature. Perhaps he fell victim to the "test" that Hongo acidly describes as follows: "If a work is adjudged meritorious by any American institution that can be characterized as 'mainstream,' then that work must necessarily be 'inauthentic' in terms of Asian American culture and, therefore, is due for condemnation by loyalists and exclusion from the reading lists of Asian American or Ethnic Studies courses" ("Questions" 4). At any rate, Mehta's absence in discussions of Asian American literature is surprising considering his prolific output, part of which details his experiences as an Indian American immigrant.

To take a more recent example, how does one characterize a writer like Abraham Verghese? He is a double diasporic, a physician by profession, author of a moving memoir of his work as an Indian American doctor treating Caucasian patients with AIDS in a small rural town in East Tennessee. *My Own Country* (1994) reveals Verghese's metaphoric search for a home through his doctoring as he compares his quest for belonging with the AIDS patients' return to their original homes from centers of gay life in San Francisco and New York. Verghese doesn't refer to himself as Asian American, but he is acutely conscious of himself as a "foreign" doctor, one of many overseas-trained physicians from South Asia and the Philippines. His work defies easy categorization, but Ruth Hsiao's essay in this volume makes a case for why it should be read as Asian American literature. Although his memoir does not primarily focus on Asian American characters, with the exception of himself, Verghese's experiences as an Asian American doctor in a southern town merit consideration as Asian American literature. Or does his being a doctor and the enthusiastic reception of his work by the mainstream press and the medical community (he was recently the commencement speaker at a graduation ceremony at

Johns Hopkins Medical School) preclude him from joining the ranks of the more "oppressed" Asian American writers struggling to find acceptance?

Recent anthologies published by non–South Asian Americans since 1993 have emulated the earlier feminist model and included writings by South Asian Americans.[17] The true test of legitimate inclusion, however, is the presence of South Asian American texts in the Asian American curriculum. What will precipitate closing the gaps between South Asian American literature and Asian American scholars and educators? Will it happen when enough South Asian Americans start educating others about themselves, representing their groups in Asian American courses, hiring committees, writers' workshops, publication editorial boards, and so on? The reconfiguration of Asian American literature must first occur in the context of classroom dynamics—in training new generations of students and scholars—and it is here that the hard questions of who belongs must be addressed.

ABOUT THE ESSAYS

This multidisciplinary collection includes eleven essays from academic scholars and community and student activists. The essays are divided between those that employ theoretical, critical, analytical modes, and those that rely on personal narratives and empirical research.

The book is organized in four sections. The first, "Limiting Names and Labels," questions the assumptions upon which the book is based. It includes two essays dealing with the problematic aspects of names and "identitarian" labels. Deepika Bahri, in her essay "With Kaleidoscope Eyes: The (Potential) Dangers of Identitarian Coalitions," discusses the role of history and memory in the formation of names and identities. She investigates the term "Asia" itself before scrutinizing the term "Asian American," and reminds us of the differences among Asians in Asia as well as among Asians in America. She insists that coalitions cannot be haphazardly formed, however well-intentioned their aims, and cautions against collective memories that erase "cracks and fissures" and simplistically close gaps between disparate groups.

Whereas Bahri reminds us of the problematic and contested genesis of the label "Asia," Lavina Dhingra Shankar's essay "The Limits of (South Asian) Names and Labels: Postcolonial or Asian American?" grapples specifically with South Asian American identity and nomenclature. By focusing on two visible South Asian literary figures in the American academy, Gayatri Chakravorty Spivak and Bharati Mukherjee, Shankar reflects on the different labels placed upon the two women and their work. Providing a brief history of "South Asians'" constantly changing nomenclature in the last two centuries, the essay addresses the complexities of naming one's "self" and "others" as both unifying and potentially divisive political strategies. Shankar finally questions whether all naming constitutes performative and essentializing acts, and compares South Asians' often self-projected "postcolonial" and "Asian American" identifications within literary and cultural studies.

The second section, "The Disconnections of Race," includes two essays that examine the perceived racial position of South Asian Americans in Asian America. Nazli Kibria's essay "The Racial Gap: South Asian American Racial Identity and the Asian American Movement" explores the "ambiguous nonwhite" racial position occupied by South Asians, in the views of Asian American and all other American communities. Although calling for South Asian American inclusion within the "pan-Asian fold," Kibria remains "pessimistic" about this possibility until race is openly discussed by all groups.

Min Song, on the other hand, seeks to establish a connection between Sikh and Japanese farmers in turn-of-the-century California. In his essay "Pahkar Singh's Argument with America: Color and the Structure of Race Formation," Song discusses the lessons provided by the story of Pahkar Singh, a Sikh farmer in California, for understanding U.S. racial, cultural, and national formation. He seeks to understand why, despite a shared historical condition, there seems to have been relatively little dialogue between Japanese and Sikh farmers; he uncovers the historical links between them and the effects of the California Alien Land Laws on both groups. He argues that despite the differences and self-imposed distance between them, the two communities occupied similar positions in the racial discourse of the United States. This shared history of racialization, Song argues, merits careful study in order to bridge the fissures within Asian America and South Asian America.

The third section, "Topologies of Activism," explores how efforts at coalition building and panethnicity are enacted in social, cultural, and political contexts. The five essays in this section chart the map of Asian American panethnicity from the vantage points of university campus student organizations, grassroots community organizations, congressional political campaigns, and gay and lesbian group activism. Vijay Prashad's essay "Crafting Solidarities," which opens this section, calls for a disbanding of all ethnic and culturally defined groups and suggests instead that we rethink and renegotiate the revolutionary category "people of color." He finds little use for coalition building under such limited labels as South Asian American and Asian American, believing that groups organized on the basis of shared phenotype or shared culture ultimately become ethnocentric.

The other four essays, however, argue that under certain conditions there is value and even necessity in bringing together disparate Asian American subgroups. In her essay "At the Crossroads: College Activism and Its Impact on Asian American Identity Formation," Anu Gupta investigates campus organizations that include and/or exclude South Asian Americans from Asian American groups—specifically those at Harvard, Yale, Brown, and the University of Pennsylvania. She urges South Asian American college students to empower themselves and their communities by embracing "dual identities as Asian Americans and as South Asian Americans."

Sumantra Tito Sinha's essay takes us from the world of campus politics to the world of grassroots community activism. "From Campus to Community Politics in Asian America" is based on his work in the Asian American Legal Defense and Education Fund, and provides insights into the position South Asians occupy within pan–Asian American legal and community organizations. Sinha's essay is an open call for panethnic coalition building; he exhorts South Asian Americans to increase their involvement in grassroots Asian American activism.

In "The Call of Rice: (South) Asian American Queer Communities," Sandip Roy describes the interactions between—and distances within—(South and) Asian American gay-lesbian-bisexual organizations. His interviews with members of the Gay Asian Pacific Alliance, Asian Pacific Sisters, Trikone, and Shamakami lead him to suggest that the "lesbian gay identity is the strongest binding force" among South and other Asian American "lesbigay groups," while the Asian connection is a secondary factor that reinforces the primary bond.

Rajini Srikanth's essay "Ram Yoshino Uppuluri's Campaign: The Implications for Panethnicity in Asian America" examines the political campaign for the United States House of Representatives by a part-Indian, part-Japanese American from Tennessee to determine the extent to which the panethnic Asian American vision operates in his political strategy. Using Uppuluri's campaign as a case study, the essay highlights some factors that facilitate or inhibit panethnic coalition building. While the essays in this section acknowledge the complexities of panethnic coalition building, they nevertheless challenge Prashad's rejection of any praxis based on ethnicity.

The last section, "Literary Texts and Diasporics," includes two essays that examine selected fictional and nonfictional writings by South Asian Americans to determine whether a diasporic consciousness enables South Asian Americans to "fit into" Asian America. Ruth Yu Hsiao's essay "A World Apart: A Reading of South Asian American Literature" argues that works by Bharati Mukherjee, Michael Ondaatje, and Abraham Verghese, who write from a diasporic viewpoint, differ from the more easily recognizably "ethnic" works by East Asian American writers, and are, hence, changing the definition of what constitutes Asian American literature. Examining the trajectory of Asian American literature over the last thirty years, Hsiao outlines the early criteria for inclusion in the Asian American literary canon and shows how the writings of three South Asian American writers both meet and depart from these criteria.

Samir Dayal, in his essay "Min(d)ing the Gap: South Asian Americans and Diaspora," states at the outset that "'Asian America' is a category into which 'South Asian America' does not and should not quite seek to 'fit.'" He argues that a productive "min(d)ing" of the gap between South Asian Americans and Asian Americans will yield rich insights into questions of nation, home, and belonging, and will, therefore, contribute to a more "civil" society. Explicating his position through a discussion of Meena Alexander's memoir *Fault Lines* (1993), Dayal rejects a complacent acceptance of the label "Asian American," seeking, instead, a shifting identity.

A PART, YET APART?

The scope of this book relates particularly to the peripheral position of South Asian perspectives within the canon of Asian American studies and within minority programs. The essays in this anthology aim to energize the overall debate on the representation of South Asian Americans within Asian America. At a simple level this book raises questions such as what constitutes Asian America today? How has the definition of this group changed since its initial articulation in 1968? To what extent have South Asian issues found their way into Asian American studies? Who decides questions of inclusion in and exclusion from Asian America? At a deeper level, the essays address other issues: How do power structures within minority groups develop? How do South Asians' postcolonial identities overlap with Asian Americanness? How do gender, class, sexuality, and generational differences among South Asian Americans affect their identification as South Asians and as Asian Americans? Are the gaps among the various Asian American subgroups created by differences in experiences of oppression versus real or perceived privilege?

A Part, Yet Apart maps the site of South Asian American inclusion within Asian American studies and complicates its terrain. Who defines what constitutes Asian American studies—should it be European Americans who still make most hiring decisions, or East Asian Americans, who gave birth to the discipline in 1968, some of "who[m] now serve as gatekeeping faculty and staff in Asian American studies programs" (Kiang

530), or South Asian Americans themselves who are beginning to develop a collective identity? Which texts get taught in the Asian American cultural and literary studies curricula? Which groups' histories get represented, and by whom? Who can be considered "authentically" Asian and, hence, "Oriental" enough to teach Asian American literature, history, politics, economics, and so on? How many generations of Americanness does it require before one can speak as an Asian American? Which part of that ancestry are South Asian Americans lacking—that they are not Asian enough, or not American enough? Under what circumstances can pan-ethnic coalitions arise? In what cases is forced ethnic-coalescing meaningless or even harmful? The essays that follow engage with these questions and call for the implementation of scholarship and pedagogy that recognizes rather than ignores the intricate significations of "Asian America."

ACKNOWLEDGMENTS

We wish to thank Rajiv Shankar for his help in rethinking and rewriting a section of this introduction, and Yuko Matsukawa and David Palumbo-Liu for their incisive critiques of earlier drafts. A brief section of this essay was presented at the MELUS International Conference in April 1997.

NOTES

1. See *The World Almanac 1990*, 539.

2. In the United States, the term "Asian American" typically refers to a person from East Asia (China, Japan, or Korea); by contrast, in Britain, "Asian" invariably refers to a person of South Asian ancestry. The differing histories of the United States and Britain with respect to Asia are, of course, responsible for this variance in the meaning of "Asian."

3. The South Asian population in America includes 815,000 Indians, "second only to the Vietnamese in the percentage increase during the decade [1980s]" (Mazumdar 1993, 284). Smaller subgroups, from Bangladesh, Bhutan, Maldives, Nepal, Pakistan, and Sri Lanka, are believed to total roughly 150,000. It is safe to assume, therefore, that South Asians in the United States number approximately 1 million (Mazumdar 1993, 284–86).

4. Even as numbers are important to achieve "critical mass," we are simultaneously skeptical of what Sandip Roy's essay in this volume terms the "numbers game" in minority group politics, and about which Sucheta Mazumdar asks provocatively, "Should we do history by the numbers and devote longer segments of the syllabi to the numerically more significant groups?" ("New Immigrants," 64). While a numbers approach may seem justifiable and even valid, its danger is that it continuously reinforces structures of centers and margins, majorities and minorities, and sets up oppositional politics. We realize that we are guilty of the same in that most of our own contributors are of Indian origin.

5. South Asia, also called the Indian subcontinent, actually rests on a separate geologic plate—the Indo-Australian—from the rest of Asia (part of the Eurasian plate). The Indo-Australian plate is pushing against the Eurasian plate, creating a chain of mountains, including the Himalayas. For a good discussion of the overall geographic, demographic, and historic coherence of this region, see *An Advanced History of India* (Madras, India: Macmillan, 1978) by R. C. Majumdar, H. C. Raychaudhuri, and K. Datta, 3–8.

6. We endorse B. H. Farmer's explanation of his use of the term "South Asia" in the introduction to his book on South Asia, as being a "neutral and inoffensive" label that does not privilege any particular country as central (1).

7. *The World Almanac 1990*, 690, 692, 718, 732, 741, 753.

8. Elaine Kim makes a similar point about the reluctance of individuals of "Chinese, Vietnamese, or Samoan" ancestry to identify themselves as Asian or Pacific American. See *Asian American Literature: An Introduction to Their Writings and Their Social Context* (Philadelphia: Temple University Press, 1982), xii.

9. However, some second-generation South Asian Americans may tend to romanticize their ancestral homelands in their eagerness to discover their "roots." Such romanticization can lead to ethnocentrism, which is always antithetical to coalition building.

10. In 1965, the number of "Asian Indians" in the United States was ten thousand; see Ronald Takaki's *Strangers from a Different Shore* (Boston: Little, Brown, 1989), 445.

11. While there are no accurate measures of the number of second-generation South Asian Americans or those immigrants who came here as children, indirect markers suggest that the under-thirty population is significant. Two factors worth keeping in mind are that between 1965 and 1974, immigration from India increased by more than 2,000 percent and immigration from Pakistan by more than 1,000 percent, and that a noticeable difference between pre-1924 and post-1965 immigration from South Asia was in gender and age composition. According to *The Asian American Encyclopedia*, edited by Franklin Ng, "At least one-third of all post-1965 Asian Indian immigrants were women, usually wives of male immigrants; a good proportion were also children, the dependents of adult immigrants" (1384).

12. South Asian migration to the United States began in the first decade of the twentieth century. Workers from the Punjab region of the Indian subcontinent, who had been lured to British Columbia by the Canadian government's promise of easy employment, began entering this western Canadian province at the rate of two thousand a year (Hess 29). In response to the rapid entry of these "brown-skinned" and culturally unfamiliar immigrants, who were seen as potential competitors to indigenous laborers, Canada imposed restrictions on immigration that made it virtually impossible for South Asians to enter Canada. Consequently, many South Asians looked southward to the United States' Pacific Coast states where they believed they would be more welcome. That they were proven wrong is now common knowledge among immigration historians. "Hindus," as all immigrants from South Asia were mistakenly called, were subjected to the vagaries of discriminatory immigration laws in the same ways in which the Chinese and the

Japanese were (Chandrasekhar 15–19; Jacoby 36; Brown 41–42); they were excluded from entering the United States (as part of the Pacific Barred Zone portion of the Immigration Act of 1917), deemed ineligible for citizenship, and described as unassimilable and uncivilized, a threat to the foundations of American culture. In 1907, in Bellingham, Washington, "six hundred lumberjacks herded some two hundred 'Hindus' out of town with many immigrants suffering serious injuries"; in 1914, a senator from North Carolina "introduced measures . . . to exclude 'Hindu' laborers" (Hess 29–30).

13. Madhulika Khandelwal of Queens College has often spoken of the dangers of mere inclusion or simple addition of new groups. Inclusion, if it is to be meaningful, must be followed by commitment to understanding the complexities of the newly included group. In the absence of such commitment, inclusion makes no improvement on invisibility. Consider this example: recently, a graduate student at Harvard University's school of public health spoke with Rajini Srikanth of the difficulties she experienced in working on public health issues with South Asian communities in California. The panethnic Asian American organization for which she was working there found that it could not get a reliable contact person from the South Asian community. Whenever an individual approached the organization and professed to speak for the entire South Asian community, some subgroup would question that individual's credibility to represent that particular subgroup. Uninformed about the heterogeneity of the South Asian American community, this graduate student and the organization for which she worked eventually "gave up" in frustration (personal conversation, November 1995). Here is a case in which outreach should have been accompanied by attempts to educate oneself about the internal dynamics of the South Asian community.

14. As some South Asian American readers may recognize, we allude to Oscar-winning filmmaker Satyajit Ray's film *Ghare Baire* to highlight the complex issues surrounding Asian American studies in both the domestic American as well as the global diasporic context.

15. Gary Okihiro and Stephen Sumida are among the scholars who have been skeptical of the West Coast bias of Asian American Studies. The development of the "East-of-California" scholarly network, with its own conference in the last decade, implicitly reveals the views of other marginalized East Coast scholars. Several South Asian American scholars we have spoken to were disgruntled about the 1997 conference theme of the Association for Asian American Studies (AAAS). Out of ninety-nine sessions at the 1994 annual convention of the Association for Asian American Studies, there were only two panels on South Asian Americans, one of which was organized by us. The 1995 AAAS convention in Oakland, California, made no significant increase to this number, and although the 1996 conference had more panels than before by or about South Asian Americans, the 1997 agenda seems to imply a reversal of the inclusive trend.

16. Chin et al.'s announcement excluded even the Korean American from Asian American literary studies, let alone South and Southeast Asians in America. It privileged American birth as a criterion for an American sensibility, dissociating the "authentic" practitioners of Asian American literature from the writers and the texts located in the ancestral countries of Asia. (The 1989 sequel, *The Big*

Aiiieeeee! An Anthology of Chinese American and Japanese American Writers, got "smaller," dropping the Filipino Americans from its contents without explanation; however, the anthology's title carefully avoided the term "Asian American," making the text's focus more precise and avoiding the politics of the term.)

17. Maria Hong's *Growing Up Asian American: An Anthology* (1993); Garrett Hongo's *The Open Boat: Poems from Asian America* (1993) and his *Under Western Eyes: Personal Essays from Asian America* (1995); Lim-Hing's *The Very Inside: An Anthology of Writings by Asian and Pacific Islander Lesbians* (1994); and Geraldine Kudaka's *On a Bed of Rice: An Asian American Erotic Feast* (1995).

WORKS CITED

Appadurai, Arjun. "The Heart of Whiteness." *Callaloo* 16.4 (1993): 796–807.

Asian Women United of California, ed. *Making Waves: An Anthology of Writings By and About Asian American Women.* Boston: Beacon Press, 1989.

Bhachu, Parminder. "New Cultural Forms and Transnational South Asian Women: Culture, Class, and Consumption among British Asian Women in the Diaspora." In *Nation and Migration: The Politics of Space in the South Asian Diaspora,* edited by Peter van der Veer. Philadelphia: University of Pennsylvania Press, 1995, 222–44.

Birkerts, Sven. "Charlie Chan Is Dead: An Anthology of Contemporary Asian American Fiction." *New York Times Book Review.* Dec. 19, 1993, 17.

Breckenridge, Carol A., and Peter van der Veer, eds. *Orientalism and the Postcolonial Predicament.* Philadelphia: University of Pennsylvania Press, 1993.

Brown, Emily C. "Revolution in India: Made in America." In *From India to America: A Brief History of Immigration; Problems of Discrimination; Admission and Assimilation,* edited by S. Chandrasekhar. La Jolla, Calif.: A Population Review Book, 1982, 41–47.

———. "A History of United States Legislation with Respect to Immigration from India." In *From India to America: A Brief History of Immigration; Problems of Discrimination; Admission and Assimilation,* edited by S. Chandrasekhar. La Jolla, Calif.: A Population Review Book, 1982, 11–28.

Chandrasekhar, S., ed. *From India to America: A Brief History of Immigration; Problems of Discrimination; Admission and Assimilation.* La Jolla, Calif.: A Population Review Book, 1982.

Cheung, King-Kok, and Stan Yogi. *Asian American Literature: An Annotated Bibliography.* New York: Modern Language Association of America, 1988.

Chan, Jeffery Paul, Frank Chin, Lawson Fusao Inada, and Shawn Wong, eds. *The Big Aiiieeeee! An Anthology of Chinese American and Japanese American Literature.* New York: Meridian, 1991.

Chan, Sucheng. *Asian Americans: An Interpretive History.* Boston: Twayne, 1991.

Chin, Frank, Jeffery Paul Chan, Lawson Fusao Inada, and Shawn Hsu Wong, eds. *Aiiieeeee! An Anthology of Asian-American Writers.* Washington, D.C.: Howard University Press, 1974.

Dayal, Samir. "Creating, Preserving, Destroying: Violence in Bharati Mukherjee's *Jasmine*." In *Bharati Mukherjee: Critical Perspectives*, edited by Emmanuel S. Nelson. New York: Garland, 1993, 65–88.

Dutta, Manoranjan. "Asian Indian Americans—Search for an Economic Profile." In *From India to America: A Brief History of Immigration; Problems of Discrimination; Admission and Assimilation*, edited by S. Chandrasekhar. La Jolla, Calif.: A Population Review Book, 1982, 76–85.

Espiritu, Yen Le. *Asian American Panethnicity: Bridging Institutions and Identities*. Philadelphia: Temple University Press, 1992.

Farmer, B. H. *Introduction to South Asia*. New York: Routledge: 1993.

Gall, Susan B., and Timothy L. Gall, eds. *Statistical Record of Asian Americans*. Detroit, Mich.: Gale Research Inc., 1993.

Grewal, Inderpal. "Reading and Writing the South Asian Diaspora: Feminism and Nationalism in North America." In *Our Feet Walk the Sky: Women of the South Asian Diaspora*, edited by the Women of South Asian Descent Collective. San Francisco: aunt lute books, 1993, 226–36.

Hagedorn, Jessica, ed. *Charlie Chan Is Dead: An Anthology of Contemporary Asian American Fiction*. New York: Penguin, 1993.

Hess, Gary R. "The Asian Indian Immigrants in the United States, 1900–1965." In *From India to America: A Brief History of Immigration; Problems of Discrimination; Admission and Assimilation*, edited by S. Chandrasekhar. La Jolla, Calif.: A Population Review Book, 1982, 29–34.

———. "The Forgotten Asian Americans: The East Indian Community in the United States." In *Asians in America*, edited by N. Hundley. Santa Barbara, Calif.: ABC-CLIO, 1976, 157–78.

Hirschman, Charles. "Problems and Prospects of Studying Immigration Adaptation from the 1990 Population Census." *International Migration Review 1994* 28.4: 690–713.

Hongo, Garrett. "Asian American Literature: Questions of Identity." *Amerasia Journal*. 20.3 (1994):1–8.

Hune, Shirley. "Expanding the International Dimension of Asian American Studies." *Amerasia Journal* 15.2 (1989): xix–xxiv.

Jacoby, Harold S. "Administrative Restriction of Asian Indian Restriction into the United States, 1907–1917. In *From India to America: A Brief History of Immigration; Problems of Discrimination; Admission and Assimilation*, edited by S. Chandrasekhar. La Jolla, Calif.: A Population Review Book, 1982, 35–40.

Jensen, Joan M. *Passage from India: Asian Indian Immigrants in North America*. New Haven: Yale University Press, 1988.

Khandelwal, Madhulika S. "Indian Immigrants in Queens, New York City: Patterns of Spatial Concentration and Distribution, 1965–1990." In *Nation and Migration: The Politics of Space in the South Asian Diaspora*, edited by Peter van der Veer. Philadelphia: University of Pennsylvania Press, 1995, 178–96.

Khandelwal, Madhulika S. Review. *Our Feet Walk the Sky: The Women of South Asian Diaspora*. *Amerasia Journal* 20.2 (1994): 98–100.

Kiang, Peter Nien-chu. "Pedagogies of Life and Death: Transforming Immigrant/

Refugee Students and Asian American Studies." *Positions* 5.2 (Fall 1997): 529–55.

Kim, Elaine H. *Asian American Literature: An Introduction to the Writings and Their Social Context*. Philadelphia: Temple University Press, 1982.

Leonard, Karen. "Marriage and Family Life Among Early Asian Indian Immigrants." In *From India to America: A Brief History of Immigration; Problems of Discrimination; Admission and Assimilation*, edited by S. Chandrasekhar. La Jolla, Calif.: A Population Review Book, 1982, 67–75.

Lim, Shirley Geok-lin. "Feminist and Ethnic Literary Theories in Asian American Literature." *Feminist Studies* 19.3 (Fall 1993): 571–95.

Lim, Shirley Geok-lin, Mayumi Tsutakawa, and Margarita Donnelly, eds. The *Forbidden Stitch: An Asian American Women's Anthology*. Corvallis, Oreg.: Calyx Books, 1989.

Lowe, Lisa. "Heterogeneity, Hybridity, Multiplicity: Marking Asian American Differences." *Diaspora* 1.1 (Spring 1991): 24–44.

Mazumdar, R. C., H. C. Raychaudhuri, and K. Datta. *An Advanced History of India*. Madras, India: Macmillan, 1978.

Mazumdar, Sucheta. "Race and Racism: South Asians in the United States." In *Frontiers of Asian American Studies: Writing, Research, and Commentary,* edited by Gail M. Nomura et al. Pullman, Wash.: Washington University Press, 1989, 25–38.

———. "South Asians in the United States with a Focus on Asian Indians." *The State of Asian Pacific America: A Public Policy Report. Policy Issues to the Year 2020*. Los Angeles: LEAP Asian Pacific American Public Policy Institute and UCLA Asian American Studies Center, 1993, 283–301.

———. "What To Do with All These New Immigrants or Refiguring Asian American History." *Building Blocks for Asian American Studies: East of California Conference*. Proceedings editors: Robert G. Lee and Lihbin Shiao. Brown University, Providence, R.I., September 25–27, 1992.

Melendy, H. Brett. *Asians in America: Filipinos, Koreans, and East Indians*. Boston: Twayne, 1977.

Nandi, P. K. "The World of an Invisible Minority: Pakistanis in America." *California Sociologists* 3 (Summer 1980): 143–65.

Ng, Franklin, ed. *The Asian American Encyclopedia*. Vol. 5. New York: Marshall Cavendish, 1995.

Okihiro, Gary. *Margins and Mainstreams: Asians in American History and Culture*. Seattle: University of Washington Press, 1994.

Omatsu, Glenn. "The 'Four Prisons' and the Movements of Liberation: Asian American Activism from the 1960s to the 1990s." In *The State of Asian America: Activism and Resistance in the 1990s*, edited by Karin Aguilar-San Juan. Boston: South End Press, 1994, 19–69.

Omi, Michael. "Out of the Melting Point and into the Fire." In *The State of Asian Pacific America: A Public Policy Report. Policy Issues to the Year 2020*. Los Angeles: LEAP Asian Pacific American Public Policy Institute and UCLA Asian American Studies Center, 1993, 199–214.

Rustomji-Kerns, Roshni. *Living in America: Poetry and Fiction by South Asian American Writers*. Boulder, Colo.: Westview Press, 1995.

Sethi, Rita Chaudhry. "Smells Like Racism: A Plan for Mobilizing against Anti-Asian Bias." In *The State of Asian America: Activism and Resistance in the 1990s*, edited by Karin Aguilar-San Juan. Boston: South End Press, 1994, 235–49.

Shankar, Lavina Dhingra. "Activism, 'Feminisms,' and Americanization in Bharati Mukherjee's *Wife* and *Jasmine*." *Hitting Critical Mass: A Journal of Asian American Cultural Criticism* 3.1 (Winter 1995): 61–84.

Sheth, Manju. "Asian Indian Americans." In *Asian Americans: Contemporary Trends and Issues*, edited by Pyong Gap Min. Thousand Oaks, Calif.: Sage Publications, 1995.

Singh, Jane, ed. *South Asians in North America: An Annotated and Selected Bibliography*. Berkeley, Calif.: Center for South and Southeast Asia Studies, 1988.

Takaki, Ronald. *Strangers from a Different Shore: A History of Asian Americans*. Boston: Little, Brown, 1989.

Wei, William. *The Asian American Movement*. Philadelphia: Temple University Press, 1993.

Westwood, Sallie. "Gendering Diaspora: Space, Politics, and South Asian Masculinities in Britain." In *Nation and Migration: The Politics of Space in the South Asian Diaspora*, edited by Peter van der Veer. Philadelphia: University of Pennsylvania Press, 1995, 197–221.

Women of South Asian Descent Collective, ed. *Our Feet Walk the Sky: Women of the South Asian Diaspora*. San Francisco: aunt lute books, 1993.

Wong, Sau-ling Cynthia. "Denationalization Reconsidered: Asian American Cultural Criticism at a Theoretical Crossroads." *Amerasia Journal* 21.1&2 (1995): 1–27.

———. *Reading Asian American Literature: From Necessity to Extravagance*. Princeton: Princeton University Press, 1993.

World Almanac and Book of Facts. New York: Scripps Howard, 1990.

I.   LIMITING NAMES AND LABELS

Deepika Bahri

1   With Kaleidoscope Eyes
The Potential (Dangers) of Identitarian Coalitions

ANY EXPLORATION of the ways in which South Asian Americans do or do not "fit into" Asian America invokes complicated array of difficult issues. The assumption of the set "Asia" is itself historically conflicted, and the notion of representational identity is increasingly seen as largely phantasmatic. To be sure, "map" names facilitate group-based social activism and make visible various and variously disenfranchised constituencies within the ongoing scene of conflict politics in America. To pursue these purposes in the absence of a historical and theoretical framework, however, is to ask for confusion on the one hand, and to promote an inherently divisive political maneuver on the other. This essay explores the shifting paths of (South) Asian American histories in the context of the temporaneity and historicity of identitarian coalitions in the United States, while suggesting that the challenges in the next stage of cultural politics are many. They include the need to investigate the potential of strategic interethnic coalitions while resisting spurious sociological solidity and the erasure of historical differences; to recognize that in such projects self-definition takes shape not simply against the center but against other marginals; to acknowledge that identity politics is a potent weapon for the right as well as the left; and to consider the historical specificity of the moment in which identity-based maneuvers become available, even sanctioned by the mainstream, as strategy.

While the affiliation of South Asians (a category whose tenuous nature has not prevented it from achieving late-blossoming but clear validation in its own right) with better-represented Asian Americans is understandable in a climate governed by the ideology and politics of difference, it must be underscored by a better understanding of their historical and cultural distinctions along with the commonalities that make for progressive and radical coalitions. The general move toward "making room" for underrepresented Others within this configuration might also serve as a useful strategy in exploring the potential for coalition with similarly segregated groups. The variant migratory patterns and economic profiles of different sorts of Asians ("the strangers from a different shore" in Ronald Takaki's words), the place of these strangers among other alienated groups

25

already present in North America, and the recent experiences of interethnic conflict in the United States—these are some of the historical realities that must inform any further developments in the discourses of difference.[1] With kaleidoscope eyes, we might then see how dangerous it can be
to forget how some achieve coalitions while others have coalitions thrust
upon them by interested parties, how coalitions shift in the winds of historic forces, and how important it is to assess these forces as strategies are
developed for the future.

The search for common cause that fueled the early movement did not
ensure participation or representation of all the groups we might think
of as constituting Asian America. If one lesson of early coalitions is that
difference could be overlooked in the interest of visible interests, another
points to the difficulty of understanding and representing differences more
inclusively. As important as it is to catalog the history of who struggled and
in what cause, it is equally important to ask, who did not speak and why?
The relative invisibility—not absence, but invisibility—of South Asians,
for instance, among the early pioneers of Asian American activism might
be, as I have suggested earlier, usefully investigated as a more inclusive
coalition is proposed. The "South Asian" case, if one might call it that,
might in fact be examined closely because it may point to the complexities
of Asian American coalitionism and its contemporary problematic. Invoking past and present histories, this essay will explore the many differences
among those labeled "Asian American," and investigate the principles on
which a coalition among them might be said to rest in the academy and
other public arenas. Eventually, I will outline what might be the beginning
of the development of a kaleidoscopic perspective that allows us to appre-
hend the benefits of coalitionism while retaining a focus on the dangers of
identitarian constructions.

Important to any discussion of identitarian movements is an understanding of memory, both collective and personal, constructed and erased,
as well as of the narratives shaped and obscured in its mobilization to
service identity affirmation. The role of memory in constructing identity is
by now so clear to social historians as to scarcely merit restatement.[2] Less
often is one reminded of the role of *identity*, or what is thought to be
cohesive identity, in constructing memory, although this is hardly a novel
observation. It is nevertheless and precisely the strategic re-memorying
and un-memorying involved in infusing identity with political charge that
should concern us when engaged in positing new identitarian coalitions.
While recovering and uncovering the shared memory of oppression and
alienation—a primary modus operandi in creating identity-based groups—
it is important to resist the eclipse of memories of difference and of privilege relative to other members of the group seeking consolidation as well

as to other groups in general. To paper over these cracks and fissures in the interest of forging a new collective memory is to risk their widening over time. Nor can a gap be effectively bridged until its measure is known. Quite apart from its dubious logic and morality, the denial of history implicit in provisional and unreflective integration is not merely a hypothetical risk but a risk that relentlessly and unavoidably concretizes itself in the materiality of quotidian conflict over resources and power; "how one is categorized," as Omi and Winant remind us, "is far from a merely academic or even personal matter" (3). Efforts to mobilize and expand notions of Asian American identity must therefore be investigated against a backdrop of some of the issues raised above, if such a move is to be valuable. R. Radhakrishnan reminds us that "we live in a society that is profoundly anti-historical" and that capitalism, assisted by technology, has the capacity "to produce a phenomenology of the present so alluring in its immediacy as to seduce the consumer to forget the past and bracket the future" (225).

One might begin by raising the much-touted question of historicity. Issuing from an acceptance of cartographic historiography, the notion of "Asian" identity, constructed or otherwise, itself depends on a constructed and perhaps empty and arbitrary signifier. I have suggested that the assumption of the set "Asia" is historically conflicted; it would be useful to explore how this is so and what its implications might be in manufacturing coalition. In his *Asia before Europe: Economy and Civilisation of the Indian Ocean from the Rise of Islam to 1750*, K. N. Chaudhuri deconstructs the concept of Asia, reminding us that "there is no equivalent word in any Asian language nor such a concept in the domain of geographical knowledge, though expressions such as the 'Sea of China' or the 'Sea of Hind' held certain analogous meaning in Arabic and some of the Indian languages" (22). As it turns out, the word "Asia" may have been derived from the Assyrian *asu*, meaning East, or it may have been the local name given to the plains of Ephesus, later extended to encompass the land mass further east. Whatever the origin, it was used by the Greeks "to designate the lands situated to the east of their homeland" ("Asia" 128). The use of the terms "Asia" and "Asiatic" (later "Asian") functioned less to accurately identify or explain a more or less homogenous group than to consolidate the notion of "Europe" on the basis of the latter's cultural homogeneity and difference from "non-European." The inversality of "Asia" with Europe is rendered historically significant if one considers that in the fifth century B.C. Herodotus provides accounts of rivalry between Europe and Asia, albeit within a much more limited context than one normally would assume when speaking of the two continents today (Thomson 426).

Of course, Chaudhuri tells us, "besides being non-European, Asia is also non-African, non-American and so on"; but significantly, "there is a sequence of exclusions of which non-European comes first" (22–23). Derived from the principles of contradiction and isomorphic mapping, "Asia" assumes in the European imagination the structural unity thought to belong to the first category, "Europe." Meanwhile, encyclopedia entries on "Asia" routinely suggest that there are multiple Asias, that it is impossible to generate a classificatory system adequate to cope with the heterogeneity of Asia, that it is more a terminological convention than a homogeneous continent, that the term is of marginal worth to serious scholars, and that it is best studied in its very different parts.[3] But, of course, one might argue, every such name is a mental construct, so why quarrel with map names? The genealogy and spirit of these usages, one responds, have had widespread ramifications in the annals of cultural history. The production of a-history [sic] is the issue under contention here. The examination in the latter half of this century of the self/other dichotomy in a great deal of postmodern, feminist, and minority discourse has served as clear-sighted recognition of the uses to which such a-historical isomorphism has been put, particularly in the context of colonialism.[4]

This discussion would be pointless if it did not explore the concomitant notion of "l'idée européenne"; it would be futile if one did not remember that "all the continents are conceptual constructs, but only Europe was not first perceived and named by outsiders. "Europa," as the more learned of the ancient Greeks first conceived it, stood in sharp contrast to both Asia and Libya" ("Europe" *The New Encyclopaedia* 522). Interestingly, while encyclopedias categorize discussions on Asia in spatial terms (dividing it according to geographic regions that are to be considered more or less culturally contiguous, however qualified this assertion might be), Europe is treated in chronological and temporal terms to suggest a progressive narrative marked by dynamic change. It is the totality of its cultural heritage that is to separate Europe from its lesser "counterparts." The notion of a unified Europe has persisted throughout both ancient and modern history, powered in the former period by vigorous empire building and in the latter by the pervasive influence of Christianity; more recently, stemming in part from the anxiety generated by the economic and political dwarfing of European nations when contrasted with the United States, Japan, and other mushrooming powerhouses in the erstwhile Third World, the idea has been resuscitated with renewed vigor. The idea of Europe necessarily raises the question of contrast and comparison, of its own cohesive superiority to others' lesser cultures; as expressed in French in the *Encyclopaedia Universalis*: "l'idée européenne . . . [evoque] le problème de savoir si . . . il n'existe pas une 'communauté supérieure' distinguant des continents massifs qui, de près ou de loin, l'entourent" ("Europe" 36).

My discussion of the "idea of Europe" has not taken into account the heterogeneity that inevitably exists in any hypothetical conglomerate; this is not so much because it is difficult to find but rather that *Europe* does not see the fractures that threaten its sense of a unified whole or the "16 million non-white Europeans who reside in Europe" and continue to be excluded from it (Alibhai, quoted in Reiss 19).[5] The variations that have existed over time and those being introduced by new immigration are still measured against a congealed sense of "Europeanness." The extension of "l'esprit européenne" to include its newest partner, the United States, completes the grand Western narrative that distinguishes itself by differentiating itself from formulated constructs like "non-Western," which are as intellectually vague and geographically imprecise as "Asia" and "the Orient." This, then, is the pseudonymic and paleonymic history of the names Asians employ to counter the very tendencies that generated them in the first place. This is the threshold obscured and made invisible in the hunger for consolidation. Those who pose "Asian" identity in opposition to the West *without* a sense of its conflicted and contradictory overtones not only purchase the false homogeneity conferred upon them but also fail to make "West-ness" visible as a construct—a far greater challenge and one that has never been seriously attempted in the context of self-affirmation narratives by cultural Others resident in the West.

While one is busy conceiving of memory and identity as a set of kinetic transformations that will contour and flesh out the invisible and relegated Other in affirming an inclusive "Asian American" identity, it is important to be aware of the static structuralism, implicit in the above-mentioned formations, that has permitted this discussion in the first place. To fail to recognize this is to deny the historic roots of contemporary problems of selective differentiation and undifferentiation.[6] To acknowledge this is to teach ourselves to examine more closely the principles by which we organize in the interest of better understanding and representing ourselves, while illuminating that what is also validated in positing Asian American identity is the empty projection of a prior identity. The chain of validation suggested in embracing further abstractions like "South Asian" and "East Indian" must also be confronted and dealt with, as must the enthusiastic acceptance of the concept of identity, which is generally thought to be peculiar to the modern Western world. Misnaming and preoccupation with identities that arise from misnaming should both be cause for concern for those attempting to make Asian American studies useful. It is tempting to wander off here into a discussion of the conceptual and transactional misunderstandings occasioned by other accidents of history—the misnaming of the native tribes of the Americas as "Indian," or the synonymification of "American" with the United States, but I will confine myself to the observation that pseudonymy functions as a potent metaphor for the a-historicizing of non-Western cultures by the West. The collusion of the non-Western world in these ventures cannot be allowed to pass unnoticed. Suffice it to say for our discussion that it is one thing to appropriate strategy consciously and another to lapse into it because it is already available. Put in their historical place, the categories available to us can be investigated to see whom they best serve. The more recent history of the usage of "Asian" as a denominator in the United States might suggest that it may have served a purpose similar to its earlier imperialist one of clumping, when convenient, and denying homogeneity or promoting division when such a "cluster" threatened to become potent and combative. The latter is an issue I will address at length later; it may be useful first to explore the principles used by groups at the center and the margin to constitute notions of identity.

All categories depend on the principle of organization; in the context of this discussion, it is necessary to examine the bases and assumptions of coalitional identity formations. Chaudhuri's invocation of set theory in his discussions on Asia before Europe might be valuable here. Georg Cantor's conception of set theory relied on the fundamental principles of differentiation, integration, and the principle of ordering or succession. The derivation of a set was, however, so enormously complex, and the search for solutions so difficult, that Cantor went insane.[7] Bertrand Russell, who subsequently continued Cantor's analysis, came to the conclusion that intuitive notions of class, sets, truth, and so forth, were, in fact, self-contradictory. Identitarian grouping, however, demands a moment of stasis, of acceptance, however apologetic, of essentialist typology, even as the group itself is struggling against it. What, then, is to be done with our analytical methods and our ideological and political quests if we are to keep our wits about us? It would be presumptuous to suggest an answer, but perhaps not unreasonable to advocate a method of coping with the numerous possibilities that confront us. In the process of systematically investigating the shifts and transformations, the continuities and ruptures in narratives of identity in general, and Asian American identity in particular, one may find, if not the answer, then at least a way of engaging contemporary issues meaningfully.

The overwhelmingly "nationalist" overtones of identity, enunciated in temporal (historical) and spatial (geographical) terms, keep returning us to national roots. "China" thus precedes the hyphenated construct "Chinese-American" (even when the hyphen is suppressed, its trace remains as the sign of hegemonic notions of national identity posing an implicit challenge to the right side of the hyphen). "Asian American," on the other hand, invokes an extranational compendious identity relying on geographical contiguities even if the construct, properly speaking, is more a conglomerate than a union. This set, in turn, is supposedly encircled by the set "American" on some occasions and "Asian" on others. "Asian American," however, is a set that is both inside and outside these sets and shuttles between these positions while sometimes overlapping partially with either or both. The multiplicity of possible affiliations, and the impact of chosen positions on the state of activism in United States, have been noted by many cultural scholars. In "Patriotism and Its Futures," Arjun Appadurai suggests that "we are in the process of moving to a global order in which the nation-state has almost become obsolete and other formations for allegiance and identity have taken its place" (421). The world itself, he would further contend, is becoming postnational and diasporic (423). Appadurai says the

> formula of hyphenation . . . is reaching the point of saturation, and the right-hand side of the hyphen [as in Asian-American] can barely contain the unruliness of the left-hand side. . . . The idea of the nation flourishes transnationally. Safe from the depredations of their home states, diasporic communities become doubly loyal to their nations of origin and thus ambivalent about their loyalty to America. (424)

The projection of an Asian identity based on national origin but at the same time transcending it to secure collective leverage is a highly complex maneuver. As Sau-ling Wong has noted, a "larger pan-Asian identity has to be *voluntarily adopted* and highly *context-sensitive* in order to work" (6). It may, therefore, be useful to examine the category of "Asian" to assess the remarkable relevance of Wong's observation.

Even cursory scholarship on "Asia" recognizes that a holistic notion of "Asia" is an agglomerate rather than an aggregate of its parts, even if usage and repetition have, over time, conjured up a sense of "Asian-ness." Relative homogeneity can be manufactured in "Asia's" constitutive parts if one applies exclusive organizational principles. Sinitic Asia might then constitute one category, based on relation to or the influence of the Chinese. Within this group, one might argue for more sameness than difference based on a selective principle. The ethnolinguistic mosaic of Southeast Asia might thus be ignored in favor of grouping based on shared climatic features and the remarkable heterogeneity of South Asia reconciled by selective cultural, political, or social principles or even the fact that "geographically, all these countries [traditionally part of the set, "South Asia"] constitute one inseparable natural region and reflects [*sic*] certain cultural identities" (Vidyarthi 1). One might then try to speculate on the number of sets that might be formulated if one varied the organizing principles and cross-fertilized them in various permutations—this would yield the layered and shifting narratives of class, gender, and social placement based on sexual orientation, religious preferences, and personal human capital. Theories of the Other have, in fact, devoted themselves in recent years to a version of the method being suggested above in their struggle against homogenizing tendencies, however benevolent. Keeping in mind that a narrative of identity based on gender, race, nationality, or geographic origin favors certain selective principles over others, one might suggest that the organizational principles used should be of paramount importance. Since identity is contingent and discursive, the context-sensitivity Wong advocates must be the mainstay of Asian American activism; this will require, of course, the ability to recognize when a set is in the process of reconfiguring and why.

A method that embraces a dynamic view of human relations can help us understand how grouping and self-grouping take place despite inconsistencies in classificatory principles as well as the extent to which such agglutination holds when based on these principles. Quite apart from the maelstrom that is Asian history, the history of "Asian" presence in the United States reveals the complexity of the task that faces us in the attempt to close visible gaps. What follows is a brief account of "Asian America" to retrieve material for contemporary purposes. Painstakingly researched and exhaustive histories of Asian Americans are available for those interested in the far greater detail than is intended for my purposes here.[8] I will confine myself to surveying it in broad strokes in order to suggest that the gaps we are seeking to bridge have a long and complex history not only in the Asian but also in the American context as well. Along with a history of divisive politics, superficial conflations of Asian American groups in popular perception and public policy—the denial of differences when expedient, in other words—moreover, can be particularly instructive for us as we attempt to negotiate the challenge of community building while remaining attentive to differences, fissures, and gaps.

In very general terms, an Asian coalition of any kind was thwarted in the early phase by several factors. Not only did the Asians bring to this continent a history of intra-Asian rivalries from their premigration days (the contentious interactions between Korea and China and then Japan for instance, or those between Japan and China, or China and India), but management policies employed in dealing with the workforce in Hawaii and the mainland fostered originary differences while creating new ones.[9] If small measures of cooperation among laborers to dupe their white overseers were common, competitive antagonism between the groups was no less so. Visible resistance occurred, but it was usually organized based on the immigrants' countries of origin.[10] The solitary instance of interethnic unity recorded by Ronald Takaki in a joint 1946 strike in Hawaii by Asian and other immigrants is all too eloquent testimony to the provisionality of a unified Asian American set.[11] What strikes one now, perhaps, with the sobriety of distance and the luxury of detachment as a uniquely unifying experience breaks apart readily to reveal overlapping, even mutually exclusive, sets that asserted themselves beyond any cohesive one that might have better served the political and economic needs of early Asian American immigrants.

Neither the inability of various Asian groups to find common cause across ethnic boundaries in this early phase nor the manipulation of their differences by employers, however, prevented them from being perceived as a fairly undifferentiated mass. When convenient, differences among groups were ignored to create the illusion of an amorphous Asian menace to mainstream society.[12] This serviceably contradictory strategy is one that we would do well to keep in mind when gauging the context in which the term "Asian American" is deployed today if we are to avoid the danger of coalition being misread as conflation or difference as implacable division.

Those of us invested in a responsive, responsible Asian American coalition must not forget the checkered history in which the politics of identity was used against our interests. Nor can we afford to ignore the fact that identitarian grouping can be a double-edged sword that must be carefully wielded. Given the divisions between the different categories of "Asian," both those that were endemic and those that were planted and fostered, it becomes somewhat difficult to assert the natural unity of the Asian American construct. Too, given the persistently unequal numerical spread and influence, how can one insist on a natural pan-Asian set or bristle at the absence of South Asians from the construct "Asian American" both in Asian American Studies and in the popular imagination? The recent call for inclusivity, of which this collection is one representation, draws our attention to some discomfort about developing hegemonies within Asian American Studies. Insisting that "South Asian" is also "Asian" invokes two modalities: one that asserts that "South Asian" is a distinct category with identifiably homogenizing qualities (itself a problematic notion), and another that effaces disparate peoples in the interest of an abstract grouping based on largely geographical nomenclature. Inserting this subset also assumes a prior, unconflicted Asian American set, in turn preceded by the set "Asian." We are confronted, then, with several layers of inconsistency in positing a unified set.

But such a set did configure itself despite the odds; an Asian American coalition did begin to develop in the 1960s. Before we move into the need for contemporary reconfigurations, we might study the circumstances of its earliest emergence. A convergence of factors contributed to the gradual bridging of many of the gaps that might have seemed insurmountable at first. The success of similar integrationist moves—the African American and the feminist movements, the belief that it is better to fight together than to fight alone, the call for nonracist education in the era of anti-Vietnam and civil rights protests, and the promise of previously denied political and economic access from such moves surface as some of the obvious reasons for the affirmation of Asian American solidarity in 1960s.

A new shared history had by then had time to develop to supplant the divided histories elided in the category "Asian." Social historians have noted that the post–World War II years constitute a watershed of sorts in the history of race relations in the United States.[13] Arthur Schlesinger Jr. contends that "if the war did not end American racism, at least it drove much racial bigotry underground. The rethinking of racial issues challenged the conscience of the majority and raised the consciousness of minorities" (40). The turning point in Asian American activism is marked by the appearance, in the interwar years, of "a sizable American-born generation"; "on the eve of World War II, among the Chinese, Japanese, and Koreans, second-generation Americans of Asian ancestry finally outnumbered their immigrant parents" (Chan 103; 118). First-generation immigrants now had to abandon "sojourner" stances and face the issue of belonging, while their children, educated in American public schools and instructed in the rights, privileges, and duties of citizenship "found themselves no better off than their parents" (115). Distanced, if not delinked, from national origins except in the cultural imaginary sustained through parental ties, "as more and more American-born Asians grew to adulthood, some among them began to see the need for collective action" (117). Recognizing "that group solidarity is a prerequisite for political power," Asians were finally learning the potential of coalitionism (Wei 271). The easily perceptible differences among the original immigrants could now be submerged in the awareness of the need for political visibility. As Chan points out, bureaucratic convenience as much as political activism served to increase the currency of this grouping: "The term *Asian American* has political and bureaucratic origins. Young activists in the 1960s popularized it in order to emphasize the commonality among the different groups of Asian Americans, while government agencies adopted it because they found it convenient to lump together the various Asian groups and people from the Pacific Islands as *Asian Pacific Americans*" (Chan xvi). Such conflation by governmental agencies not only recalls earlier erasures of difference among Asians when deemed convenient but also predicates the reactionary use to which such grouping could be put in the future.

In her introduction to a South Asian American Studies bibliography, Rosane Rocher observes that a 1976 collection on the Asian American experience included a piece on "The Forgotten Asian Americans: The East Indian Community in the United States." "Twenty years later," she continues, "it remains the case that the Indian American experience in the United States has received less attention than that of some other Asian Americans" (64).[14] Jane Singh's foreword to *Our Feet Walk the Sky: Women of the South Asian Diaspora*, a 1993 publication, underscores the same problem: "As one of the least studied groups in the United States, people of South Asian origin have been overlooked by historians and social scientists as well as by scholars of Ethnic and Women's Studies" (vii–vii).

Such omissions, however, are best understood in light of our historical legacy. It is not accidental that mention of the word "Asian" conjures up in the American mind a Far Eastern Asian rather than South Asian presence. In numbers and historical primogeniture, the former have always played a more significant role in this country, largely because of geographical proximity between countries on the Pacific ocean and the American West. In the second half of the nineteenth century, large numbers of Chinese *gastarbeiters* came into the country, to be joined by successive waves of Japanese, Korean, and Filipino sojourners. In the extremely small window of opportunity available to them before the 1924 quota-based legislation was passed, only 6,400 Asian Indians came to America as opposed to about 430,000 Chinese, 380,000 Japanese, and 150,000 Filipinos (Takaki 62; 65).[15] The South Asian component of "Asian America" remained relatively insignificant until the floodgates opened in 1965, when race, religion, and nationality were eliminated as criteria for immigration and the quota system in the United States was phased out.[16] Because a pan-Asian identity was forged under local pressures, it is not surprising that South Asian Americans would need to cycle through a gestation period before moving toward a South Asian or Asian identity.

A recent count of various constituencies suggests some of the reasons for the current state of Asian American identity, with certain groups much more dominant than others. At last count, of the 6,908,638 individuals of Asian ancestry, Asian Indians numbered a mere 815,447, or a mere 11.8 percent.[17] If one added the number of other South Asians (from Bangladesh, Burma, Pakistan, and Sri Lanka—as made available by the U.S. Census), the percentage creeps up to 13.4, with the figures totaling 925,803. It is not surprising that the nations of South Asia have come together in the interest of gaining visibility, despite remarkable differences, chiefly in religion and political structure. The dominance of India within this construct has been evident both to those of Indian and non-Indian extraction; the analogous dominance of the Chinese within the Asian American construct might be explained by their greater numbers since they total 1,645,472, and thus account for 23 percent of the Asian population, although Filipino Americans are close behind. "By the year 2000 the Filipino body count will surpass the two million mark" to total nearly 21 percent of all Asians in the United States.[18] The East Asian component together adds up to almost 84 percent of the total Asian population in the United States, helping to explain the historic reasons for the synonymity of Asian with East Asian in the history of race relations in the United States. Also significant here are figures on the geographical spread of Asian Americans across the country, the East Asians among them being largely concentrated on, though certainly not restricted to, the West Coast. This proximity and a continuing history from the earliest immigration of these ethnic groups to Hawaii and the Pacific Coast to the present day have certainly also contributed to their prominence in Asian American activism.[19]

Although numbers or timing alone are hardly the only significant factors in an examination of coalitional politics or visible gaps in the Asian American fabric, both have played a crucial role in the current gaps in Asian America. Because they have come to this country in substantial numbers only since 1965 or so, South Asians, like other new immigrants, face the relative absence of a continuous history that promotes a forgetting of histories different from the present. For the same reason, many South Asians, particularly those who came in the later phase, are apt to maintain stronger ties to the homeland and to homeland concerns—the latter might include the relatively "fresh" memory of antagonistic relations with other Asian countries, discouraging them from perceiving members from those countries as their fellows in the American context.[20] At the same time, diasporic groups may discover or find reinforced narrower communal and linguistic identities. This is particularly true of Asian Indians who often cling to a more regional sense of identity. Shifting between multiple and themselves dynamic identities, South Asians, again like many other minority groups, "seek to define both their historical legacies and their present geographic and social realities" (133).[21]

The limited presence of South Asians on the Asian American scene is largely a function of numerical imbalances, but it is also attributable to a complex variety of other factors as well. Demographic histories indicate clearly the paucity of subcontinental Asians in the United States till 1965. But even in later years, while their presence has made itself known in various ways in public and social life as well as in the field of education, South Asians have been slow to assume their place within Asian America as such.[22] There are several possible explanations for the lower level of political involvement of South Asians as compared with their fellow Asians. Perhaps because of their newer status in the States or because of ways of thinking entrenched in a long colonial history, South Asians perceive themselves as very different from other peoples of color here. The historical conflation of "Oriental" with Asian and of Asian with East Asian also serves to consolidate this intransigent sense of difference from other Asians. Amritjit Singh observes in "African-Americans and the New Immigrants" that the diasporic South Asians have been heavily invested in projects directed toward homeland nationalisms of one kind or another—political, religious, ethnic, or regional. The net effect of these tendencies is to reinforce "national" or religious identities and impede any progress toward global citizenship or active participation in American life (96).[23]

He asks that South Asians cultivate an awareness of other ethnic histories in the United States as a necessary basis for interethnic coalitions. Pointing out that "new [South] Asian immigrants cannot become 'White,' so they seek overcompensation in real estate and material goods," Singh argues that many of them "make up for this lack of whiteness by acquiring a consciousness which is often as 'White' and assimilationist and 'mainstream' as that of most whites" (100). The class makeup of a large number of South Asians is an important factor here. The early wave of South Asian immigrants would have belonged, barring a small number of middle-class students, elites, and political refugees, to the laboring and farming class without the advantage of much education (Sheth 171).[24] Conversely, the profile of the second wave of South Asian immigrants suggests that "they were highly educated, English-speaking, had come to the United States for economic reasons, and had immigrated together as a family."[25] Sheth comments that "the new Indian immigrants consist mainly of college-educated, urban, middle-class professional young men and women of religious, regional, and linguistic diversity (169). Although the earlier influx was from rural areas, "post-1965 Indian immigrants have generally come from large cities in all parts of India," and "most of them are fluent in English" (Sheth 174). Mazumdar, speculating on the reasons for interethnic solidarity among South Asians and blacks in Britain, South Africa, and to some extent, Canada, suggests that "this coalition may have been more possible because South Asians in these countries are, by and large, also members of the working class. In the United States, in contrast, where the urban professional bourgeoisie still are numerically the larger percentage, it is too early to tell whether segments of the South Asians in the United States will become sufficiently politicized to form similar alliances with blacks and other people of color" ("Race" 36). Although a shared class background is not the only criterion for finding common ground, the early history of Asian American activism suggests that it can be a potent factor at least in the initial stages.

As the preceding discussion suggests, if South Asian invisibility in Asian American politics and activism is due in part to the group's own failure to make connections, the reasons are also historical. I have not so far mentioned the concomitant failure of traditionally dominant groups among Asian Americans to seek more aggressively the inclusion of newer or numerically weaker groups. The twin failures of both groups and the presence of other historical factors emblematically underscore the difficulties in developing a responsible pan-Asian coalition.

The ideological rifts between South Asians and more established activist groups in the United States suggest the various forms of disconnection from local politics and culture not only in the case of South Asian Americans but also among segments of other minority groups: the temporary and selective loyalties of permanent residents, many of them from India, who long to return to their "homes" and always defer commitment to local concerns; the exclusive preoccupation with homeland nationalism and the retreat into ethnic ghettoes among immigrants ill-equipped financially and otherwise to face the challenges outside; the self-styled segregation of the economically advantaged and a blindness to those in need; as well as the difficulty in gaining a forum for expression among more dominant groups.[26] Moreover, since they are a minority among minorities, the relative invisibility of South Asians should alert us to the similar relegation of other such groups like the Vietnamese, Khmer (Cambodian), lowland Lao, Hmong, Mien, and other Laotian and Vietnamese highlanders who lack the visibility guaranteed by large numbers and longer histories. These fractures exemplify the larger fractures in the social fabric of the country, but they need not, and do not, in fact, prevent coalitional social and political action. The presence of gaps and differences has not thwarted the persistent quest for a pan-Asian coalition. The motivating factors for this desire thirty years after it first surfaced, albeit with many new constituents, are the lingering problems of prejudice and feelings of *unheimlichkeit* among nonwhite immigrants despite attempts at economic, if not cultural, assimilationalism.

In a discussion on the reasons why "South Asianism" was being mobilized in Anglo-America in recent years, Mary Vasudeva and I listed the following in the introductory chapter of our collection *Between the Lines: South Asians and Postcoloniality*:

> to gain visibility in the socio-political arena; to speak against racism and misrepresentation from a position of collectivity; to initiate social action for the economically depressed and systemically alienated among the group; to open up an avenue for the exploration of lost or receding cultural ties with the country of origin; to provide a forum for expressing and investigating one's experiences and feelings of displacement, alienation, and other forms of cultural anxiety; as well as to gain a more equal footing, perhaps even an advantage, in terms of market value and economic opportunity. (7)

Many of the same reasons might be said to characterize most ethnic coalitions, and it is clear that some of these have to do with the public face of a group while others address more internal needs. Forged under the pressure of local contexts and stimuli, identity in this sense is always fluidly constituted. Xenophobia in the new homeland and the struggle for economic ground and political visibility, as much as anxiety at the loss of tradition, offer incentives for seeking coalition. Often the reasons merge into one another and are not always distinguishable from one another. Through the operation of complex factors, new immigrants find themselves confronting Hobson's choice: simultaneously made to feel different and beginning to perceive the need to identify as separate from others, they are often obliged to take the identity they are given and try to reclaim and redefine it for productive purposes. Immigrants will thus form groups as a response to being grouped. The history of Asian American activism suggests that a more comprehensive sense of Asian identity became necessary as a defense against mainstream perceptions of the group as homogeneous and undifferentiated; the progression from a shared sense of political vulnerability in American life to the cultivation of racial pride as a result of being perceived as part of a racial collective thus occurs in an organic and concurrent manner.

Besides, newer Asian American immigrants tend to represent the academic and technological elite at home and abroad, and thus carry, along with second- and third-generation immigrants, a greater sense of entitlement than earlier generations of immigrants. Since "foreign-born Asian Americans," in fact, "now outnumber their native-born counterparts," and they enter the country with a greater degree of confidence on account of their superior credentials, they are more apt to want to fight for their rights and join up with their more experienced confrères (Nee and Sanders 78). The resurgence of identity politics also accounts for a boost in ethnicity and race-based strategies, and this resurgence, in turn, is partly attributable to the fact that although legislation following World War II seems uncharacteristically liberal and egalitarian in its treatment of minority races, racial lumping and divisive strategies still play a role in interethnic politics. On the one hand, nonwhite races are coalesced into one minority group when it comes to employment, funding, and cultural polarities; on the other, they are still being cast opposite one another. In a throwback to earlier strategy, the myth of "Asian American" as the model minority, for instance, which first surfaced in the mid-1960s and has since been challenged statistically and otherwise, has been used in recent years to criticize African American demands for more resources and support as well as to withhold funding for social service programs from those within the model minority group who do not match its composite profile.[27] Most significant, violence and antipathy against Asians remain abiding realities of American life. In other words, the need for concerted political and social action remains.

This is why in more recent years, South Asians, despite their newer status, internal divisions, and charges of apathy to local concerns, have begun to muster a political presence on the landscape of American cultural politics. The extent of South Asian presence might be gauged by the fact that "Asian Indians have started imprinting their culture on American schools, residential streets, and marketplaces" by giving Indian names to areas where they live or do business with the support of local politicians; they donate funds to universities, politicians, and hospitals "which help to increase their clout" (Sheth 176). "All but ignored between 1930 and 1965, the South Asians in the United States and Canada are now starting to write and research their own social and historical role in North America's cultural mosaic" ("South Asians in North America" 11). The numerical growth in their ranks has already prompted the current call for South Asian participation by other Asian Americans and South Asian assertions of an Asian American identity. The heightened consciousness of South Asians might indeed propel them to seek wider coalition.[28]

The pan-Asian movement has gained considerable momentum, the struggle of less represented groups within the collectivity for a stronger voice is escalating, and efforts to construct a more inclusive and meaningful pan-Asian ethnicity are resurgent in light of an increasingly diversifying Asian American population and persistent racism. It is thus more important than ever to maintain a kaleidoscopic vision that can encompass past and present histories, relationality and individuality, sameness and difference. The issues of different migratory patterns, numerical inferiority, ideological schisms, and class differentials among all Asians must be openly addressed to better place them within the set being proposed. The relative economic disenfranchisement of certain groups within the aggregate (the Vietnamese, for instance) might be highlighted to prevent the kind of undifferentiation that characterizes mainstream perceptions of "Asian American" as economically privileged. Distinctions between the needs of older and newer immigrants might be carefully uncovered to better address the needs of both. The minimalization of Thai, Malay, and Indonesian presence in Asian America should also command our attention. In order to properly address gender-based needs, it is also necessary to confront the fact that reliance on national identity as a basis for political activism often eclipses the role of gender differences.

Most important, at least one of our perspectives on the viability of pan-Asianism should consider the much more sophisticated deployment of racial lumping in operation in the current climate of liberal multiculturalism. "When a cultural identity is thrust upon one because the center wants an identifiable margin," Gayatri Chakravorty Spivak reminds us, "claims for marginality assure validation from the center." [29] If official racial lumping was pursued for bureaucratic convenience in the 1960s, it seems now to have given way to the congratulatory rhetoric of identity and difference in the mainstream academic industry. As the cultural expressions of peoples of color are increasingly "celebrated" and disseminated through changing school and university curricula, it seems important to recall that if conflation can be used in some contexts for overtly racist purposes, its more benevolent face is not without its problems.

As I have been arguing in this essay, the Asian American coalition, forged as it was under historical pressures, involves elements of foisted choice. That it is foisted and nevertheless is a choice is a meaningful ambiguity to keep in mind. If we cannot discount the importance of a coercive dynamic that makes resistive coalition necessary, neither should we minimize the significance of responding to this pressure *in the terms defined by the dominant rather than dominated group*. Historically, resistance has been mounted in reactive rather than proactive ways. The victim must play the game according to rules instituted by the oppressor. The diasporic individual thus "discovers" the identity that he or she has already been given for purposes of containment and management. While this identity is reshaped and retooled for particular purposes, as might be evident in the remaking of "Oriental" as "Asian American" identity, or even in the use of a faux category like "Asia," it is nevertheless reliant on categories that cannot challenge completely the divisive and managerial ideology that produced them. A kaleidoscopic vision can allow us to recognize that if an oppressive history has obliged us to seek the same categories that were used to oppress, the new cultural politics must include measures of protest against them. Performance of categorical identity for strategic political purposes may indeed be unavoidable but cannot be the goal for the long term. Even as we use these categories to combat the problems of the moment, we cannot ignore the reification that is inherent in their deployment. Our goal ultimately must be to transcend the categories imposed by colonial and imperial hegemonies, to strive to be free of constructions that consolidate the power of the center by defining the margins. In this same vein, we must consider that ethnic coalitions based on the criterion of "sameness," however that might be defined, are also foundationally dependent on a declaration of difference—certainly from the dominant society, but from other minority groups as well. While groups like "Asian American" carve out their sociopolitical niches in Anglo-American cultural politics, they are also defining themselves within the same categorical grooves that have thwarted considerations of sameness with other minoritized groups. The net result of overreliance on such cultural identities is capitulation to diversionary politics that obscure the principles at stake, compound our complicity, and leave us vulnerable to manipulative constituencies. This danger is most visible in political arenas: "Social scientists are quick to remind us that ethnic voting behavior was and is important in American politics and often transcends class or regional lines" (Dinnerstein and Reimers 152). It seems gratuitous to point out that not all members of our tribe are our friends, nor those of others our natural enemies, but this is precisely the danger of coalitional grouping without careful examination of organizational criteria. Likewise, it may seem entirely too obvious, but perhaps therefore most easy to overlook, that in the face of persistent racism, the history of "Asian America" will tell us, it is not unnatural to define oneself away from the group most commonly targeted.

A principled activism requires that our responsibility to other minorities in this country be faced alongside our concerns as "Asian" minorities, that differences not be forgotten in our preoccupation with sameness,[30] that we distinguish among our various reasons for grouping,[31] and that our short-term and long-term objectives be considered together. A dynamic view of interethnic relations, the ability to nimbly spot moments when differences can and must be dissolved into a principled unity *for the moment*, the abjuration of easy dichotomies and too casually and unproblematically yoked coalitions, and the ability to keep in sight the ultimate goal of undoing categories designed to keep us in place—these are the materials that make for kaleidoscopic and futuristic vision.

ACKNOWLEDGMENTS

Some of the ideas developed in this essay originated in and are addressed in a 1993 interview I did of Gayatri Spivak which appeared in *Between the Lines: South Asians on Postcolonial Identity and Culture*, eds. Deepika Bahri and Mary Vasudeva.

NOTES

1. It would be well to acknowledge that a total capture of history is an impossibility. As David Lowenthal observes, "No historical account can recover the totality of any past event, because their content is virtually infinite. The most detailed historical narrative incorporates only a minute fraction of even the relevant past; the sheer pastness of the past precludes its total reconstruction" (214–15). As a "narrative," history becomes a repository of the artifacts of collective memory. There are other memories beyond the public and the collective, often cathected by social influences. That it may not be possible to retrieve them all should not prevent us from continuing to excavate what we can.

2. See Benedict Anderson, Thomas Butler, Paul Connerton, John R. Gillis, and Jacques Le Goff for discussions on this subject.

3. See *The New Encyclopaedia Britannica: Macropaedia, Collier's Encyclopaedia*, the *Encyclopaedia Americana*, and *Encyclopaedia Universalis*.

4. As Edward Said puts it, "Without examining Orientalism as a discourse one cannot possible understand the enormously systematic discipline by which European culture was able to manage—and even produce—the Orient politically, sociologically, militarily, ideologically, scientifically, and imaginatively during the post-Enlightenment period" (3); Richard Fung contends that "it is worth remembering that Asia is not in fact a natural entity but exists only in relation to notions of Europe and Africa developed in the West. These are political and economic demarcations closely tied to the colonial project" (163).

5. See Timothy J. Reiss for a discussion of the idea of Europe.

6. Karen Aguilar-San Juan reminds us that "there is no 'Asian essence,' no genetic quality that makes us inherently distinct from individuals of other races" and that "we should view our identity as Asian American as a product of a particular historical period and a myriad of economic and social events, and not a biological fact. So we are left with the task of both asserting race and *at the same time* challenging its categorization of people by skin color" (8).

7. Chaudhuri points out that "the search for solutions to intractable and impossibly difficult questions raised by his own work proved too much for Cantor and he became insane" (27).

8. See Sucheng Chan and Ronald Takaki for detailed and useful histories of Asian presence in the United States.

9. Plantation owners in Hawaii aggressively pursued a divisory policy in the recruitment and treatment of labor, housing different ethnic groups separately and often paying different wage rates to different nationalities for the same work, in addition to condoning interethnic riots. The sojourner status of early Asian immigrants would also have hindered any commitment to a burgeoning sense of solidarity; too, the active hostility of white Americans would have forced a group to eschew identification with the Asian group that functioned as the target *du jour* and to distance and separate itself carefully from it; the spontaneous retreat of minority groups into ethnic enclaves to prevent majority antagonism must have afforded the only measure of comfort and security. Divided by the majority, it would have seemed dangerous to gather for fear of inviting the same antagonism experienced by other minority groups played off against each other. Disunited by language, food habits, history, and cultural traditions, the members of the "Asian" contingent, the East Asian included, fulfilled, for the most part, their employers' expectations that diversity would ensure division. No significant coalitions among the groups themselves have been recorded in the first phase of Asian immigration, apart from extremely rare interethnic strikes arising from a provisional sense of common exploitation and a vague spirit of anticapitalism.

10. As Chan notes, "Asians in America have a long, though until recently unrecognized, tradition of engaging in political action, but they never did so on a publicly visible scale until the 1960s" (171). Chan cites several specific examples of organized labor resistance by Chinese, Japanese, and Filipino workers in Ha-

waii, for instance, but a unified interethnic revolt of any major proportions is conspicuous by its absence in the early history of Asian Americans.

11. A statement from the International Longshoremen's and Warehousemen's Union (ILWU) Territorial Sugar Negotiating Committee noted that this was the "first time in the history of Hawaii that a strike of sugar workers has been conducted where there has been no split among racial groups" (quoted in Takaki 409).

12. The Chinese could thus be lumped with the blacks and Asian Indians as morally inferior, or with native Indians as barbaric and in need of control; Asian Indians were lumped with other Asians as another version of the "yellow peril," while the Japanese could be dismissed as "Chinks," and Koreans and Chinese confused with "Japs." A recent instance of such confusion was the tragic murder of Chinese American Vincent Chin in Detroit by disgruntled White auto workers in 1982. See Omi and Winant, 181n. Expressed in more "innocuous" popular cultural forms—films and fiction—neo-anti-Japanese resentment in the wake of depressed economic conditions in the United States has the potential to instigate further tragedies of this sort.

13. Mazumdar notes in "Asian American Studies," "the year [1968] marked the crest of a worldwide struggle against racism, against capitalism, against bureaucratic socialism, struggles which exploded with the escalation of the Vietnam war" (39). See also Takaki, Chan, William Wei, Arthur M. Schlesinger Jr.

14. Rocher's conflation of "Indian" with "South Asian" is fairly common in South Asian discourse. While it undoubtedly points to the preponderance of "Indian" within the construct "South Asian," it should not be taken to imply an exclusion of other constituencies. See the bibliography contributed by Rosane Rocher to *Sagar: South Asia Graduate Research Journal* 2.1 (Spring 1995): 64–95. On the lack of attention to Indian and South Asian Americans, see also P. K. Nandi's "The World of an Invisible Minority: Pakistanis in America," *California Sociologists* 3 (1980): 143–65.

15. The scanty nature of early Asian Indian presence is catalogued by Bhardwaj and Rao in "Asian Indians in the United States: A Geographical Appraisal": "From 1820, when a solitary Indian was admitted to the United States, through the next half a century, fewer than ten Asian Indians arrived per year on average. . . . This trickle of Indians, all told, amounted to fewer than 700 over a period of 80 years from 1820 to 1900" (Bhardwaj and Rao 197).

16. See "South Asians in North America" in *South Asians in North America: An Annotated and Selected Bibliography,* Occasional Paper Series 14 (Berkeley, Calif.: Center for South and Southeast Asia Studies, 1988) 5–14.

17. Bureau of the Census. *1990 Census of Population: General Population Characteristics, United States.* (Washington, D.C., 1992).

18. See E. San Juan Jr. "The Predicament of Filipinos in the United States: 'Where Are You From? When Are You Going Back?'" 206.

19. The appearance of the earliest programs in Asian American Studies in West Coast universities because of this concentration has also had the effect of promoting such geographical concentration.

20. The Sino-Indian war of 1965 and a continuing history of confrontation with China might be an obvious example.

21. Calvin Reid, "Caught in Flux: Transatlantic Aesthetics in the Museum," *Transition: An International Review* 5.1 (Spring 1995): 131–39.

22. For information on the growing visibility of South Asian Americans see "South Asians in North America"; Manju Sheth's "Asian Indian Americans"; Arthur W. Helweg and Usha M. Helweg's *The Immigrant Success Story: East Indians;* and Jayjia Hsia's *Asian Americans in Higher Education and at Work.*

23. Deepika Bahri and Mary Vasudeva, eds., *Between the Lines: South Asians and Postcoloniality* (Philadelphia: Temple University Press, 1996) 93–110.

24. See also Takaki, and "South Asians in North America."

25. Amarpal K. Dhaliwal, "Gender at Work: the Renegotiation of Middle-class Womanhood in a South Asian-Owned Business" in *Reviewing Asian America: Locating Diversity*, edited by Wendy L. Ng, Soo-Young Chin, James S. Moy, and Gary Y. Okihiro (Pullman, Wash.: Washington State University Press, 1995), 75–85, 84n5.

26. The various "layers" of South Asian presence in the United States—the pre- and post-1965 immigrants, the various generations, the more- and the less-educated and well-trained professionally—indicate both the diversity that is characteristic of Asian Americans and the difficulty that lies in the path of building an inclusive Asian American coalition that can address and reflect all its constituencies.

27. See Chan, 167.

28. In New York City, where as many as 60 percent of cab drivers are new immigrants of South Asian origin, the potential for wide coalition as a powerful counter to police brutality has already brought together a significant Lease Drivers Coalition of the Committee Against Anti-Asian Violence. A show of this strength in the recent dismissal of charges against Islamabad-born Saleem Osman has been attributed to "community pressure" on the District Attorney's office to drop a racist and weak case. Osman, a staff organizer for the Lease Drivers Coalition, plans to continue his fight for justice while the committee has been active in protesting the "significant harassment and violence [toward cab drivers of Asian origin] at the hands of police" (19)."Charges Dropped: DA's Office Backs down under Community Pressure," *India Today* 9.10 (Aug. 1995): 19.

29. *Outside in the Teaching Machine, 55.*

30. I quote here Rita Chaudhry Sethi's eloquent and analogous sentiment: "If we are to achieve a community, we must educate ourselves about our common denominator as well as our different histories and struggles. Ranking and diminishing relative subjugation and discrimination will only subvert our goal of unity" (237).

31. Mary C. Waters defines symbolic ethnicity as "subjective identity invoked at will" (7) and suggests that it persists "because of its ideological 'fit' with racist beliefs" (147), while Karen Aguilar-San Juan warns that "we often make the dangerous mistake of equating the process of acquainting ourselves with our ethnic, linguistic, religious, or historic roots with activism against racism" (8).

Works Cited

Aguilar-San Juan, Karen. "Linking the Issues: From Identity to Activism." In *The State of Asian America: Activism and Resistance in the 1990s,* edited by Karen Aguilar-San Juan. Boston: South End Press, 1994, 1–15.

Anderson, Benedict. *Imagined Communities: Reflections on the Origin and Spread of Nationalism.* New York: Verso, 1991.

Appadurai, Arjun. "Patriotism and Its Futures." *Public Culture* 5.3 (1993): 411–29.

"Asia." *The New Encyclopaedia Britannica: Macropaedia.* 1994 ed.

Bahri, Deepika, and Mary Vasudeva, eds. Introd. *Between the Lines: South Asians on Postcolonial Identity and Culture.* Philadelphia: Temple University Press, 1996.

Bhardwaj, Surinder M., and Madhusudana Rao. "Asian Indians in the United States: A Geographical Appraisal." In *South Asians Overseas: Migration and Ethnicity,* edited by Colin Clarke, Ceri Peach, and Steven Vertovec. Cambridge: Cambridge University Press, 1990, 197–217.

Butler, Thomas, ed. *Memory: History, Culture and the Mind.* Oxford: Basil Blackwell, 1989.

Chan, Sucheng. *Asian Americans: An Interpretive History.* Boston: Twayne, 1991.

Chaudhuri, K. N. *Asia Before Europe: Economy and Civilization of the Indian Ocean from the Rise of Islam to 1750.* Cambridge: Cambridge University Press, 1990.

Connerton, Paul. *How Societies Remember.* Cambridge: Cambridge University Press, 1989.

Dinnerstein, Leonard, and David M. Reimers. *Ethnic Americans: A History of Immigration and Assimilation.* New York: Dodd, Mead & Co., 1975.

"Europe." *Encyclopaedia Universalis.* 1993 ed.

"Europe." *The New Encyclopaedia Britannica: Macropaedia.* 1994 ed.

Fung, Richard. "Seeing Yellow: Asian Identities in Film and video." *The State of Asian America: Activism and Resistance in the 1990s.* Ed. Karen Aguilar-San Juan. Boston: South End Press, 1994, 161–71.

Gillis, John R., ed. *Commemorations: The Politics of National Identity.* Princeton, N.J.: Princeton University Press, 1994.

Helweg, Arthur W., and Usha M. Helweg. *The Immigrant Success Story: East Indians.* Philadelphia: University of Pennsylvania Press, 1990.

Hess, Gary R. "The Asian Indian Immigrants in the United States: The Early Phase, 1900–65." In *From India to America: A Brief History of Immigration; Problems of Discrimination; Admission and Assimilation,* edited by S. Chandrasekhar. La Jolla, Calif.: Population Review, 1982.

Hsia, Jayjia. *Asian Americans in Higher Education and at Work.* Hillsdale, N.J.: Erlbaum, 1988.

Jensen, Joan. *Passage from India: Asian Indian Immigrants in North America.* New Haven: Yale University Press, 1988.

Le Goff, Jacques. *History and Memory.* Translated by Steven Rendall and Elizabeth Clamon. New York: Columbia University Press, 1992.

Lowenthal, David. *The Past Is a Foreign Country.* Cambridge: Cambridge University Press, 1985.

Mazumdar, Sucheta. "Asian American Studies and Asian Studies: Rethinking Roots." In *Asian Americans: Comparative and Global Perspectives,* edited by Shirley Hune et al. Pullman, Wash.: Washington University Press, 1991. 29–44.

———. "Race and Racism: South Asians in the United States." In *Frontiers of Asian American Studies: Writing, Research, and Commentary,* edited by Gail M. Nomura et al. Pullman, Wash.: Washington University Press, 1989, 25–38.

Nee, Victor, and Jimy Sanders. "The Road to Parity: Determinants of the Socioeconomic Achievements of Asian Americans." In *Ethnicity and Race in the USA: Toward the Twenty-First Century,* edited by Richard D. Alba. New York: Routledge, 1989.

Omi, Michael, and Howard Winant. *Racial Formation in the United States from the 1960s to the 1980s.* New York: Routledge, 1986.

Radhakrishnan, R. "Is the Ethnic 'Authentic' in the Diaspora?" In *The State of Asian America: Activism and Resistance in the 1990s,* edited by Karen Aguilar-San Juan. Boston: South End Press, 1994, 219–33.

Reiss, Timothy J. "Introduction: Literature and the Idea of Europe." *PMLA* 108: 1 (Jan. 1993): 14–29.

Russell, Bertrand. *My Philosophical Development.* London: Allen and Unwin, 1959.

Said, Edward W. *Orientalism.* 1978. New York: Vintage-Random, 1979.

San Juan, E., Jr. "The Predicament of Filipinos in the United States: 'Where Are You From? When Are You Going Back?'" In *The State of Asian America,* edited by Karen Aguilar-San Juan. Boston: South End Press, 1994, 206.

Schlesinger, Arthur M., Jr. *The Disunity of America: Reflections on a Multicultural Society.* New York: Norton, 1992.

Sethi, Rita Chaudhry. "Smells like Racism: A Plan for Mobilizing against Anti-Asian Bias." In *The State of Asian America: Activism and Resistance in the 1990s,* edited by Karen Aguilar-San Juan. Boston: South End Press, 1994. 235–50.

Sheth, Manju. "Asian Indian Americans." In *Asian Americans: Contemporary Trends and Issues,* edited by Pyong Gap Min. Thousand Oaks, Calif.: Sage, 1995, 169–98.

Singh, Amritjit. "African-Americans and New Immigrants." In *Between the Lines: South Asians on Postcoloniality,* edited by Deepika Bahri and Mary Vasudeva. Philadelphia: Temple University Press, 1996, 93–110.

"South Asians in North America." In *South Asians in North America: An Annotated and Selected Bibliography,* edited by Jane Singh et al. Occasional Paper Series 14. Berkeley: Center for South and Southeast Asia Studies, 1988. 5–14.

Spivak, Gayatri Chakravorty. *Outside in the Teaching Machine.* New York: Routledge, 1993.

Takaki, Ronald. *Strangers from a Different Shore: A History of Asian Americans.* New York: Penguin, 1989.

Thomson, David. "Europe." *Collier's Encyclopedia.* 1994 ed.

Vidyarthi, L. P. *South Asian Culture: An Anthropological Perspective*. Delhi: Oriental, 1976.

Waters, Mary C. *Ethnic Options: Choosing Identities in America*. Berkeley: University of California Press, 1990.

Wei, William. *The Asian American Movement*. Philadelphia: Temple University Press, 1993.

West, Cornel. *Race Matters*. Boston: Beacon, 1993.

Wong, Sau-ling Cynthia. Introduction to *Reading Asian American Literature*. Princeton, N.J.: Princeton University Press, 1993, 1–17.

LAVINA DHINGRA SHANKAR

2   The Limits of (South Asian) Names and Labels

Postcolonial or Asian American?

SOUTH ASIAN immigrants have had difficulties associated with being named and with naming themselves ever since their arrival in North America in the eighteenth century. In various contexts they have been called, or have called themselves, East Indians, Asian Indians, Caucasians, Dark Aryans, Hindoos or Hindus, Pakis, Indo-Paks, Indian Subcontinentals, Indo-Americans, and South Asians, among other appellations.

This essay explores the complex issue of South Asians' constant renaming and, specifically, the discrepancies between their "postcolonial" and "Asian American" identifications within literary and cultural studies.[1] By raising broad theoretical questions, this chapter examines the significance and the inherent problems of naming, especially within North American academic discourse. What follows is an investigation of how the act of naming involves political and strategic choices—both by minority writers and critics and the mainstream academy, which is governed by larger ideological and political apparatuses. Specifically, the essay analyzes the positioning of two women, Gayatri Chakravorty Spivak and Bharati Mukherjee, who are among the best-known South Asians in American literary circles, to illustrate the complications surrounding nomenclature. This article does not examine Spivak's or Mukherjee's oeuvre per se. But rather, it views their (self-)representation in the American academy as epitomizing the problematics of the naming, visibility, and lack of recognition of South Asian Americans.

South Asian Americans' religious, racial, geographical, and nationalist nomenclatures have historically often been conflated; thus there have been numerous gaps between onomastics, or the issues surrounding the origins of names for South Asian Americans, and their group identification as Asian Americans. H. Brett Melendy provides a history of the 1911 definition of "Hindus" in the United States and clarifies his own usage of the term "East Indians." The United States Immigration Commission's 1911 *Dictionary of Races or Peoples* broadly defined an "East Indian as any native of the East Indies . . . from the inhabitants of the Philippines to the

Aryans of India" (Melendy, 186). Of course, the definition did not take into consideration the fact that Filipinos were being wrongly categorized as Indian, and that not all Indians were "Aryan." According to the commission, any native of India was called "Hindu," even though the term had originally applied to "Aryans" from northern India (186). Furthermore, the term "Hindu" was a misnomer since the religious name referred to a group in the United States most of whom, in the early part of the twentieth century, were not Hindus, but Sikhs. Simultaneously, Indian Parsees (a group of adherents to Zoroastrianism) were viewed as "white" and of the "Aryan race" (217–19).[2] As these examples reveal, the problems of naming Indian subcontinentals remained unresolved in the early twentieth century and have continued until the present.

Sharon M. Lee's essay "Racial Classifications in the U.S. Census: 1890–1990" (1993) provides the census categorization table documenting that the 1930 and 1940 census added "Hindus" to the classifications; the 1950 census returned South Asians to their earlier designation as "Whites," converted them to "Other" in 1960 and 1970, "Asian Indian" in 1980, and "Asian and Pacific Islander" in 1990 (78). Yen Le Espiritu's essay "Census Classification: The Politics of Ethnic Enumeration" (1992) recounts the many transformations of census classification for South Asian Americans. In the 1970 census, "Asian Indians" were first identified as "Other" and then reclassified as "Whites" to return to the 1950 definition. But in 1974, the Association of Indians in America (AIA) lobbied to be categorized as "Asian American," so that they could claim economic benefits as minorities (124–25). This decision followed Manoranjan Dutta's recommendation at a congressional hearing that Indians from Asia be reclassified as "Asian" rather than as "Whites" (125).

Manoranjan Dutta himself clarifies the adoption of the category "Asian Indian" in the 1980 U.S. Census in his essay "Asian Indian Americans: Search for an Economic Profile." He explains that terms such as "Indic, South Asian, East Indian, Hindustani" were also considered, but that "Indian" was chosen to reflect the majority of the population from South Asia (77). Dutta's own nationalist bias as an Indian and his easy acceptance of representation by majority status is ironically revealed. In co-opting the term "Indian," he immediately effaces the visibility of other South Asian "minorities" such as the Pakistanis, Bangladeshis, Sri Lankans, Nepalese, and Bhutanese. As these historical details reveal, the various constituencies involved in naming South Asians in America have not yet found common ground.

Can Subalterns Name Themselves?

Names essentialize. Yet we cannot operate without them. Personal names signify individual personal identity, making one human being distinct from another; in other words, names grant subjecthood; family names signify legal identities as well as lineage, breeding, class status, and often ethnic and national identities.

The subject names; the object is named. Who has the power to name? Which individuals and groups have had the privilege of choosing their own names? Servants, slaves, and the colonized subjects have always been nameless, faceless groups, not individualized by proper names. In her introductory essay "Friday on the Potomac," in the volume *Racing Justice, En-gendering Power* (1992), Toni Morrison reminds us that Defoe's Robinson Crusoe does not think of asking his black slave his given name, but rather names him Friday. And in a typically imperialistic manner, Crusoe himself wishes to be accorded the title of "master" (xxiv). "Friday's" father's name is not solicited either; he is instead referred to as "the old savage" (xxvii). Morrison, who chooses her own fictional characters' names carefully thus exposes the complex power relations involved in naming others and oneself.

In his essay "What's in a Name? Some Meanings of Blackness," Henry Louis Gates Jr. illustrates the problematics of names and self-naming as he recounts the gripping first sentence of his Yale college application essay: "My grandfather was colored, my father is Negro, and I am black" (137). And he further questions whether his daughters will identify themselves as African Americans in the future, or whether "they'll be Africans by then, or even feisty rapper-dappers. Perhaps, by that time, the most radical act of naming will be a return to 'colored'" (137). Gates's remark thus suggests that self-naming and renaming have been necessary in forming African American group identity. Since African slaves had historically been known by their masters' names, it is critical for them to assert their authority by renaming themselves both as individuals, and as a group.

The significance of self-naming with respect to the group identity of Americans of African descent is further emphasized in Kenneth Ghee's essay "The Psychological Importance of Self Definition and Labeling: Black Versus African American" (1990). Nomenclature applied to African Americans over the centuries includes "*African . . . negro, nigger, colored, Negro, black, Black, Afro-American, Afric-American* and *African American*" (81, Ghee's emphasis). In his cogent argument in favor of displacing the name "black" with "African-American" in "Black, Negro, or Afro-American? The Differences Are Crucial!" Halford H. Fairchild avers that "race names have long been associated with the development and main-tenance of racial attitudes" (47), that research in racial and ethnic psy-chology has proven that ethnic groups' identity is partly "a function of the racial or ethnic label associated with that group." Thus recent "minority consciousness movements" have led to a "Negro-to-Black conversion ex-perience"; Mexican-Americans are now "politically sensitive 'Chicanos'"; and Asians have undergone a "movement of 'Yellow power' and 'Asian' identity" (Fairchild 48). As Fairchild further explains, the "'Negro-to-Black' conversion is critical because it relates to the underlying identity and consciousness of black people." He regrets, however, that "black Americans remain somewhat schizophrenic (multiple personality is a bet-ter analogy) when it comes to using own-race descriptors and labels." Names in current use include "'Black' (capitalized or uncapitalized, which is an important issue in its own right), 'Afro-American,' 'African-American' (hyphenated or unhyphenated), 'Negro,' 'colored,' 'nigger' (al-though often used as a term of endearment according to Gettone, 1981), and so on" (Fairchild 54). Like African Americans, South Asians in America, too, might be considered to have "multiple personalities," to use Fairchild's term, resulting in the gaps between their names and their iden-tification as (non)–Asian American.

The issue of nomenclature is thus important within a larger framework of who names whom? who is named by whom? who is the subject who names the Other? and which is the object that is named? To rephrase a question posed by Gayatri Chakravorty Spivak in another context, we might ask, can subalterns name themselves?[3] Or, do individuals or groups who reveal their agency by naming themselves forfeit their subordinated status? If individuals or groups are enfranchised enough to be able to cre-ate an identity, does that imply they are no longer marginalized? Does the act of self-naming signify that those who (can) name themselves are al-ready empowered? Or is the act of self-naming itself the first step toward self-assertion and an attempt to move from the margin to the mainstream, to *create* a sense of self by first naming it into existence. So, if South Asian Americans' voices are now being heard in the academy, does it signify that they are being invited (or allowed) to speak? That somebody wishes to listen to them? If so, who listens and why? And, under what categories— South Asian, postcolonial, or Asian American—must their voices be clas-sified in order to be heard?

To what extent are names, then, a precondition to identity formation? Is South Asian Americans' act of self-naming a response to a preassigned identity, or is the act itself the process of *performing* and, hence, constitut-ing a new identity merely as an arbitrary attempt to close real or imagined gaps between South Asians and the rest of Asian America? I will apply this line of questioning to examine South Asians' performance, so to speak, of their postcolonial and Asian American identities, first, as reflected in Spivak's and Mukherjee's self-naming, and as projected in the title of this book.

SPEAKING IN (M)OTHER TONGUES

Since the terms "postcolonial" and "(South) Asian American" define marginalized groups while presuming the Anglo-American identity as the center, they have limited significance outside Western academic circles. Indians, Pakistanis, Bangladeshis, and others from the general populace in South Asia do not consider themselves "postcolonial" while resident in their home countries; doing so would obliterate their indigenous histories before European colonization. It is obviously misleading for peoples from civilizations that have thrived for many millennia before the birth of Anglo-Saxon Great Britain or Euro-America to describe themselves as postcolonial. Aijaz Ahmad effectively argues that "the conceptual apparatus of 'postcolonial criticism' privileges as primary the role of colonialism as the principle of structuration in that history, so that all that came before colonialism becomes its own prehistory and whatever comes after can only be lived as infinite aftermath" (7).[4]

What do the classifications Asian American and postcolonial as employed within the North American academy signify, anyway? David Palumbo-Liu's essay "Theory and the Subject of Asian America [*sic*] Studies" challenges "'Third World intellectuals' (largely signifying South Asian metropolitan academics)" (62) role within postcolonial and/or Asian American studies. Although Palumbo-Liu doesn't name anyone in particular, his questions might apply to South Asians, including Gayatri Chakravorty Spivak, Homi Bhabha, Arjun Appadurai, Aijaz Ahmad, Sara Suleri Goodyear, Partha Chatterjee, and Dipesh Chakrabarty—none of whom are identified with Asian American studies. Palumbo-Liu is rightly apprehensive about the "problem of who speaks for whom," since there is "a correlate relationship between the cultural and institutional politics of postcolonialism and U.S. minority discourse" (62). I would like to extend his concern further to speculate about academic disciplines that are rapidly being redefined: Are certain fields (such as postcolonial theory) associated with more academic prestige than others (such as Asian American/ethnic studies)? What does it mean for South Asians to maintain positions of privilege and authority in postcolonial criticism in North America? What do they stand to gain or lose by engaging with Asian American Studies? How might their entrance into the discipline of Asian American Studies alter South Asians' visibility within Asian America? Alternatively, is there a threat to Asian American Studies—which has mostly been centered around American minority discourse—of being appropriated or silenced by foreign-born, often British-accented, middle- and upper-class South Asian postcolonial critics? Is there perhaps a resistance, therefore, among proponents of Asian American Studies to invite (somewhat privileged) postcolonial South Asian Americans within their disciplinary fold? As Ella Shohat cautions in "Notes on the 'Post-Colonial,'" postcolonial theory has formed a "contested space, particularly since some practitioners of various Ethnic Studies feel somewhat displaced by the rise of post-colonial studies in North American English departments . . . the 'post-colonial' is privileged precisely because it seems safely distant from 'the belly of the beast,' the United States" (108).

Or does South Asians' own hesitation to join an already existing minority American group arise out of their inability to identify with the discrimination and persecution many East and Southeast Asians have historically experienced in America? For instance, in her essay "Is the United States Postcolonial? Transnationalism, Immigration and Race," Jenny Sharpe tries to distinguish between the objectives of Asian American studies and postcolonial studies. She seems to reprimand "Diasporic South Asian intellectuals who demand representation within Asian-American studies [and hence] abandon issues of postcoloniality in favor of United States multiculturalism" in order to "form alliances with other minorities" (196). Skeptical of their intentions, Sharpe asks, "To what end? If it is to sanction a claim to marginality or racial minority status, I must interject the reminder that Third World immigrants do not constitute 'the new empire within' the United States." In her conclusion, Sharpe seems to privilege postcolonialism over ethnic studies as "the study of transnationalism and differential power rather than marginality and oppression" (196). Perhaps this valorization of transnationalism (and poscoloniality) as the preferred mode of analysis, which devalues the emphasis on American minorities' oppression, is what Sau-ling Wong cautions against in her essay "Denationalization Reconsidered." It might even be safe to infer that a conflation of postcolonial and Asian American studies would dramatically alter South Asians' invisibility within Asian America.

Two Examples: Spivak and Mukherjee

Following the current interest in postcolonial studies and multicultural discourse, the work of Gayatri Chakravorty Spivak and Bharati Mukherjee has recently been embraced by many American literary circles, in contrast to the earlier invisibility of South Asian Americans within Asian American literary studies. Both upper-class Bengali (and upper-caste Brahmin) "women of color"[5] from Calcutta, India, who entered the United States for doctoral study in English literature in the early 1960s, Spivak and Mukherjee are unlike the majority of early South Asian American immigrants. They can be viewed as early Indian "feminists," single women who traveled to the West for higher education. It is significant that unlike most other female immigrants of their generation, Spivak's and Mukherjee's passages to America did not result from marriage to South Asian male immigrants.[6] Themselves members of an extremely privileged minority in their birth land, Spivak and Mukherjee have ironically enough been adopted by progressive English departments in the American academy as representatives of the "Third World" presence in the United States. Spivak is considered an authority on Third World or non-Western feminism, postcolonial theory, and in her own words as a "feminist, Marxist deconstructivist" (*In Other Worlds,* 117). Spivak is one of the most cited voices in "minority" literary and cultural criticism. Numerous interviews, and book-length studies of her work have appeared within the last five years marking, commodifying, and essentializing her as "The Post-Colonial Critic"—strategically the title of her book-length collection of interviews.[7]

In the North American academy, Spivak first received acclaim, not as an Asian or an Indian scholar, but because of her European connection as the translator of Jacques Derrida's *Of Grammatology* from French into English. And yet, in the last decade, she has been appropriated, or has reconfigured herself, as a postcolonial critic. Despite her prominent position as a South Asian academic in America, Spivak has not been identified with, or identified herself with, Asian American Studies. I realize it is dangerous to essentialize Spivak's identity by questioning why she is not intellectually engaged in scholarship on what she herself "is," that is, a member of an Asian minority in America. And yet, such speculations and assumptions are regularly being made in decisions about who should teach what in the contemporary academy.[8]

Bharati Mukherjee's fiction has recently been included in multicultural literature and composition anthologies, and within Asian American and Ethnic/Women's Studies curricula as that of a representative (South) Asian American.[9] She is the only fiction writer of South Asian descent whose work is analyzed in Ruth Yu Hsiao's "A Practical Guide to Teaching Asian-American Literature" (1992) and in Sau-Ling C. Wong's *Reading Asian American Literature: From Necessity to Extravagance* (1993).

Seeking to understand Spivak's and Mukherjee's affiliations with Asian American studies, I realize that Asian American identity may not be essential to Spivak and Mukherjee and to their speaking as South Asian Americans. Yet both women have been interested in the position of Asian women vis-à-vis mainstream middle-class "white" European/American feminism, and have spoken vehemently against the inapplicability of Western feminist solutions for "non-Western" women's power struggles.[10] In her essay "French Feminism in an International Frame," Spivak makes a trenchant attack on Julia Kristeva's condescending attitude toward Asian women in the French feminist's book *About Chinese Women*. In an interview with Ellen Rooney, Spivak claims to be "repelled by Kristeva's politics," her "Christianizing psychoanalysis," and "ferocious western European-peanism" ("In a Word" 145). In her critiques of Western/Eurocentric/white feminism, Gayatri Chakravorty Spivak has, along with other Asian American women, including Trinh T. Minh-ha and Chandra Talpade Mohanty, given birth, so to speak, to "non-Western," "Third World," "postcolonial" feminist theory.

Like her Bengali sister Gayatri Spivak, Bharati Mukherjee also defends her "non-white, *Asian*" sisters against the "imperialist" "white, upper-middle-class women's tools and rhetoric" (Mukherjee to Connell, 22; emphasis added). In fictional portrayals and in explicit interview statements, she censures "white" American feminists of the mid-1970s.[11] Although both Spivak and Mukherjee have been active participants in the American academy for nearly three decades, their gaining recognition recently among Asian American feminist scholars, including Lisa Lowe and Sau-ling C. Wong, might be related to their having identified themselves as feminists from Asia.

IN/OUT/SIDE ASIA, OUT/IN/SIDE AMERICA

Some of the differences between Spivak's and Mukherjee's positions in "postcolonial" and "Asian American" literary criticism, respectively, arise out of their tendencies to identify with either Asians *in Asia* or with Asians *in America*. In her cogent argument on the dangers of denationalization and the influence of diasporic imperatives on Asian American studies, Sau-ling C. Wong argues in favor of "claiming America," which was a crucial part of the Asian American cultural politics two decades ago ("Denationalization Reconsidered" 16). Wong critiques minority and, implicitly, postcolonial diasporic critical discourse that focuses on the powerlessness not of America's domestic Asian minorities, but of Asians in Asia. Wong's paradigm provides a useful framework for my discussion of the difference between postcolonial criticism and Asian American studies vis-à-vis Spivak's and Mukherjee's work and self-projected identities.

Despite her advocacy of ever-shifting, transnational identities, Gayatri Chakravorty Spivak presents herself as strongly Indian- and, especially, Bengali-identified in much of her work as well as interviews. Spivak avows that the mother tongue determines identity: "The feeling of cultural identity almost always presupposes a language. In that sense, I suppose I feel a Bengali" (*Outside* 54). Elsewhere, she identifies herself as "we educated Bengalis" (*Worlds* 186). To put it in simple terms, Spivak's work in the last decade is grounded more with (South) *Asians in Asia* than with (South) *Asians in America*. This includes her projects with the Subaltern Studies group in India, her translation and/or interpretation of Bengali texts such as Rabindranath Tagore's *Didi* ("Burden"), or Mahasweta Devi's works including "Draupudi," and "Stanadayini" (*In Other Worlds; Imaginary Maps* [1993]), and her work on Hindu widow self-immolation in her landmark essay "Can the Subaltern Speak?" In an interview with Ellen Rooney, Spivak thus defends herself and her fellow postcolonial theorists in America, Homi Bhabha and Abdul Jan Mohammed, against being branded as elitist deconstructionists, since they are "native, too, . . . The post-colonial is the old colonial subject . . . I *am* one of the subalternists; I don't work *on* them" ("In a Word" 141, Spivak's emphasis). Claiming her colonial connection to the Subaltern Studies group in India, Spivak thus explicitly aligns herself with colleagues in South Asia.

To be sure, citizenship must both influence the immigrants' identities and be influenced by their cultural identifications. In other words, whether writers/scholars feel as if they belong more in Asia or in America may determine their choice of legal identity and citizenship. In numerous interviews, as well as in critical essays, Spivak often describes herself as an "outsider" and as a "resident alien," and specifically, as a citizen of postcolonial India, not of the United States ("Postmarked" 76, 78). In *In Other Worlds*, she acknowledges that even after living in the United States for nineteen years, she feels like an "outsider" (102); the title of her book *Outside "in the" Teaching Machine* clearly implies the inside-outside dichotomy. In her 1993 interview with Sara Danius and Stefan Jonsson, she refers to herself as "a Europeanized postcolonial" (48). Elsewhere, rather eagerly, Spivak acknowledges her designation as an "expatriate English Professor," in the December 1990 issue of the leading Indian news magazine *India Today* (quoted in Spivak, "Burden," 153). The self-identifying label she uses thus is expatriate, not immigrant; an outsider, not an insider.

In contrast, Mukherjee's authorial viewpoints, her fictional protagonists, and her personal views as stated in interviews are explicitly American-immigrant-identified. Unlike Spivak, Mukherjee doesn't represent herself as a subaltern/ist or colonized "native," but rather as an immigrant whose fiction depicts (South and other) Asians recreating the American Dream. Some of the difference between Spivak's and Mukherjee's self-positioning might thus be the difference between an Asian *in* America and an American *from* Asia; perhaps between the postcolonial expatriate, and the Asian American immigrant.

Like Spivak, Mukherjee acknowledges the power of language in according identity. However, Mukherjee claims English as her own language, which she has appropriated since age three. And it is not Bengali that Mukherjee chooses to speak out in: "Language gives me my identity. I am the writer I am because I write in North American English about immigrants in the New World" (Mukherjee to Hancock, 35). She even acknowledges her adopted status in America with "North American English as my step-mother-tongue" (38). Again the Asian American writer's attitude seems to sharply contrast with that of the postcolonial critic, Spivak, who repeatedly reminds her readers that her mother tongue is Bengali and that she is glad she attended a school where the medium of instruction was in Bengali, not the colonizer's English ("Postmarked Calcutta" 87, 89; *Outside* 11). Mukherjee's unhesitating adoption of the imperial master's "voice" echoes the American-born writer Frank Chin's earlier insistence on English (as opposed to native languages such as Chinese or Japanese) as a requisite for claiming space within the rubric of Asian American and, ultimately, American literature (*Aiiieeeee!*).

Names and Cultural Identity

Both Mukherjee and Spivak are aware of their varied nomenclature and of the liminality of their position in different parts of the "West": England, the United States, and Canada. In her essay "Marginality in the Teaching Machine," Spivak posits that "presumed cultural identity often depends on a name" (*Outside* 54). She discusses the starkly varied implications of the same name when employed in different locales. She differentiates between the British and the U.S. use of the label "Asian." Spivak explains that while speaking to academics in England in July 1988, her identity was presumed to be Asian, irrespective of the label's underclass implications. In contrast, "In the United States, 'Asians' are of Chinese, Japanese, Korean, and of late, Vietnamese extraction. . . . In the United States, she is 'Indian'" (54). Thus Spivak recognizes her lack of affiliations with (East?) "Asians" in America, as well as the tenuousness of "Indians'" Asian heritage within mainstream American consciousness. Mukherjee, too, laments that (particularly in Canada) she was often ascribed an "origin" she herself did not recognize:

> I have no country of origin. In polite company, I am an "East Indian" (the opposite presumably, of a "West Indian"). The East Indies, in my school days, were Dutch possessions, later to become Indonesia. In impolite com-

pany I'm a "Paki"... . For an Indian of my generation, to be called a "Paki" is about as appealing as it is for an Israeli to be called a Syrian. ("An Invisible Woman" 38; quoted in Tapping 46)

Mukherjee does not wish to be called a Paki or Pakistani and, thus, unconsciously exposes internal fissures within South Asia. Whereas Spivak claims to be a transnational postcolonial diasporic who is at home everywhere and nowhere, Mukherjee's sense of herself as an American immigrant whose "home" is New York, is explicitly unproblematic: "I am an immigrant, living in a continent of immigrants" who devours "voraciously the literature of deracination and assimilation" (Mukherjee to Hancock, 32). The emphasis on "assimilation" might distinguish the immigrant from the expatriate and, perhaps, if stretched further, "Asian American-ness" from "postcoloniality."

Openly critiquing her native country,[12] Mukherjee figuratively claims American geographical and literary territory as her own. This pioneering spirit—which Elaine Kim describes with respect to East Asian American writers as "claiming America" (170) and as "claiming an American, as opposed to an Asian, identity" ("Defining Asian American Realities" 147)—is probably what binds Mukherjee's work to the more mainstream Asian American writers such as Maxine Hong Kingston, Cathy Song, and Amy Tan, whose classics *The Woman Warrior, Picture Bride,* and *The Joy Luck Club* have been adopted into Asian American literary studies curricula.[13] Like Kingston, Song, and Tan, Mukherjee's "ethnic" writing has been acclaimed by mainstream critics; her book *The Middleman and Other Stories* (1988) won the National Book Critics Circle Award for short fiction. Described by her South Asian interviewer Ameena Meer as "simply a New Yorker of Mediterranean origin" whose "midwestern accent doesn't give her away," Mukherjee appropriates a position for herself in the American literary canon by describing her novel *Jasmine* (1989) as "the making of the American mind" (Meer 26). In a Whitmanesque claiming of America, Mukherjee explains that "I see myself as an American writer in the tradition of other American writers whose parents or grandparents had passed through Ellis Island" (*Darkness,* "Introduction" xv), one who is emphatic in her self-identification as American:

I totally consider myself an American writer . . . writing about . . . a new kind of pioneer here in America. *I'm the first among Asian immigrants to be making this distinction between immigrant writing and expatriate writing.* Most Indian writers prior to this, have still thought of themselves as Indians, and their literary inspiration, has come from India. India has been the source, and home. Whereas I'm saying, . . . *my roots are here and my emotions are here in North America.* (Mukherjee to Meer, 27, emphasis added)

These appropriative gestures of self-definition—in Kim's terms, the Asian American's transformation from "sojourner to immigrant searching for a permanent place in America" (154)—have become Mukherjee's passport into the Asian American literary canon. By critiquing previous Indian writers for having identified themselves as Indian and not as American, Mukherjee is perhaps unwittingly pointing to the distinction between postcolonial diasporics, expatriates from Asia, and immigrants whose homelands are not the imaginary South Asian ones, but who have reincarnated themselves as Americans of Asian descent, who urgently desire to connect with other (Asian) Americans. Mukherjee, like her counterpart Spivak, is aware of the advantages of strategic self-representation and fully cognizant of how she wishes to be recognized, not as a postcolonial, but rather as an American of Asian descent.

STRATEGIZING SELF-NAMING

To return to the problematic issue of South Asians' performative names with respect to the objectives of this collection of essays, it is worth asking whether this volume is itself an example of a Spivakian "strategic essentialism," that is, the "*strategic* use of positivist essentialism in a scrupulously visible political interest" (*Worlds* 205, Spivak's emphasis)—the political interest being South Asian Americans' staking a claim for self-representation within Asian America. Or, by vying with East and South East Asians for representation, are South Asians in America making themselves vulnerable to the majority's "divide and conquer" strategy, which leaves minorities to fight among themselves? In her frequently cited essay "Heterogeneity, Hybridity, Multiplicity: Marking Asian American Differences," Lisa Lowe warns against essentialized Asian American identities that efface differences of national origin, generation, gender, political party, and class. Lowe powerfully argues that "the grouping 'Asian American' is not a natural or static category; it is a socially constructed unity, a situationally specific position that we assume for political reasons. It is 'strategic' in Gayatri Spivak's sense" (39). Lowe's paradigm for constructing Asian group identity can be applied to the case of South Asian Americans, in order to reveal the strategic essentialism at stake in projects such as this book:

> The concept of "strategic essentialism" suggests that it is possible to utilize specific signifiers of ethnic identity, such as Asian American [read South Asian American], for the purpose of contesting and disrupting discourses that exclude Asian Americans [read South Asian Americans], while simultaneously revealing the internal contradictions and slippages of Asian American [read South Asian American] so as to insure that such essentialisms will

not be reproduced and proliferated by the very apparatuses we seek to dis-empower (39).

Acts of self-identification and self-nomination are thus not without the risks and dangers of also essentializing and fixing identities by naming and performing them into existence. This collection's basic tenet, in trying to bridge the gaps between South Asian Americans and all other Asian Americans, reifies the binary schema. Must the label "South Asian Americans in/and/versus Asian American" establish an either/or proposition? Does being one preclude being the other? The binary schema seems to set up a nationalist politics of identity. But South Asia is not one nation; in fact, India, the largest and most populous country in South Asia is not a unified, homogeneous nation, either. How, then, can South Asians in America reconcile their conflict-ridden histories in Asia and at the same time attempt to be united in America? Can we forget that our histories of coalitions forged and betrayed in Asia are older than the birth of the United States of America itself? [14]

(SOUTH) ASIAN AMERICAN "PARTITIONS"?

Even as I question the validity of bridging the gulf between South Asian Americans and other Asian Americans, I realize that the category "South Asian" is, like all other labels, entirely inadequate in describing an extremely heterogeneous group. Of course, this self-naming of peoples from the Indian Subcontinent, based on geographical, rather than cultural, racial, political, national criteria, unites disparate groups and forms coalitions against common "hegemonic" powers, whether majority Euro-American, or minority Asian American. It is, however, necessary to heed Bangladeshi American scholar Naheed Islam's warning that "the use of the term 'South Asia' has become interchangeable with the term 'India'" (244).[15] The "Indian" Subcontinent, it must be remembered, is not merely Indian; India, though often referred to as Hindustan, is not merely Hindu; South Asia is not merely the (Indian) Subcontinent.

I will end with some questions, some of which can be answered only with the passage of time. Will this new title—South Asian Americans—appease South Asian scholars, critics, and authors who have felt excluded from the Asian American literary canon and Asian American Studies programs? Or will this attempt to close gaps between certain constituencies create further schisms within minority American groups by importing communalism and nationalist struggles across three continents? Will the process of self-representation within Asian America reunite South Asians to their cohesive pre-British colonization identity (partitioned by the British in 1947 into India and Pakistan, and further subdivided into Bangladesh in 1971)? Or are yet other partitions of Subcontinental Studies as well as of Asian American Studies imminent in the academy?

Notes

1. For an argument critiquing the use of the term "postcolonial" in literary theory, see Aijaz Ahmad's "The Politics of Literary Postcoloniality." Despite its complicated implications, I continue to employ it for lack of another word for what "postcolonial" signifies in contemporary literary criticism.

2. Sucheta Mazumdar cites the results of a survey of twenty-four South Asians in New York City in 1975: fifteen people identified themselves with the terminology of "Aryan." Five considered Indians as "Caucasians," six thought just the opposite, and five others thought "some Indians are white" ("Race and Racism" 31).

3. See Gayatri C. Spivak, "Can the Subaltern Speak?"

4. For other useful critiques of the term "postcolonial" as well as of the dangers of postcolonial studies, see, for instance, Shohat, Sharpe, Frankenberg, and Mani.

5. I endorse Hazel Carby's reading of the complicated nature of the term "women of color" ("Multicultural Wars" 13), but use it critically because of its prevalence in contemporary literary discourse.

6. See Sucheta Mazumdar's "General Introduction: A Woman-Centered Perspective on Asian American History" in *Making Waves* for a brief history of Asian women's immigration. Also see Joan Jensen for South Asian American women's history (281).

7. The recent publication of *The Spivak Reader* is a case in point.

8. I do not believe that one's scholarship should necessarily be based on identity. For my argument that one should not be obliged to teach only what one's identity "is," see my essay "Pro/(con)fessing Otherness: Trans(cending)national Identities in the 'English' Classroom."

9. See also her stories in *Sudden Fiction International* (1989), ed. Robert Shapard and James Thomas; *The Story and Its Writer: An Introduction to Short Fiction*, ed. Ann Charters (4th ed. 1995). Also see collection of literary critical essays on Mukjerjee's fiction in *Bharati Mukherjee: Critical Perspectives*, edited by Emmanuel S. Nelson (1993).

10. Another problematic term that reinforces the idea that "Western" is normative.

11. For a detailed analysis of Mukherjee's complicated relationship to white feminisms of the mid-1970s in her novels, see my article "Activism, Feminisms and Americanization in Bharati Mukherjee's *Wife* and *Jasmine*."

12. Mukherjee explains that she realized her commitment to the "New World" while writing *Days and Nights in Calcutta* since the "old world was dead for me. Emotionally and inspirationally. There were just so many aspects of India that I disliked by then" (Mukherjee to Connell, 15).

13. Excerpts from these popular works are also to be found in short fiction and composition anthologies. See Ruth Yu Hsiao's "A Practical Guide" for a fairly representative selection of texts popular in Asian American literature courses. Significantly, popular female authors such as Maxine Hong Kingston have been chastised by Frank Chin in his essay "Oh Come All Ye Asian American Writers" in *The Big Aiiieeeee,* for pandering to majority American audiences (26–27); there are some resonances of similar charges made against Mukherjee, especially by Indian critics. See Emmanuel Nelson, ed., *Bharati Mukherjee* (1993).

14. For instance, contemporary communal tensions among Hindus, Muslims, and Sikhs in India have roots that go back many centuries.

15. Islam, Naheed. "In the Belly of the Multicultural Beast I am Named South Asian," in *Our Feet Walk the Sky* (San Francisco: aunt lute, 1993).

Works Cited

Aguilar-San Juan, Karin, ed. *The State of Asian America: Activism and Resistance in the 1990s.* Boston: South End Press, 1994.

Ahmad, Aijaz. "The Politics of Literary Postcoloniality." *Race and Class* 36 (1995).

Asian Women United of California, ed. *Making Waves: An Anthology of Writings By and About Asian American Women.* Boston: Beacon Press, 1989.

Carby, Hazel. "The Multicultural Wars." *Radical History Review* 54 (1992): 7–18.

Chan, Jeffrey Paul, et al., eds. *The Big Aiiieeeee! An Anthology of Chinese American and Japanese American Literature* (New York: Meridian, 1991).

Chandrasekhar, S., ed. *From India to America: A Brief History of Immigration; Problems of Discrimination; Admission and Assimilation.* La Jolla, Calif.: Population Review, 1982.

———. "A Bibliography of Asian Indians in the United States: History of Immigration and Immigrant Communities in the United States" in *From India to America*: 93–106.

Charters, Ann, ed. *The Story and Its Writer: An Introduction to Short Fiction* (Boston: St. Martin's Press, 1995).

Cheung, King-Kok, and Stan Yogi. *Asian American Literature: An Annotated Bibliography.* New York: MLA, 1988.

Chin, Frank. "Come All Ye Asian American Writers of the Real and the Fake." In *The Big Aiiieeeee!,* edited by Jeffrey Paul Chan et al., 1–92.

Chin, Frank, Jeffery Paul Chan, Lawson Fusao Inada, and Shawn Hsu Wong, eds. *Aiiieeeee! An Anthology of Asian-American Writers.* Washington, D.C.: Howard University Press, 1974.

Connell, Michael. "An Interview with Bharati Mukherjee." *Iowa Review* 20.3 (Fall 1990): 7–23.

Danius, Sara, and Stefan Jonsson. "An Interview with Gayatri Chakravorty Spivak." *boundary 2* (Summer 1993): 24–50.

Dutta, Manoranjan. "Asian Indian Americans: Search for an Economic Profile" in S. Chandrasekhar, ed. *From India to America*: 76–85.

Espiritu, Yen Le. "Census Classification: The Politics of Ethnic Enumeration" in *Asian American Panethnicity: Bridging Institutions and Identities*. Philadelphia: Temple University Press, 1992: 112–33.

Fairchild, Halford H. "Black, Negro, or Afro-American? The Differences Are Crucial!" *Journal of Black Studies*. 16.1 (1985): 47–55.

Frankenberg, Ruth and Lati Mani. "Crosscurrents, Crosstalk: Race, 'Postcoloniality' and the Politics of Location." *Cultural Studies*. 7 (1993): 292–310.

Freedman, Diane P., Olivia Frey, and Frances Murphy Zauhar, eds. *The Intimate Critique: Autobiographical Literary Criticism*. Durham, N.C.: Duke University Press, 1993.

Gates, Henry Louis, Jr. "'What's in a Name?' Some Meanings of Blackness." In *The Intimate Critique: Autobiographical Literary Criticism*, edited by Diane P. Freedman, 135–50.

Ghee, Kenneth. "The Psychological Importance of Self Definition and Labeling: Black Versus African American." *The Journal of Black Psychology*. 17.1 (Fall 1990): 75–93.

Hancock, Geoff. "An Interview with Bharati Mukherjee" *Canadian Fiction Magazine* 59 (1987): 30–44.

Hsiao, Ruth Yu. "A Practical Guide to Teaching Asian-American Literature." *Radical Teacher* 41 (1992): 20–23.

Islam, Naheed. "In the Belly of the Multicultural Beast, I Am Named South Asian." In *Our Feet Walk the Sky: Women of the South Asian Diaspora*, edited by the Women of the South Asian Descent Collective. San Francisco: aunt lute, 1993, 242–45.

JanMohamed, Abdul R., and David Lloyd, eds. *The Nature and Context of Minority Discourse*. New York: Oxford University Press, 1990.

Jensen, Joan. *Passage from India: Asian Indian Immigrants in North America*. New Haven: Yale University Press, 1988.

Kim, Elaine. "Defining Asian American Realities Through Literature" in *The Nature and Context of Minority Discourse*, edited by Abdul R. JanMohamed and David Lloyd. New York: Oxford University Press, 1990: 146–70.

Landry, Donna, and Gerald MacLean, eds. *The Spivak Reader: Selected Works of Gayatri Chakravorty Spivak*. New York: Routledge, 1996.

Lee, Sharon M. "Racial Classifications in the US Census: 1890–1990." *Ethnic and Racial Studies*. 16.1 (1993): 75–94.

Lowe, Lisa. "Heterogeneity, Hybridity, Multiplicity: Marking Asian American Differences," *Diaspora* 1:1 (1991): 24–44.

Mayberry, Katherine J., ed. *Teaching What You're Not: Identity Politics in Higher Education*. New York: New York University Press, 1996.

Mazumdar, Sucheta. "General Introduction: A Woman-Centered Perspective on Asian American History." In *Making Waves: An Anthology of Writings By and About Asian American Women*, edited by Asian Women United of California : 1–22.

———. "Race and Racism: South Asians in the United States." In *Frontiers of Asian American Studies: Writing, Research, and Commentary*, edited by Gail Nomura et al. Pullman: Washington University Press, 1989: 25–38.

Meer, Ameena. "Bharati Mukherjee" [An Interview]. *Bomb*: 29 (1989): 26–27.

Melendy, H. Brett. *Asians in America: Filipinos, Koreans, and East Indians*. Boston: Twayne, 1977.

Mohanty, Chandra Talpade. "Under Western Eyes: Feminist Scholarship and Colonial Discourses." In *Third World Women and the Politics of Feminism*: 51–80.

———, ed. *Third World Women and the Politics of Feminism*. Bloomington: Indiana University Press, 1991.

Morrison, Toni. "Introduction: Friday on the Potomac" in *Race-ing Justice, En-gendering Power*, vii–xxx.

———, ed. *Race-ing Justice, En-gendering Power: Essays on Anita Hill, Clarence Thomas, and the Construction of Social Reality*. New York: Pantheon, 1992.

Mukherjee, Bharati. *Darkness*. New York: Fawcett Crest, 1992.

———. *Jasmine*. New York: Fawcett Crest, 1989.

———. *The Middleman and Other Stories*. New York: Fawcett Crest, 1988.

Nelson, Cary, and Lawrence Grossberg, eds. *Marxism and the Interpretation of Culture*. Urbana: University of Illinois Press, 1988.

Nelson, Emmanuel S., ed. *Bharati Mukherjee: Critical Perspectives*. New York: Garland, 1993.

———, ed. *Reworlding: The Literature of the Indian Diaspora*. New York: Greenwood, 1992.

Palumbo-Liu, David. "Theory and the Subject of Asian America [*sic*] Studies." *Amerasia Journal* 21.1 and 21.2 (1995): 55–65.

Shankar, Lavina Dhingra. "Activism, Feminisms, and Americanization in Bharati Mukherjee's *Wife* and *Jasmine*." *Hitting Critical Mass: A Journal of Asian American Cultural Criticism*. 3.1 (Winter 1995): 61–84.

———. "Pro/(con)fessing Otherness: Trans(cending)national Identities in the 'English' Classroom. In *Teaching What You're Not: Identity Politics in Higher Education*, edited by Katherine J. Mayberry, 195–214.

Shapard, Robert, and James Thomas, eds. *Sudden Fiction International: Sixty Short Stories*. New York: Norton, 1989.

Sharpe, Jenny. "Is the United States Postcolonial? Transnationalism, Immigration, and Race." *Diaspora*. 4.2 (1995): 181–99.

Shohat, Ella. "Notes on the 'post-colonial.'" *Social Text* 31/32 (1992): 99–113.

Spivak, Gayatri Chakravorty. "The Burden of English." In *Orientalism and the Postcolonial Predicament: Perspectives on South Asia*, edited by Carol A. Breckenridge and Peter van der Veer. Philadelphia: University of Pennsylvania Press, 1993.

———. "Can the Subaltern Speak?" In *Marxism and the Interpretation of Culture*, edited by C. Nelson and L. Grossberg. Urbana: University of Illinois Press, 1988, 217–313.

———. *In Other Worlds: Essays in Cultural Politics*. New York: Routledge, 1988.

———. *Outside "in the" Teaching Machine*. New York: Routledge, 1993.

———. *The Post-Colonial Critic: Interviews, Strategies, Dialogues*. Edited by Sarah Harasym. New York: Routledge, 1990.

———. "Postmarked Calcutta, India." In *The Post-Colonial Critic*, edited by Sarah Harasym, 75–94.

————, trans. *Imaginary Maps: Three Stories by Mahasweta Devi.* Introduction by G. C. Spivak. New York: Routledge, 1995.

Tapping, Craig. "South Asia/North America: New Dwellings and the Past." In *Reworlding*, edited by Emmanuel S. Nelson: 35–49.

Trinh, T. Minh-ha. *Woman, Native, Other: Writing Postcoloniality and Feminism.* Bloomington: Indiana University Press, 1989.

Wong, Sau-ling C. "Denationalization Reconsidered: Asian American Cultural Criticism at a Theoretical Crossroads." *Amerasia Journal* 21:1 (1995): 1–27.

————. *Reading Asian American Literature: From Necessity to Extravagance.* Princeton, N.J.: Princeton University Press, 1993.

II. THE DISCONNECTIONS OF RACE

Nazli Kibria

3   The Racial Gap
South Asian American Racial Identity and the Asian American Movement

SEVERAL FRIENDS had been urging me to watch *Late Night with David Letterman* to see the two Bangladeshi brothers who have become a semipermanent feature of the show. (I am of Bangladeshi origin.) On one Fourth of July holiday, Sirajul and Mujibur, operators of a small convenience store in New York, were shown holding American flags in front of the White House. In their familiar-sounding "accented" English, they responded in polite monosyllables ("yes," "no," "very nice") to Letterman's pesky questions as the audience screamed with laughter, often for no apparent reason. I watched transfixed, feeling disturbed and perversely fascinated. Who are these men? Do they feel themselves to be the objects of ridicule or of affectionate amusement? And how did the audience view and socially identify Sirajul and Mujibur? As naive greenhorn immigrants? As clever entrepreneurs cashing in on the American penchant for foreign oddities? As "Bangladeshis"? As "Indians"? As "South Asians"?[1] As "Asians"?

As South Asian Americans become a more visible presence in the United States, the need for analysis and dialogue about questions of South Asian American identity has become more pressing than ever. I would like to explore questions of South Asian racial identity in the United States, questions that lie at the heart of the gap between South Asians and the larger Asian American community, and to consider how this gap may be closed, if only in a limited way.

As a Bangladeshi immigrant, I realize that as a signifier of identity, the term "South Asian" is itself highly problematic, masking deep divisions of nationality, culture, religion, and language;[2] however, I use the term "South Asian" here because in the United States, persons of South Asian origin are not generally distinguished from one another in racial terms. Although there are some signs of change, I believe that the racial identity of South Asians in the United States is ambiguous in certain respects, and this ambiguity has resulted in a sense of marginality for South Asian Americans in a variety of social contexts.

SOUTH ASIAN AMERICANS AS "AMBIGUOUS NONWHITES"

My own awareness of this ambiguity was reinforced when I was teaching a small undergraduate class on the sociology of race and ethnic relations. The highly diverse group was unusually gregarious and frank. We were discussing the meaning of race, and at one point I casually asked, "Well, what race do you think I am?" I waited, fighting the urge to break the awkward silence. After several minutes, I was rewarded for my patience with a barrage of comments:

"Aren't Indians Caucasians? I remember reading somewhere that Indians from India are from the same racial stock as Europeans. Their features are white; except for their skin color they're basically white."[3]

"But the skin color is what matters. Asian Indians have dark skin. No one in America would ever look at Professor Kibria and say that she is white."

"The only thing I know about this is from watching *Mississippi Masala*. And from that it seemed to me that Indians don't see themselves as black."

"As far as race, it's clear that you're not white or black or Asian. So what does that leave us with? How do you feel about Latino?" (followed by laughter)

"It's a ridiculous question. I don't see why we have to put these labels on people. We don't have to accept the system."

Such situations serve to remind me constantly of the questions that surround the racial classification of South Asians in the United States. Especially apparent is the breach within the racial category of "Asian." It is interesting that not one of my students described me as Asian.

In the United States, race is a commonsense aspect of reality, one that serves as a basic frame of reference by which to order and interpret social relations and encounters (see Outlaw). Race is, furthermore, viewed as "pure," and thus adequately defined by a limited and discrete set of categories (see Lee). Those persons who lack a clear-cut "race" because they are not easily placed into available racial categories (such as "Black," "White," or "Asian") are likely to be a source of some unease to others, who wonder about the exact social identity of the person they have encountered. Such situations create a sense of uncertainty about "racial etiquette" or the rules of "correct" race behavior. For such "raceless" persons, more important perhaps than the danger of causing social discomfort and awkwardness is the risk of being ignored, of being invisible because of their inability to fit into established racial schemes. As Omi and Winant observe, "Without a racial identity, one is in danger of having no identity" (62).

Studies of racial attitudes in the United States show that South Asians are clearly perceived to be racially distinct from the white population. There is, however, considerable confusion about the exact "race" of South Asians, who are inconsistently categorized by the majority population as members of any of the major racial groupings in the United States (see Fisher and Dworkin). So while it would be going too far to say that South Asian Americans have no "race," I believe that ambiguity is a prominent element of current South Asian racial identity in the United States. For lack of a more elegant term, South Asian Americans can be considered ambiguous nonwhites.

A fundamental dynamic of the U.S. racial system arises from the racial division of people into a dichotomous scheme of white and nonwhite, based loosely on skin color (see Lee and Root). South Asian Americans are clearly nonwhites within this scheme. Historically, for example, despite the fact that South Asians were "scientifically" classified to be "Caucasian," the U.S. courts judged them to be "nonwhite" in popular U.S. understanding and thus ineligible for the privileges of white status, such as the acquisition of citizenship, and, along with that, the right to own land (Jensen). The racial ambiguity of South Asians does not then stem from the question of whether they are white or nonwhite, but rather, who exactly they are as nonwhites.

As I have mentioned, U.S. racial thinking is characterized by an understanding of race as "pure" and is thus easily divided into a series of limited and mutually exclusive categories. In the United States, the established racial categories that are popularly used today in everyday social encounters to classify nonwhites include Asian ("Oriental"), Black, Native American ("Indian"), and Hispanic. Although South Asians do not fit well into any of these categories, they, like everyone else, encounter a social dynamic that insists on pigeonholing people into a "race." As a result, South Asian Americans are, in a certain sense, racially marginalized. This position of racial marginality is not unique to South Asian Americans, but is shared by growing numbers of "biracial" and "multiracial" persons, as well as groups such as Arab Americans. The very conception of race as consisting of a neat set of categories is one that inevitably marginalizes some groups and persons.

In some complex ways, South Asian Americans have themselves exacerbated the ambiguities of their racial identity. Like other minority groups in the United States, South Asian Americans view issues of identity in ways that are influenced by conceptions of race that originated in their home countries. Because South Asian American communities are transnational in character—maintaining active relations among multiple countries of origin and settlement—the influence of these "native" conceptions of race may be particularly sharp for them. For South Asian Americans, these "native" conceptions of race may provide a frame of reference by which to resist the dominant society's racial thinking. At the same time, these concepts contribute to the group's racial ambiguity by facilitating South Asian American efforts to ignore or bypass the issue of South Asian racial status in the United States.[4]

Unfortunately, empirical research on how South Asian Americans understand their racial identity is currently limited. Existing studies suggest that there is considerable resistance to both the categorical character and skin color logic of U.S. racial thinking. For example, in her study of Asian Indians in New York City, Maxine Fisher describes the lack of consensus among Asian Indian immigrants about an appropriate racial designation for their group; instead, they suggested a wide range of possible racial terms, including Aryan, Dravidian, Indo-Aryan, Indian, Oriental, Asian, and Mongol. Fisher further describes the consistent separation of race from skin color among Asian Indians, in contrast to U.S. racial thinking, in which skin color is a major indicator of race. The Asian Indians she interviewed emphasized the diversity of skin color among Asian Indians, as well as the lack of relationship between skin color and race: "My uncle is very dark and my aunt is very fair. Their son is very fair and one daughter is very dark; one is in the middle. Their colors are different, but the race is the same" (126).

Such conceptions of race, which are so different from the principles of U.S. racial thinking, have helped South Asian Americans to remain ideologically disengaged from the U.S. racial order. In other words, when confronted with the fact of their nonwhite ambiguity, South Asian Americans can turn to alternative conceptions of race to interpret their identity. Perhaps further reinforcing the tenacity of this response is the historical South Asian experience with white colonialism, which has fostered a powerful tradition of cultural resistance to colonial ways of thinking.

The changing composition of the South Asian American community is, however, making it increasingly difficult to maintain this position of ideological disengagement from the U.S. racial order. South Asian Americans are collectively experiencing a heightened sense of their nonwhiteness. Over the course of the past decade or so, South Asian Americans have moved from being a relatively invisible and benign presence to one that is increasingly visible as well as economically and culturally threatening to portions of U.S. society. Underlying this ongoing transformation are structural shifts within the South Asian American communities. On the one hand, there are the sheer numbers. The 1990 census, for example, showed the Asian Indian population to have grown 125.6 percent in the 1980s, from 387,223 to 815,447 (Mazumdar, "South Asians"). There is, furthermore, the growing socioeconomic diversity of the South Asian American communities. In the immediate aftermath of the 1965 Immigration Act, South Asian immigrants to the United States were largely professionals who were sheltered by the privileges of their class status from the most blatant forms of racism against nonwhites in the United States. Today, however, a growing number of South Asian Americans are to be found in labor-intensive and high-risk enterprises, such as the operation of convenience stores, gas stations, taxicabs, and motels, where they are highly vulnerable to racial hostility.

Besides socioeconomic diversity, there is also the growing generational diversity of the South Asian American communities. "Native" conceptions of racial identity are likely to have far less meaning for second-generation South Asian Americans than they do for the immigrant generation. Particularly given their socialization into a post–civil rights political environment, an environment characterized by its heightened consciousness of race, second-generation South Asian Americans may find it more necessary than their parents did to confront directly the dynamics of U.S. racial thinking. For the South Asian American communities, a posture of distance from issues of race in the United States will become harder to maintain.

As the historical record makes abundantly clear, racial definitions and categories are not fixed in stone but are shifting, emergent, and contested in character. All of these developments suggest that for South Asian Americans, processes of "racialization" (Omi and Winant) will become more intense in the years to come and will be influenced by external forces as well as by the group's own efforts. From the perspective of the larger U.S. society, as South Asians become a force to be reckoned with, the need to racially define them becomes pressing. This is true on a variety of levels, ranging from institutional procedures that call for keeping track of minorities to the realm of everyday social encounters, with their informal but powerful rules of "correct" race behavior. We can also anticipate that among South Asian Americans, efforts to gain a political voice in the United States will result in a growing movement toward racial self-definition and positioning.

As South Asian Americans become an increasingly racialized presence in the United States, questions about their relationship to the larger Asian American community will also come to the fore. What is the relationship of the Asian American movement to South Asian racialization? What part will the movement play in this process? Once again, I believe that the issue of South Asian racial identity is a central part of this puzzle.

RACE, SOUTH ASIANS, AND OTHER ASIAN AMERICANS

I was at a fund-raising reception for Asian American student scholarships where I was introduced to a bright young Korean American college student. We talked for a while about the courses she was taking and her career plans. Quite abruptly, she asked me if I consider myself "Asian." A little taken aback, but curious about her thinking on the issue, I replied that I did indeed, consider myself Asian. But what had prompted the question?

"Quite frankly, you're the only Indian person here, so it got me thinking about the whole thing. I mean, there's a natural bond among most of the Asian groups because of the way we look, everyone sees us as 'Oriental.' But that's not the case with Indians. The only bond with Indians is geographical—we're all from Asia. And maybe there are some cultural similarities with us, although I don't know because India's not really a Confucian-based society like a lot of the Asian ones. It's really very hard to figure out. I've wanted to ask someone about these things for a while, but I'm usually too embarrassed."

Incidents such as this highlight the power and depth of the issue of race for South Asians—there are significant cultural differences among all Asian Americans, but for South Asians there is a racial difference, as well. Despite this racial gap, there is little doubt that in the course of the past two decades or so, the pan–Asian American movement has provided an important political platform for South Asian Americans, one from which to voice their concerns and interests within the larger U.S. political arena. South Asian Americans, who are largely post-1965 immigrants (or their children), share many concerns with other Asian American groups, especially those who have entered the United States under similar circumstances. Many of the issues that concern other Asian American groups—immigration, hate crimes, the glass ceiling—are also of vital interest to South Asian Americans. Reflecting this, South Asian Americans have in recent years been an important part of various pan-Asian political efforts, especially those in which the competitive advantage of unity and larger numbers has been clear. For example, the demand for a revision of the 1980 census so that Asian-origin groups were more accurately represented was an instance when South Asians joined with other Asian groups. In recent years South Asian American college students have joined with other Asian students to protest college and university admission policies affecting Asian Americans.

In Detroit, Asian Indians were part of the Vincent Chin campaign, which is often cited as a watershed event in the history of the Asian American movement, especially in its involvement of a wide range of Asian ethnic communities. Vincent Chin was a Chinese American who in 1982 was beaten to death with a baseball bat by white auto workers who were angry at the Japanese for their negative impact on the U.S. car industry. Acknowledging the ethnically indiscriminate nature of the attack, a number of different Asian-origin communities banded together to protest the extraordinarily light sentences (a fine of $3,780 each and probation) meted out to the perpetrators of the crime. At a time of increasing violence toward them, Asian Indians joined and supported the campaign.

These and other instances of successful solidarity suggest that the pan–Asian American movement will play an important and supportive role for South Asians as they collectively experience racialization. That is, the movement will be a place from where South Asians can both give and receive support as they negotiate their place and position in U.S. society. At the same time, a deep sense of uncertainty marks the relationship of South Asians to the larger Asian American community. Race is at the heart of this gap.

In her analysis of the Asian American movement, Yen Espiritu shows the importance of the political context to its development, in particular a post–civil rights environment in which race has become a point of political organization for minorities as well as a means of access to the resources of the state. But also important to the development and strength of the movement has been the shared experience of racial "lumping" or being judged by the larger society to look and thus be alike. The point is that an experience of common race has been an important element in bringing Asian Americans together. The ongoing immigration from Asia following the 1965 Immigration Act has increased the ethnic, generational and class diversity of the Asian population in the United States. As Espiritu and others have observed, the new immigration has thus challenged the pan-Asian movement by enhancing potential sources of division and conflict. As exemplified by the experience of South Asians, one of the most important but least-talked-about of these axes of diversity is racial difference.

While once again there is limited scholarly empirical evidence on this question, I think it is fair to say that South Asian Americans have a sense of profound racial difference from other Asian Americans, reflecting both the prevailing racial conceptions and categories in the United States as well as immigrant "native" conceptions of race among South Asians. The racial gap felt by South Asians is suggested by Sinha's observation (in this volume) that many South Asians do not realize that they are among the client groups of Asian American service organizations. This sense of a racial gap with other Asian Americans may be enhanced for South Asians when they participate in pan–Asian American forums.

Within the Asian American academic circles with which I am familiar,

South Asians tend to feel like outsiders, in ways that are somewhat similar to the experiences of Southeast Asians and Filipinos. This marginality reflects, in part, the more recent immigrant character of the South Asian American population and concurrently, its shorter history of involvement with the Asian American movement. But beyond all of this is the issue of perceived racial difference between South Asians and other Asian Americans. A number of South Asian American scholars that I have talked to feel that they are marginalized and the objects of suspicion in Asian American forums. These suspicions are driven in part by questions regarding intent: what motivates the South Asians to join in the Asian American fray? Is it pure self-interest? At the heart of these questions about motivation and integrity is the issue of who is a *real* Asian American. South Asian claims to legitimate "Asian Americanness" are suspect because of perceived racial difference.

Given the power of racial categories, the racial gap is not likely to disappear. This does not mean that there is no common ground or that important and supportive cross-cutting alliances cannot be formed. As I have mentioned, South Asian Americans share many common concerns with other Asian American groups. The racial gap does, however, point to some of the limitations of the alliance.

At times when interests collide, the racial gap may add to the divisions and conflicts that are part of any alliance. An example of this is provided by the 1991 debate in San Francisco about whether or not South Asians should be included as Asians in the city's minority set-aside programs. In this now infamous incident, the effort to exclude South Asians (eventually overruled) was supported by a segment of the Chinese American business community which felt "it would be wrong to mix two groups who were clearly different physically" (Vora). In summary, as South Asians negotiate their racialization into U.S. society, the particular role played by the Asian American movement in their efforts will not be constant but will ebb and flow over time and circumstances.

ACKNOWLEDGMENTS

I would like to express my thanks to Naheed Islam, Madhulika Khandelwal, Lavina Shankar, and Rajini Srikanth for their comments on earlier drafts of this essay.

NOTES

1. "South Asia" includes Bangladesh, Bhutan, India, Pakistan, Maldives, Nepal, and Sri Lanka. Most of the empirical studies that I cite in this paper relate to

the Indian population because of the absence of research on the other groups. This chapter draws on materials that appear in an earlier article, "Not Asian, Black or White? Reflections on South Asian American Racial Identity," *Amerasia Journal* 22.2 (1996): 77–86.

2. See Islam for further discussion of the problem of the "South Asian" category.

3. Like other non-Indian South Asians, I am frequently referred to as "Indian." This reflects both the dominance of India in popular American perception of the South Asian region as well as the dynamic of being lumped into one group, which all South Asians experience.

4. For an analysis of the South Asian unwillingness to come to terms with the U.S. racial order, see Mazumdar, "Race and Racism."

WORKS CITED

Almaguer, Tomas. *Racial Fault Lines: The Historical Origins of White Supremacy in California.* Berkeley: University of California Press, 1994.

Cornell, Stephen. "Land, Labour and Group Formation: Blacks and Indians in the United States." *Ethnic and Racial Studies* 13.3 (1990): 368–88.

Dworkin, Rosalind. "Differential Processes in Acculturation: the Case of Asiatic Indians in the United States." *Plural Societies* 11 (1980): 43–57.

Espiritu, Yen. *Asian American Panethnicity: Bridging Institutions and Identities.* Philadelphia: Temple University Press, 1992.

Fisher, Maxine. *The Indians of New York City.* New Delhi, India: Heritage Publishing, 1980.

Islam, Naheed. "In the Belly of the Multicultural Beast I am named South Asian." In *Our Feet Walk the Sky: Women of the South Asian Diaspora,* edited by Women of South Asian Descent Collective. San Francisco, Calif.: aunt lute books, 1993, 242–45.

Jensen, Joan. *Passage from India.* New Haven, Conn.: Yale University Press, 1988.

Lee, Sharon. "Racial Classifications in the U.S. Census: 1890–1990." *Ethnic and Racial Studies* 16.1 (1993): 75–94.

Lowe, Lisa. "Heterogeneity, Hybridity, Multiplicity: Marking Asian American Differences." *Diaspora* 1.1 (1991): 24–44.

Mazumdar, Sucheta. "Race and Racism: South Asians in the United States." In *Frontiers of Asian American Studies,* edited by Gail Nomura, R. Endo, S. H. Sumida, and R. C. Leong. Pullman, Wash.: Washington State University Press, 1989, 25–39.

———. "South Asians in the U.S. with a Focus on Asian Indians." In *The State of Asian Pacific American: A Public Policy Report.* LEAP Asian Pacific American Public Policy Institute and UCLA Asian American Studies Center, 1993, 283–302.

Omi, Michael, and Howard Winant. *Racial Formation in the United States.* New York: Routledge, 1986.

Outlaw, Lucius. "Toward a Critical Theory of 'Race.'" In *Anatomy of Racism,* edited by David T. Goldberg. Minneapolis: University of Minnesota Press, 1990, 58–82.

Root, Maria. "Within, Between, and Beyond Race." In *Racially Mixed People in America,* edited by Maria Root. Newbury Park, Calif.: Sage Publishing, 1992, 3–11.

Vora, Batuk. "Indians Win Minority List Battle." *India West,* June 28, 1991.

MIN SONG

4 Pahkar Singh's Argument with Asian America

Color and the Structure of Race Formation

ON APRIL 2, 1925, the multiracial residents of southern California's Imperial Valley—made up mostly of Europeans, Japanese, Mexicans, and Indians from the Punjab region—woke up to the following
sensational headline in the *Imperial Valley Press*: "Hindu murders 2 in
Rage—Attacks 3rd." The day before, a handsome young farmer by the
name of Pahkar Singh grew angry during a heated argument with two
men, Victor Sterling and John Hagar, before pulling out a gun and shoot-
ing them. He then bludgeoned the men on the head with an ax. The
double murder was witnessed by a handful of Mexican packers and a
white truck driver. Singh drove to the nearby town of Calipatria and
threatened to shoot another man, William Thornburg, in his office until
the latter's wife literally stepped in front of his gun. She was eight months
pregnant at the time and must have presented a formidable sight, for as
soon as she intervened, Singh relinquished his gun and gave himself up to
the waiting sheriff outside. Using the authority of a new law designed to
discriminate against Japanese and Indian immigrant farmers alike, these
three men had conspired to usurp a large crop from Singh and to dispos-
sess him of his leased property. Singh's violent behavior would have immense repercussions on race relations in Imperial Valley for decades to
come, and he is reported to have told the arresting sheriff that he killed the
men "because they robbed me." These words hardly begin to explain what
provoked Singh to this desperate act. What part did race have to play in
the unfolding of this tragedy? Was race the only actor, or did class also
have a part? How did the legal grouping together of Indians and Japanese
affect the outcome?[1]

By raising these questions, I hope to draw attention to the way traditional discussions about Asian Americans have tended to focus on immigration from East Asian countries at the expense of South Asian immigrant histories. These oversights are methodological problems in the
practice of Asian American studies that need redress.[2] What is at stake is
not the exposition of an underlying a priori characteristic that necessitates
the formation of an Asian American racial category, but rather the expo-

sition of an identity that has developed out of a historical process. I do not, in other words, wish to frame this debate in terms of whether South Asian Americans, as a subject for study, belong in a larger discussion on Asian America. This formulation depends upon the unexamined belief that East Asians naturally fit into such a category while South Asians, as well as other Asian groups, do not. It should be axiomatic that the identity of Asian America has evolved historically from a set of structural relationships with no preconceived notion of who belongs and who does not. There is no one group that fits naturally into such a category for there is nothing natural, meaning essential or transhistorical, about the category Asian America. This rather unexceptional point will lead me to a more theoretical and speculative discussion on what can be learned from Singh's story about race formation, and indeed about U.S. cultural and national formation in general. More specifically, I will attempt to address directly the issue of the internal tensions and marginalizations within a discourse about an already marginalized group. What follows is an analysis of the immigration history of the early South Asian American community that led up to and postdated the Singh incident as the playing out of a certain structural logic that depended upon and drew in the immigration history of other Asian communities. The analysis of this history demands that we pay special attention to the importance of South Asians in the emergence of an Asian American race.

Any cursory inspection of the categories used to define Asian Americans as a race reveals the instability of the categories themselves. Even the government publication documenting a national overview of 1990 U.S. Census results reveals the difficulty of ascertaining who fits into such a category. Of the four pages in an appendix describing the criteria used to demarcate respondents to the race question, most are dedicated to determining who belongs. At one point, a quarter-page-long table is presented, breaking down the various nations of origin that might make up the Asian and Pacific Islander category; this table is, in turn, further qualified by three footnotes.[3] It should be noted that inclusion is based on nations of origin, as opposed to the more biological or linguistic concerns used to determine assignment in other racial categories. Partly, this results from the diversity of languages, (so-called) phenotypic characteristics, and cultural practices among what has come to be known from within this group as Asian America. This diversity is so prominent that one wonders what criteria were used to define an Asian American identity that pulled together such seemingly unrelated national groups? Something close to an answer appears in the historical context of late-nineteenth- and early-twentieth-century America.

These were the crucial years of a nation beginning to cut its teeth as a coherent political entity. The United States had just asserted itself against a foreign nation a few decades before the Singh double murders in the Spanish-American War, resulting in the acquisition of overseas possessions; federal Reconstruction had heartrendingly given way to concentrated industrial growth and the concomitant emergence of a militant white-ethnic working class; a host of populist organizations had finally reached their peak in a long campaign of nativist politics, with the passage of tough immigration legislation; and the courts upheld the solidifying of a national racial identity via exclusion of elements deemed incompatible.[4] For people like Singh, these events, when put together, meant a flowering of hostilities. Such immigrants found themselves increasingly being treated as if their respective differences were negligible, regardless of how prominent such differences might appear from within individual groups. All that seemed to matter was the view that they were essentially foreign.

Pahkar Singh, himself, belonged to a relatively large wave of fellow travelers from the Punjab region of northern India who first went to British Vancouver and, when anti-Indian sentiments led to immigration restrictions there, found their way south to California.[5] These immigrants represented one of the first examples of a South Asian presence in the United States. Unfortunately, little has been written about the historical conditions and experiences leading up to this first miniwave of immigration from South Asia. The immigrants were mostly Sikhs belonging to Punjabi Jat families (Bhardwaj and Rao 198); many had made their way to North America's Pacific Coast after serving as "British military or police in India and overseas" (Leonard, "Punjabi" 107); their actual presence in California was a "by-product of Indian emigration to Canada" (Hess 80); and the primary stream of immigrants to Vancouver took place immediately "following the Boxer Rebellion in Peking, China" (Melendy 187). To make our understanding of these early immigrants even more sketchy, scholars disagree about how to characterize this group. Verne Dusenbery, for example, questions Karen Leonard's insistence on talking about a Punjabi diasporic identity, as opposed to a Sikh one:

> In phrasing the issue in the terms of whether this was a Punjabi or a Sikh Diaspora, McLeod and Leonard themselves appear to be overly constrained by high modernist sensibilities that anticipate "clear-cut normative identities"—including radical distinctions of religion and secular identities . . . and unambiguous mappings of peoples and their cultures on places." (18–19)

Setting aside objections to Dusenbery's sweeping dismissal of "high modernism," the debate inaugurated here points out, more than a methodological failing on Leonard's part, an overall lack of concentrated study on the background of South Asian immigration, specifically to the United

States, by relevant scholars. Even Ronald Takaki, perhaps the most determined historian of America's multicultural past and of its pan-Asian contributors, has nothing to say about where and for what reasons these
South Asians "suddenly began appearing in the lumber towns of Washington and the agricultural fields of California" (294). This lack of interest in
the origins of these immigrants is particularly surprising considering the
recent upsurge of academic interest in British imperialism, especially
among cultural critics, and the obvious connection between British imperialism and the appearance of South Asians in the United States.[6] I will
briefly return to this connection later on in the discussion.

Amongst these immigrant farmers who found their way to Imperial
Valley, Pahkar Singh was one of the more successful. At the time of the
double murders, he had been leasing about 320 acres and was in the process of harvesting a crop of lettuce worth about fifty thousand dollars. By
any estimation, this was a small fortune at the turn of the century and a
relatively large farming operation for an independent concern. Singh was
dependable and hardworking, and every indicator pointed toward the
likelihood that he would one day become a respectable landholder and
perhaps even what one might call a pillar of his community. He had been
living in Imperial Valley for ten years, and was well liked by many of his
neighbors, Indian and non-Indian alike. The men that he shot, on the
other hand, were agricultural agents who arranged for the transportation
and distribution of produce for the region's farmers. Most likely, there was
little love lost between them and the other small farmers, and many probably felt sympathy for Singh when these men seized his crops.[7]

At the start of the twentieth century, there were many compelling legal
and linguistic reasons why South and East Asians might think of themselves as a single race. Though the boundaries around such a racial group
would not have been clearly drawn, the connections between the member
ethnicities were plainly visible. The year before the Singh incident, the
jurisdiction of the California Alien Land Law, first passed in 1920 to apply
to Japanese farmers, was expanded to include "Hindus," an insultingly
generic term referring to anyone of South Asian descent living in the
United States at the time. The insult was also a misnomer, because most
of the Indian immigrants were "85 percent . . . Sikhs and another 10 percent Muslims" (Leonard "Pahkar" 122). Only 5 percent, in other words,
were actually Hindus. This designation followed the guidelines outlined
by the United States Immigration Commission's 1911 *Dictionary of Races
or Peoples*, where "Hindu" not only referred to immigrants from India
but also the Philippines, as well as all lands in between (Melendy 186).
Even in the early indiscriminate use of this term, we can see evidence of an

unwillingness to acknowledge the differences inherent among the Asian immigrant populations.

For the Punjabis and the Japanese, these connections would have been difficult to ignore after they were lumped together by the Alien Land Law for the purposes of taking away their property rights. But the existence of these commonalities does not mean that they would have moved immediately to join forces. What would have been the point of making alliances with people who were just as powerless under the law as oneself? Rather, the preferred course of action was to make compromises with those who had more power. The Punjabis, like the Japanese immigrant farmers they suddenly found themselves resembling, tried to get around the law by making informal and illegal arrangements with white Americans in the area, whose ability to attain citizenship gave them the privilege of ownership. Pahkar Singh made such an agreement with the agents Sterling, Hagar, and Thornburg. But, because the Alien Land Law made it illegal for Singh to own or benefit in any direct way from farmland, the agreement he made with these agents was not legally binding. These apparently foolhardy agents, therefore, felt as if they had a legal basis for claiming the entire harvest as their own and telling Singh to leave the valley with only his blanket in tow (Leonard "Pahkar" 125).

An examination of the racial dynamics that came into play in the wake of the double murders has much to reveal about the way South and East Asian immigrants were being treated by the white majority. Though these dynamics reveal little group consciousness between the Punjabis and Japanese, they do suggest that to ignore the way their identities overlapped and developed in connection with each other leads to grave gaps in our understanding of historical events. As Asian Americanists and Americanists, we need to move toward remedying such gaps in our understanding of the way various Asian immigrant groups came into contact with each other. If the Punjabis and the Japanese in Imperial Valley did not actively acknowledge their similarities and seek to forge themselves into a common identity, neither could they successfully cut themselves off from each other or from an inchoate sense of self created by their entangled structural positions.

When the facts of the case came out, public sentiment in Imperial Valley, white and nonwhite, appears to have been mixed. Most surprising of all was the number of white neighbors Singh could count among his supporters. Leonard points out:

> As could be expected, Hindus from all over California rallied behind Pahkar Singh during his trial. What is surprising is that local farmers and even a

banker and a judge from his locality gave him support. At the time of the double murders, Indian farmers had only been in the valley for ten years. Yet Pahkar Singh had been able to develop strong ties with financial and political leaders in his part of the valley. Even more surprising, and ironic in view of the instigation of the Alien Land Law by small farmers' pressure, many small farmers in the Imperial Valley felt sympathy for Singh's violence against the big growers and shippers and spoke out in his defense. ("Pahkar" 130–31)

Obviously race played a large part in the tragedy that transpired and in the way that tragedy was interpreted by the greater community. Especially among the other Indian immigrants of the region, there was a sense of pulling together to form a protective circle around one of their own. Yet, as the more mixed response of the white community suggests, race was but one aspect, albeit an important one, of the sentiments this sensational event elicited, much as race is a very essential element in understanding the reception of the O. J. Simpson verdict. Leonard outlines at least three factors that played a part in the splintered loyalties among the white residents of Imperial Valley which a narrow focus on race partly occludes.

First and foremost was the question of class: "In 1925, however, Pahkar Singh and other small growers were very much at the mercy of the consignment system and the shippers who were often big growers as well. Thus some Anglo farmers viewed Singh's action sympathetically—he acted on behalf of their interests" (Leonard "Pahkar" 129). In other words, Singh had come along at the right moment. His act of violence became concurrently understood as an act against the unfair racial policies of his day and an act against the unfair economic system that put the small farmers at the mercy of the larger business concerns. Who is to say that Singh himself did not act for both reasons? Perhaps he was maddened by the liberties the distribution agents were taking in pricing his crops and dumping the losses on his shoulders. When they finally decided to take everything, his response was the flash point at the end of a long-burning fuse. Regardless of whether this characterization of Singh's motives is accurate or mere conjecture, what is important is that the small white farmers could conceivably attribute such motives to him. Because of the overlapping symbolism surrounding Singh's moment of murderous rage, the allegiances of the small white farmers were split between a racial identification, which they must have thought would allow them freer reign in the region but which only meant less economic competition for the big growers, and a class awareness, which made them sympathize for another person experiencing the same kind of exploitation that they themselves were feeling. Neither of these factors, pushing the small white farmers in conflicting directions, was completely free of racial and class implications. Underlying everything was a sense of racial superiority and the unavoidable fact of the small farmers' economic inferiority at the hands of the big growers.

Another factor affecting the whites' complicated loyalties was the splintering of support along geographic lines. The northern end (where the murders took place), primarily made up of Calipatria and Brawley, and the southern end, comprising El Centro and Holtville, were traditional rivals. It was Holtville's town newspaper that published articles in sympathy with the then incarcerated Singh, drumming up support for him during the trial. The newspaper's open cheerleading for Singh could not have helped matters between the two halves of the valley. This geographical animosity only grew worse over the years to come, polarizing the entire valley even after Singh was released from San Quentin, where he spent fifteen years after the murders. His violent act seems to have deepened a wound that had been festering for years. Even within a group of racially and economically homogeneous people, there are fissures that, while not apparent from the outside, can powerfully influence the way people react to an incident. Indeed, one of the pitfalls of a heightened awareness of race is its capacity to obscure other concerns. At the same time, one must ask what fueled these regional animosities if not race and class? No clear answer appears in the historical record, though the term ethnicity might offer some interesting avenues of future study.

Finally, unlike the Japanese farmers who had very little day-to-day contact with other communities, the Punjabi farmers played an interactive role in shaping opinion about themselves among the local whites in Imperial Valley. As Leonard again points out, they were notorious for the frequency with which they appeared in court to sue not only whites but also each other. By turning to the judicial system to settle their disputes so often, something perhaps learned through the exigencies created by living under a British colonial administration, they became familiar to the court personnel and this may, in turn, go a long way in explaining why a judge gave Singh his backing.[8] Familiarity, of course, does not always create allies, but this seems to have been the case for at least one individual. As for the banker, his support can be illuminated by the Punjabi farmers' dependence on local banks for immediate capital to bolster their farming activities. They apparently borrowed a great deal, and even when the laws stated in no uncertain terms that their presence in the farming communities were no longer welcome, bankers continued to lend money to the Punjabis and to argue for their right to exist in the community (Leonard "Punjabi" 119).

In addition to their reliance on the court system and lending institutions, the Punjabi farmers further insinuated themselves into the life of the community by marrying outside their group. Because of the disproportionate number of males to females, many of the remaining single men chose exogamy, especially to Mexican women, though some also married black and white women. Imperial Valley, especially, appears to be the most salient example of this miscegenating phenomenon, where sixty of the seventy-three such recorded marriages taking place in southern California before 1924 occurred—fifty-two to Hispanic women, five to white women, and three to black women (Leonard "Marriage" 71). Even Pahkar Singh, after his release from prison, eventually returned to Imperial Valley and settled down with a Hispanic widow named Mota Singh, who had been married to an ex-partner and village mate. Their marriage soon ended in divorce. Singh again married a Hispanic woman, this time of eighteen years of age, and produced four children in seven years (Leonard "Pahkar" 81). At least one commentator attributes this tendency toward intermarriage between Punjabi men and Hispanic women to their appearance: "Owing to similarities in physical appearance and socioeconomic status, the East Indians were frequently identified with Mexicans who generally accepted them into their community" (Hess 32). This suggests that differences in appearance between the Japanese and the Punjabis created one barrier to their perceiving the similarities in their circumstances. This explanation, however, ignores the fact that the gender ratio among the Japanese was quite equitable and thus they could marry within their own group. The Punjabi farmers of southern California, being primarily men, did not have this option, and thus if they wanted to marry (or at least mate, since some were already married to women in India), they had to seek out partners from outside their group.

Perhaps this emphasis on the physical differences between the Punjabis and the Japanese shows the extent to which polarized racial explanations, confined only to the American national context, have dominated such analyses and also the ambiguity with which Indian immigrants were treated as a result. Then, as now, race in the United States was perceived largely as a matter of black and white skin color, with little room for people who do not fit into this Manichaean view. Hence, most people are treated as if they are either black or white, regardless of whether they fit into such divisions. Indeed, this is the general pattern of reception for all Asian immigrant groups, if not all new immigrant groups at one time or another in the United States.[9] When individuals like Singh refused to be easily categorized, they either became invisible or their racial status became a topic requiring compulsive discussion.

This compulsion becomes even harder to break when one couples the ambiguity of a figure like Singh with the tendency among some Asian Americanists to separate skin color from race. In a country that tends to equate race with skin color, to insist that race and color are two different concepts is to make race a more confusing system of classification than it already is. At the same time, the confusion that inevitably arises out of this conflict of definitions leads to the possibility of forming affiliations, willingly or unwillingly, with peoples of different races, as for instance between South Asians and blacks. As Sucheta Mazumdar points out:

> While foreign-born South Asians may be able to overcome color prejudice to some extent, through unusually high levels of professional training typically acquired abroad, they cannot be certain that their U.S.-born sons and daughters will fare as well. Like the dilemma facing the black bourgeoisie . . . they cannot escape identification with people of the same skin color who, as part of the working class, are more directly assaulted by the cruder manifestation of racism. (34)

This implied elision between South Asian Americans and blacks highlights the possibility of making a distinction between skin prejudice, which both middle-class South Asians and middle-class blacks face, and racism, which involves a closer connection to economic and structural modes of power inequalities. This distinction enables one to see how racism, as separate from color prejudice, involves an inescapable link to issues of class, geographical and provincial animosities (which may merely designate some kind of ethnic cleavage), and social interaction. All of these issues are inextricably woven together with conceptualizations of race to form a dense, labyrinthine weave, as one can see in the reception of the Singh double murders in Imperial Valley. Holding this weave together, at its base, are the twin concerns of race and class that permeate all the events and motivations discussed thus far. Defining racism as a structural concern gets us around the problem of making phenotypical differences the bases for excluding South Asians from Asian American studies; if the latter is about race, it must pursue its research by looking at historical and structural similarities and not by relying on perceived physical differences.

By focusing on these different factors, I do not mean to marginalize the impact of racism but rather to acknowledge that race plays a central role in the life of an American community's understanding of itself as a social entity. The study of racism, as a result, cannot be separated out from these other concerns, for that merely has the effect of ghettoizing the importance of race and race discrimination from the context that gives them meaning. To concentrate on race outside of these other concerns marginalizes the importance of the Punjabis and other Asian immigrants within the daily lives of the more general American culture. Even, for example, the inclusion of Indians under the punitive authority of the California Alien Land Law cannot be understood as a discrete historical occurrence. It should, rather, be studied in the light of past precedents, of which it is only a small but crowning product, and as precedent for future developments. At the same time, one should understand race as it complements and is complemented by class consciousness, which is also another way of delineating structural inequalities of power between different groups within a given community. In order to explicate this claim, I continue by looking at past legislative "reforms" before moving on to discuss judicial proceedings that were designed to test, but only upheld, the decisions already made. It is interesting to note how much attention distinctions between race and color receive, if only implicitly, in U.S. court history.

Sripati Chandrasekhar, in a thorough if schematic investigation of the history of Indian immigration to the United States and the legislation that restricted it, points out: "Since the adoption of the Constitution in 1789 the U.S. did not have any immigration laws and it was presumed [by whom, he does not indicate] that open doors and open borders were the natural order of things" (11). The passage of the Chinese Exclusion Act of 1882 ended this one-hundred-year-old federal precedent. Naturalization, however, had been impossible for Chinese, and presumably other Asian, immigrants long before their actual physical entrance was prohibited.[10] Most of the immigration that took place before 1882 was from northern Europe and Africa. While one cannot compare the experiences of Africans torn from their land to European settlers, one might still point out fruitfully that "half to two-thirds of these whites to migrate to North America before the American revolution were indentured servants who had contracted away their freedom for up to seven years in return for passage" (Crosby 295). Only from 1820 onward, when Indian immigration amounted to a trickle, did large numbers of "free" Europeans cross the Atlantic. At about the same time (circa 1825), Hawaii began attracting Chinese laborers. When gold was discovered in California just before the start of the Civil War, Chinese workers from the southern provinces—made hungry by European imperialism's one-sided trade and corruption in the Qing ruling class—began to appear on North America's West Coast in increasingly large numbers.[11] This coincidence of dates would place Chinese immigration squarely within the large wave of immigration that swept over and repopulated North America, beginning from the early nineteenth century and lasting until the beginning of the First World War. Indeed, this wave of European immigration was so large that it makes immigration from other places seem comparatively negligible. Of the 50 million Europeans who immigrated to what Alfred Crosby calls Neo-Europes during this period, about two-thirds traveled to the United States (301). In stark contrast, Indian immigration to the United States "amounted to fewer than 700 over a period of 80 years from 1820 to 1900. In fact, no Asian Indian was admitted to the United States between 1893 and 1898"

(Bhardwaj and Rao 197). But, as we will shortly see, such numbers are misleading.

The end of this seemingly idyllic tradition of open immigration affected non-Europeans much more violently and directly than it did arrivals from the fringes of Europe. Northern European mobs, including the much-reviled Irish, roved the streets of San Francisco, beating up Chinese laborers and quoting from newspaper editorials about the unalterable foreignness of the Chinese; these Europeans failed to acknowledge that most of them had only been there for a few years and were themselves foreigners (Saxton 104–9). California in the mid-nineteenth century needed labor, and the Chinese filled that need with great vigor, to the point where Alexander Saxton, with great acumen, could call these early Asian immigrants the "indispensable enemy." Saxton was one of the first historians to point out how much labor the Chinese actually supplied:

> The 1870 census estimated California's gainfully employed as 239,000 in a population of somewhat over 570,000. There were, by the same count, slightly fewer than 50,000 Chinese, almost all of whom were gainfully employed. But even this figure is too small. The census category included entrepreneurs, independent farmers, supervisors, businessmen—and these we can assume to have been more numerous among non-Chinese than among Chinese. If then our concern is primarily with wage workers, it would probably not be far wrong to estimate that *one-quarter of all available for hire in the early seventies must have been Chinese.* (7; my emphasis)

So, on the eve of the Chinese Exclusion Act, Chinese immigrants constituted a major presence in the smooth running of California's economy and, by extension, social formation. No wonder white laborers saw the Chinese as a threat that needed to be contained.

If Saxton is correct in arguing that population figures do not reflect the actual level of significance, wouldn't this observation also hold true for other Asian groups? While their actual numbers might not be impressive, such immigrant groups probably constituted a greater part of the workforce and, hence, a greater level of significance to California and the nation than is usually ascribed to them.[12] According to the U.S. Census, in 1920, there were 111,010 Japanese in the entire United States, of whom 71,950 were in California (Daniels 115). But many of these immigrants were farmers, and fairly successful ones at that. In 1919, they either leased or owned a total of 458,156 acres (144). As historian Roger Daniels concludes:

> In 1919 the Japanese controlled acreage amounting to about 1 percent of California's land used in agriculture, but this is a misleading figure because much of that land was used for grazing and was then of little value. . . .

More indicative of the significance of Japanese in California agriculture was the fact that in 1919 the gross income from their crops was computed at more than $67 million, or about 10 percent of the total value of all California's agricultural production that year. (143–44)

Similarly, there were 1,723 immigrants from India living in California at the same time, a high proportion of them making a living as successful farmers. Success, of course, is not always the easiest adjective to quantify, but the numbers seem to bear out this characterization. Just in Imperial Valley alone, they worked 32,380 acres in 1919—a third of "all California land leased and owned by the Punjabis at the time" (Leonard "Pahkar" 122). This would mean that they worked a total of 97,140 acres in California, or roughly a fifth of the land farmed by the Japanese. This is an amazing figure if one keeps in mind that their population totaled only a minute fraction of the Japanese population, making them quite productive indeed for their small size. If immigration had continued to infuse their community with new members and they had continued to prosper the way they did in southern California, they would no doubt have become as visibly successful as their Japanese counterparts, not to mention their white counterparts.

Considering the country's racially charged atmosphere, buttressed by a scientific establishment bent on disseminating theories of racialized physical difference,[13] is it any surprise that the insurgence of anticoolie sentiments near the end of the nineteenth century would eventually affect other Asian immigrants besides the Chinese, or even immigration as a whole? As one Californian senator proclaimed, "We don't want these Hindus . . . and they should be barred out just as the Chinese are excluded" (quoted in Brands 3). Having had some success in keeping people out and hence exerting some control over the racial composition of the nation, the Asiatic Exclusion League and similar groups pressured Congress to pass the Immigration Act of 1917 that aimed its discriminatory agenda at the non–Northern European. First, it slowed down the rate of immigration from Southern and Eastern Europe by establishing a literacy test requirement, though immigration from these regions was never strictly prohibited and quotas always allotted (Hess 30). Second, and with great efficacy, it created a "Pacific Barred Zone" that criminalized immigration from all of Asia and the Middle East (Chandrasekhar 18).[14] This sweeping piece of legislation determined the pattern of immigration to the United States until after the Second World War and almost guaranteed that the official racial identity of the nation—an unstable concept at best but within a certain set perimeter—would reflect the actual majority of the population.

The Asiatic Exclusion League was one significant political force at the time pushing for these legislative measures. Originally called the Japanese and Korean Exclusion League, it changed its name in response to the arrival of the Punjabi immigrants after 1900. Thus, even as early as 1900, Indian immigrants were being categorized alongside other Asian groups by quasi-governmental organizations. This is important to remember when thinking about the census's current attitude toward demarcating people originating from Asia; it is a tradition that goes back almost a hundred years and is rooted firmly in the advocacy of xenophobia. The existence of this tradition compels us to close the gap in our study of Asian Americans, if this study proposes, even in part, to understand the history that has created this group. This tradition of grouping these particular non-European immigrants under one rubric, after all, led to the "Pacific Barred Zone" in the 1917 Immigration Act. As Chandrasekhar explains:

> Critics who examined the Act in some detail at the time offered two plausible explanations for the barred zone. One was that the U.S. Government, having discriminated against two important countries, China and Japan, did not wish these countries to feel that they had been singled out for discrimination and so they added India and the rest for the sake of fairness! (18)

Because they had all been excluded together to maintain a semblance of "fairness," they would also be recognized as belonging to the same racial category for their shared experience of exclusion. Even at the level of federal policy, what emerges is a coherent picture of racial thinking that groups South, Southeast, and East Asians, as well as Pacific Islanders, together into one large category that needs to be dealt with as if they were one large (and perhaps even homogenous) racial group.[15]

Regardless of how convenient overlooking the differences between various Asian immigrant groups might have been for federal policy makers, and their tiptoeing around British imperialist policy, those differences did exist and were made use of by local politicians. As Saxton argues, anti-Asian agitation was essential to organizing white workers and the white underemployed to keep union leaders in power while diverting their attention away from the social problems that plagued them, such as low wages, long workdays, and the sporadic availability of jobs: "The only real danger was that the Chinese might finally leave or die out; but happily the Exclusion Act had been written only against the Chinese, and there remained a parade of Asian menaces—Hindoos, Filipinos, Japanese—waiting in the wings to provide employment for subsequent generations of craft union officials and labor politicians" (264). This is why, perhaps, the history of exclusionary legislation followed such an orderly sequence: the Chinese Exclusion Act of 1882, the "gentleman's agreement" with the Japanese in 1907, and finally the "Pacific Barred Zone" in 1917.

As an added incentive, such inflammatory anti-Asian immigration rhetoric allowed politicians and labor leaders to conceal their own foreignness. Many of these leaders and their constituents were immigrants themselves—about 15 percent of the entire American population was foreign-born just before World War I (Crosby 301) and, as noted earlier, immigration figures were significantly higher among the working classes in California—and no doubt had as good a reason to flee their native lands as the Asian immigrants they denigrated. As a result, we should not be surprised that racial tension, which was based on, and even encouraged, economic competition among the working poor, would be pushed to the limits of violence, desperate as they all were to hold onto what little advantages migration had conferred upon them. By using the rhetoric of xenophobia, European settlers were able to position themselves as a racially undefined majority; they become visible as "nativist" by identifying another group as being even more foreign than themselves.

Yet, the differences between the European and Asian immigrants were not as large as contemporary rhetoric suggested. For example, Alfred Crosby identifies three motivations driving the 50 million Europeans who "crossed the oceans to the Neo-Europes between 1820 and 1930": their home countries were overly populated and undernourished, the means of travel were readily available, and they believed there were more opportunities abroad (296). These same motivations could also be attributed to Asian immigrants with equal accuracy. Perhaps what disturbed European immigrants most about their Asian cousins were not their differences but their similarities. The latter had come to America for the same reasons and wanted the same opportunities, but still they remained recalcitrantly different from the European majority in physical appearance, social practices, language, and history (no doubt, differences made more pronounced by political mercenaries and pundits of the time to further their own personal agendas). As a result, they were aggressively alienated from their dreams of a better life. For Europeans, looking at Asian immigrants must have felt too much like looking into a fun-house mirror—the same image but perversely out of proportion. At the same time, they could not actually pin down the irreducible causes of the distortion. This must have perturbed them to no end. It was this distortion, being made the negative reflection of a racially undefined majority's aspirations, that made the experiences of the diverse Asian immigrant groups so similar to each other even while one could not see this similarity from within the insularity of the respective groups. It was a racial identity imposed from, and made attractive to, a white working majority haunted by its own fears of not belonging. We should keep in mind, however, that many European immigrants came to the United States with anti-Asian attitudes acquired in their homelands. In the Old World countries, most of which had homogeneous populations, Asians were frequently perceived to be dangerous and undesirable "others."

The term "Asian American," then, can be reserved to describe those who belong to groups that came to the United States for reasons similar to their European counterparts, but who did not share the same cultural history and were forcibly prevented from identifying themselves as Americans. This latter term was exclusively reserved for an evolving racial category known today as "white," which signified a whole array of surprisingly divergent and frequently antagonistic ethnic groups who before entering the United States probably would not have considered themselves as such.

This last claim becomes more substantial when we examine the different Supreme Court decisions handed down around this same turn-of-the-century period that dealt with the racializing of Asian Americans as one pan-ethnic population group. The gentleman's agreement of 1907, which effectively halted male immigration from Japan even before passage of the 1917 Immigration Act, had been refined in 1920, closing the loophole that allowed the practice of "picture brides." Not content with this legislation, the Supreme Court ruled in 1922 that Takao Ozawa was not qualified for citizenship because he was not "Caucasian" and therefore not "white" (Takaki 208; Daniels 151). In the next year, Supreme Course Justice George Sutherland, the very same person who delivered the majority decision in the Ozawa case, gave this opinion denying Bhagat Singh Thind his claim to citizenship—a claim upheld by lower courts:

> In the endeavor to ascertain the meaning of the statute we must not fail to keep in mind that it does not employ the word "Caucasian" but the words "white persons," and these are words of common speech and not of scientific origin. . . . The words of the statute are to be interpreted in accordance with the understanding of the common man from whose vocabulary they were taken. (Chandrasekhar 20)

Hence, having stopped the infusion of new immigrants from a broadly defined Asia and having restricted the existing immigrant population's access to their chosen livelihoods, a final piece of tortured logic deprived this population the opportunity of becoming a participatory member of their adopted nation. Ronald Takaki's argument about the fears motivating passage of the Alien Land Law seems to ring true here: "The concern of many exclusionists was not so much miscegenation as settlement. As Japanese immigrants became landholders, they increasingly became settlers— immigrants with families" (204).

What is striking about these twin decisions presided over by Chief Justice Sutherland is the unchanging need to recognize the difference of the Japanese and the Indian as racial and legal. In other words, there was a need to reify their ontological status in the United States as a palpably definable other. Judge Sutherland's overriding compulsion to solidify into law his difference from these claimants, even at the expense of contradicting himself, was one thing Ozawa and Thind had in common. This contradiction would permanently bind Ozawa's name with Thind's in the historian's mind, and to talk of one without the other is to tell a grossly incomplete and perhaps incomprehensible story.[16]

But what about the nature of this contradiction? Undoubtedly, the Chief Supreme Court Justice at the time was an intelligent and thoughtful person who saw no contradiction in what he was saying. There must have been some internally coherent logic which he could make out and which remains invisible thus far in this discussion. The distinction between race and color is useful here. If we analyze Sutherland's opinion in the Thind case, we can see that the terms race and color align themselves ideologically with the distinction "Caucasian" and "white persons," which he in turn aligns with "scientific" and "common speech." The crux of his decision centers around these distinctions. At the same time, he plays on the confusion between these two positions to decide against Ozawa and Thind without seeming, at one level, to contradict himself. He does so by replacing one position with the other whenever it suits his needs.

In the former case, the Supreme Court was able to base its decision on a scientific, especially (pre–Franz Boas) anthropological, discourse that reaffirmed and expressed the logic of a racialist hierarchy. Ozawa could not be a citizen because the law stated quite clearly that one needed first to be a racial "Caucasian." Regardless of his skin color, he could not be deemed "white" because "whiteness" was a function of race rooted in a larger semiotic meaning, including a scientific meaning, which the law intended. The Supreme Court ruled, in other words, that there was no distinction between race and color. In the latter case, the Supreme Court makes this distinction between race and color by ruling that while, scientifically, Thind may be a racial "Caucasian," he is not white by the "common man's" understanding. The judges declared that the law made a distinction between racial prejudice and color prejudice and explicitly intended to uphold the latter without any consideration of the former. These twin decisions, seen from this perspective, are clearly contradictory. But this contradiction is not self-evident until one can make the distinction between race and skin color.

With this important distinction in mind, I want to examine what race might mean on a theoretical level incorporating the insights afforded by a historical analysis. Michael Omi and Howard Winant, two sociologists whose work focuses primarily on theories about race, try to define race in ways that intentionally foreground the many contradictions pitting its articulation. First, they take a current scientific view as their starting point:

> race is a concept which signifies and symbolizes social conflicts and interests by referring to different types of human bodies. Although the concept of race invokes biologically based human characteristics (so-called "phenotypes"), selection of these particular human features for purposes of racial signification is always and necessarily a social and historical process. . . . There is no biological basis for distinguishing among human groups along the lines of race. (55)

Part one of their definition seems straightforward. They are debunking the kind of argument made in the Ozawa case, based on a biologistic understanding of human difference which reinforces and reifies preexisting hierarchies. This is an easy enough argument to make; as Howard Winant points out elsewhere, "Even the KKK stalwarts claim to be antiracist today" (*Racial Conditions* 6). Though antiracism does not entail a critique of biological racial difference, the two ideas are yoked together in their work so that one position appears to entail the other. While it may be prudent to approach the Klan's claim with a great deal of skepticism, the point is well taken. Race as a concept has been under attack for so long that it is not difficult to show how inadequate it is in describing the world's population. Nevertheless, by insisting upon the critique of a biological racial distinction, they make it more difficult for us to elide science and race as the Supreme Court does without any hesitation in its ruling on *Ozawa v. the U.S.* and *Thind v. the U.S.*

At the same time, because of the powerful presence of race (vis-à-vis phenotypic markers) with its inescapable historical and current impact on the formation of our society, it would be inaccurate to displace the concept race with another structure of human relationships that is supposedly more real or material. Omi and Winant have the difficult task of incorporating this conceptual bind within their analytic framework. Here is the second part of their definition: "Thus we should think of race as an element of social structure rather than as an irregularity within it; we should see race as a dimension of human representation rather than an illusion" (55). Struck by the powerful presence of race, obviously still alive in everyday discourse and made palpable as a prejudice of skin color, with its very real historical heritage, they find themselves incapable of reducing race to a concept that must either be thrown out or exploded. This latter argument, after all, is the centerpiece of neoconservative writers who would not only prohibit one from talking about race all together but would also label one a racist if one continued to do so. While perhaps slightly expressive of an enlightened sentiment about color prejudice, this is nothing more than de facto racism: it allows existing forms of discrimination to proceed and even fester unchecked by commentary or critique while allowing the far right to prey on the electorate's economic worries through the use of subtexts and open race-baiting for political gain.[17] The alternative that Omi and Winant offer is to place race at the center of their thinking.

They explain the thorny situation they find themselves in by pointing toward what they might call the far right's and the neoconservative's strengths—though these positions are certainly not the sole provinces of consciously political conservatives—before defining their own position:

> There is a continuous temptation to think of race as an *essence*, as something fixed, concrete, and objective. And there is also an opposite temptation to image race as a mere *illusion*, a purely ideological construct which some ideal non-racist social order would eliminate. It is necessary to challenge both these positions, to disrupt and reframe the rigid and bipolar manner in which they are posed and debated, and to transcend the presumably irreconcilable relationship between them. (54)

In other words, they are asking their readers both to deny that race has an "essence" and to admit simultaneously that it is more than an "illusion," that it is both not-real and real. Is this Judge Sutherland's "common man" argument yet again? While one might intellectually disqualify racialist discourses, this does nothing to address the kinds of social and economic disequilibrium that exist in the present nor to redress the historical developments that have perpetuated such disequilibrium. What one must deal with, then, is the viewpoint of the common person from whose vocabulary the concept of race was taken. While Sutherland wanted to appeal to this viewpoint, and even to use it as source of authority, Omi and Winant want to combat it by making everyone first admit that such a viewpoint exists— that the expressions of skin color prejudice, or other phenotypic prejudices, point toward a more deeply underlying form of inequality and outright repression. While finding their argument highly unstable, as unstable as any ideology, I believe they envision the only stand available to the present discussion in defining a usage of race: *it is historically real but scientifically chimerical.*

However, I insist on at least one provision. What a close study of the Singh double murders and its reception shows is how disputes over racial suitability, regardless of how overdetermined the motivation or reception, are always accompanied by a debate over property. It is this latter debate that underlies the application of the Alien Land Law to both the Japanese and Indians and rationalizes a discourse that would group such diverse groups under the same racial heading. As Omi and Winant put it: "The U.S. has confronted each racially defined minority with a unique form of despotism and degradation. The examples are familiar: Native Americans faced genocide, blacks were subjected to racial slavery, Mexican Americans were invaded and colonized, and Asians faced exclusion" (1). Africans were property, Native Americans and then Mexicans had property, and Asians were trying to compete for the same property that the Europeans wanted. I do not mean to suggest that, because all people of color are bound together by the experience of racism, this is the only bond between South and East Asians living in the United States. The distinctive nature of the racial oppression these groups suffered must also be taken into account. It is this difference of historical treatment that led to five separate racial categories in the 1990 U.S. Census.

This crude division of racialized groups and their experiences in North America, while perhaps too general to account for their experiences with any kind of historical specificity, helps to define rhetorically the kinds of shockingly reductive distinctions racism has had to make in order to divide an extremely heterogeneous population into manageable, racially charged subgroups. This entrenched logic has shaped the structure of race formation and subsequently the character of the American nation as it emerged into coherence during the turn of the nineteenth century. This emergence of a structure of race formation that goes beyond the veneer of phenotype explains how South Asian immigrants came under the purview of Asian American Studies, and perhaps disappeared discursively as a result. The perception of Asian Americans as foreigners, as others that need to be excluded because they could not become assimilated, was important to the development of a national identity based on a normative whiteness. At the present moment there are two options available to academics and activists to remedy the "disappearance" of South Asians from an Asian American scholarly discourse: either accept the pull of a history that carelessly throws different groups together and make what alliances one can with each other, or insist upon ever narrowing definitions of group differences and look for less historically conditioned coalitions elsewhere. No doubt, both approaches will be taken (if academics and activists alike are not already well along each path), though it is still too early to determine how well each approach alone and in dialogue with the other will amend this gap in the study of race in America.

ACKNOWLEDGMENTS

In writing this paper, I have received advice and encouragement from a large number of people. While I do not have enough space to recognize everyone, I would like to thank Rajini Srikanth, Lavina Shankar, Emma Teng, and Modhumita Roy. I also wish to mention the great intellectual debt this paper owes to Karen Leonard, whose work on the Punjabi farmers of Imperial Valley has proven an invaluable source of historical information.

Notes

1. See Karen Leonard's "The Pahkar Singh Murders: A Punjabi Response to California's Alien Land Law," referred to in parenthetical citations as "Pahkar." Leonard's "Punjabi Farmers and California's Alien Land Law" is referred to in parenthetical citations as "Punjabi," and her "Marriage and Family Life among Early East Asian Immigrants" as "Marriage."

2. For examples of such exclusions, compare Michael Omi's "It Just Ain't the Sixties No More: The Contemporary Dilemmas of Asian American Studies"; William Wei's *The Asian American Movement* (especially x); and Elaine Kim's *Asian American Literature* (especially xiii). For attempted remedies of such exclusions, see Karin Aguilar-San Juan, ed., *The State of Asian America: Activism and Resistance in the 1990s*, especially preface.

3. See United States Department of Commerce, Economics and Statistics Administration, and Bureau of the Census, B-20.

4. On the Spanish-American War, compare Amy Kaplan's "Black and Blue in San Juan Hill"; on the end of Reconstruction, compare Barbara Fields's "Ideology and Race in American History" and David Roediger's *The Wages of Whiteness: Race and the Making of the American Working Class*; on populist organizations, see Alexander Saxton's *The Indispensable Enemy* and the discussion of his book later in this paper.

5. See Gary Hess's "The Asian Indian Immigrants in the United States, 1900–1965."

6. There are too many prominent studies in this field to list all of them here, and so the following should be read only as a partial list: Patrick Brantlinger's *Rule of Darkness: British Literature and Imperialism 1830–1914*; Edward Said's *Culture and Imperialism*; Aijaz Ahmad's *In Theory: Classes, Nations, Literatures*; Mary Louise Pratt's *Imperial Eyes: Travel Writing and Transculturation*; and Anne McClintock's mostly synthetic *Imperial Leather: Race, Gender, and Sexuality in the Colonial Conquest*. Of course, there has always been a sustained critical interest in imperialism, though few assumed that the experience of British imperialism was inextricably woven into the entire social fabric alongside issues of, for example, aesthetics, textuality, race, gender, sexuality, and class. Early examples of this changing approach to the study of imperialism and culture are Martin Green's *Dreams of Adventure, Deeds of Empire* and Said's *Orientalism*.

7. For more details, see Leonard's "The Pahkar Singh Murders."

8. Compare with Leonard's analysis in "Punjabi Farmers and the Alien Land Law" (107).

9. In Susan Lanser's remarkable essay "Feminist Criticism, 'The Yellow Wallpaper,' and the Politics of Color in America," she claims the existence of a third

racial classification called "yellow," which contained anyone who did not belong to the other two classifications. Unlike "negro" and "white," which were viewed as being unusually stable, this third classification was most notable for its extreme instability, reserved as it was for more recent groups of immigrants. Being "yellow" also seems to have acted as a sign for one's unassimilabilty and irreducible foreignness, again indicating how there was room for only two racial colors in America's perception of itself, all other considerations having to be viewed as outside this self-image.

In a related vein, Virginia Domínguez in *White by Definition* notes how the Registrar's Office in Louisiana did not know how to classify Filipinos, whose birth certificates alternated between calling them white and colored. According to one person at the Registrar's Office whom Domínguez quotes, his successor "would always record Filipinos as 'colored' and . . . would not record them as Filipinos unless they insisted on being registered as white" (35–36).

10. . At least one scholar, Hyung-Chan Kim, in *A Legal History of Asian Americans, 1790–1990*, traces the urge to control and restrict immigration all the way back to colonial times: "Early debates on immigration during Colonial America centered around the concept of quality of the immigrant. Most colonies passed legislation to keep out the morally undesirable. These debates continued to persist into Revolutionary America and finally found their way into legislation; first, regulating naturalization, and later excluding undesirable aliens" (8).

11. Compare Joseph Esherick's *The Origins of the Boxer Uprising* (94–95); Anthony Chan's *Golden Mountain: The Chinese in the New World* (25–29); and *From China to Canada: A History of the Chinese Community in Canada* (ed. Harry Con et al. 7–10).

12. Compare Gail Nomura's "Significant Lives."

13. See Stephen Jay Gould's *The Mismeasure of Man* for a cogent and in-depth discussion of such theories and the episteme that informed them; also, compare with Thomas Gossett's classic work in this field, *Race: The History of an Idea in America.*

14. The barred zone "included most of China (the Chinese were already excluded, as were the Japanese), India, Siam, the Malay State, the Asian part of Russia, and most of Arabia, Afghanistan, the Polynesian Islands and the East Indian Islands (present Indonesia)" (Chandrasekhar 18). Melendy argues this provision of the 1917 Immigration Act was mainly aimed at eliminating Indian immigration (200–201).

15. As Chandrasekhar goes on to argue, even this apparent domestic policy decision has the imprint of the "nefarious hand of British imperialism": "The lack of independence in American judgment and a need to hang onto British skirts on this subject, occasioned by a determination not to hurt the sensitivities of her closest ally, which were very delicate wherever British colonials were concerned, had been pointed out by more than one critic" (18). In tracing the importance of British imperialist interests in the development of a pan-Asian racial category, albeit unwittingly, it seems relevant to recall how the early Punjabi immigrants served as part of Britain's military presence in China, mainly as an imperialist police force (Leonard "Punjabi" 107). Before arriving in Imperial Valley, Pahkar Singh himself

had spent some time in China, though we do not know what his occupation was there (Leonard "Pahkar" 125).

16. For a more complete treatment of the interconnections between these two cases, see Ian Haney Lopez's well-researched *White by Law: The Legal Construction of Race* (79–110).

17. For a lucid discussion of this phenomenon, see Winant (especially 24–36). Because of space constraints, I have elided the distinction Winant makes between "far right" and "new right," while maintaining his sense of "neoconservatism."

WORKS CITED

Aguilar-San Juan, Karin, ed. *The State of Asian America: Activism and Resistance in the 1990s*. Boston: South End, 1994.

Ahmad, Aijaz. *In Theory: Classes, Nations, Literatures*. London and New York: Verso, 1992.

Bhardwaj, Surinder, and N. Madhusudana Rao. "Asian Indians in the United States: A Geographical Appraisal." In *South Asians Overseas*, edited by Colin Clarke. New York: Cambridge University Press, 1990, 197–218.

Brands, H. W. *India and the United States: The Cold Peace*. Boston: Twayne, 1990.

Brantlinger, Patrick. *Rule of Darkness: British Literature and Imperialism, 1830–1914*. Ithaca, N.Y.: Cornell University Press, 1988.

Chan, Anthony. *Gold Mountain: The Chinese in the New World*. Vancouver: New Star Books, 1983.

Chandrasekhar, Sripati. "A History of United States Legislation with Respect to Immigration from India." In *From India to America,* edited by Sripati Chandrasekhar, La Jolla, Calif.: Population Review, 1982, 11–28.

Chandrasekhar, Sripati, ed. *From India to America: A Brief History of Immigration; Problems of Discrimination; Administration and Assimilation*. La Jolla, Calif.: Population Review, 1982.

Con, Harry, et al., eds. *From China to Canada: A History of the Chinese Community in Canada*. Toronto: McClelland and Stewart, 1982.

Crosby, Alfred. *Ecological Imperialism: The Biological Expansion of Europe, 900–1900*. London and New York: Cambridge University Press, 1986.

Daniels, Roger. *Asian America: Chinese and Japanese in the United States since 1850*. Seattle: University of Washington Press, 1988.

Domínguez, Virginia. *White By Definition: Social Classification in Creole Louisiana*. New Brunswick, N.J.: Rutgers University Press, 1986.

Dusenbery, Verne. "A Sikh Diaspora? Contested Identities and Constructed Realities." In *Nation and Migration: The Politics of Space in the South Asian Diaspora*, edited by Peter van der Veer. Philadelphia: University of Pennsylvania Press, 1995.

Esherick, Joseph. *The Origins of the Boxer Uprising*. Berkeley: University of California Press, 1987.

Fields, Barbara. "Ideology and Race in American History." In *Region, Race, and Reconstruction: Essays in Honor of C. Vann Woodward*, edited by J. Morgan

Kousser and James M. McPherson. New York: Oxford University Press, 1982, 143–78.

Gossett, Thomas. *Race: The History of an Idea in America*. Dallas: Southern Methodist University Press, 1963.

Gould, Stephen Jay. *The Mismeasure of Man*. New York: Norton, 1981.

Green, Martin. *Dreams of Adventure, Deeds of Empire*. New York: Basic, 1979.

Haney Lopez, Ian. *White by Law: The Legal Construction of Race*. New York: New York University Press, 1996.

Hess, Gary. "The Asian Indian Immigrants in the United States, 1900–1965." In *From India to America*, edited by Sripati Chandrasekhar, La Jolla, Calif.: Population Review, 1982, 29–34.

Ignatiev, Noel. *How the Irish Became White*. New York and London: Routledge, 1995.

Kaplan, Amy. "Black and Blue in San Juan Hill." In *Cultures of United States Imperialism*, edited by Amy Kaplan and Donald Pease. Durham, N.C.: Duke University Press, 1993.

Kim, Elaine. *Asian American Literature*. Philadelphia: Temple University Press, 1982.

Kim, Hyung-Chan. *A Legal History of Asian Americans, 1790–1990*. Westport, Conn.: Greenwood, 1994.

Lanser, Susan. "Feminist Criticism, 'The Yellow Wallpaper,' and the Politics of Color in America." *Feminist Studies* 15:3 (Fall 1989): 415–41.

Leonard, Karen. "Marriage and Family Life among Early Asian Indian Immigrants." In *From India to America*, edited by Sripati Chandrasekhar, La Jolla, Calif.: Population Review, 1982, 67–75.

———. "The Pahkar Singh Murders: A Punjabi Response to California's Alien Land Law." *Amerasia* 11 (1984): 75–87. Reprinted in *Asian Indians, Filipinos, Other Asian Communities and the Law*, edited by Charles McClain. New York: Garland, 1994, 121–34.

———. "Punjabi Farmers and California's Alien Land Law." *Agricultural History* 59 (1985). 549–62. Reprinted in *Asian Indians, Filipinos, Other Asian Communities and the Law*, edited by Charles McClain. New York: Garland, 1994, 107–20.

McClintock, Anne. *Imperial Leather: Race, Gender, and Sexuality in the Colonial Conquest*. New York and London: Routledge, 1994.

Mazumdar, Sucheta. "Race and Racism: South Asians in the United States." *Frontiers of Asian American Studies: Writing, Research and Commentary*. Proceedings of the Association for Asian American Studies Conference, March 1989, Washington State University. Edited by Gail Nomura, et al. Pullman, Wash.: Washington State University Press, 1989, 25–38.

Melendy, Howard Brett. *Asians in America: Filipino, Koreans, and East Indians*. Boston: Twayne, 1977.

Nomura, Gail. "Significant Lives." *Western Historical Quarterly* 25 (1994): 69–88.

Omi, Michael. "It Just Ain't the Sixties No More: The Contemporary Dilemmas of Asian American Studies." *Reflections on Shattered Windows: Promises and Prospects for Asian American Studies*. Proceedings of the Association for Asian

American Studies Conference, 1987, San Francisco State University, edited by Gary Okihiro. Pullman: Washington State University Press, 1988, 31–36.

Omi, Michael, and Howard Winant. *Racial Formation in the United States: From the 1960s to the 1990s.* 2d ed. New York: Routledge, 1994.

Pratt, Mary Louise. *Imperial Eyes: Travel Writings and Transculturation.* New York: Routledge, 1992.

Roediger, David. *The Wages of Whiteness: Race and the Making of the American Working Class.* London and New York: Verso, 1993.

Said, Edward. *Culture and Imperialism.* New York: Knopf, 1993.

———. *Orientalism.* New York: Vintage, 1979.

Saxton, Alexander. *The Indispensable Enemy.* Berkeley: University of California Press, 1971.

Takaki, Ronald. *Strangers from a Different Shore: A History of Asian America.* New York: Penguin, 1989.

United States. Department of Commerce, Economics and Statistics Administration, and Bureau of the Census. *1990 Census of Population and Housing-1-1: Summary of Population and Housing Characteristics, United States.* Washington: GPO, 1992.

Wei, William. *Asian American Movement.* Philadelphia: Temple University Press, 1993.

Winant, Howard. *Racial Conditions: Politics, Theory, Comparisons.* Minneapolis: University of Minnesota Press, 1994.

III. TOPOLOGIES OF ACTIVISM

Vijay Prashad

5   Crafting Solidarities

Azia, Red Star Youth Project, Leicester, 1980s: "We come from all kinds of families, but when it comes to our rights we are black."

—Pnina Werbner and Muhammad Anwar, *Black and Ethnic Leaderships in Britain*

Asian Indian, New York City, 1970s: "I can't call myself white. But Caucasian, that's the blood, I think, as far as racial things go. . . . On forms, I put myself down as brown, I can't help it—I can't write myself down as white and I can't write myself as black."

—Maxine Fisher, *The Indians of New York City*

MANY PEOPLE adhere to the idea that political interests must be based on a *single* conception of identity (whether of gender, race, class, or sexual orientation). This theory, which operates under the omnibus label "identity politics," wallows in parochialism and rejects any attempt to formulate universal categories (considered to be "totalitarian"). This tradition fails to acknowledge the dialectical relationship between parochialism and universality. I argue that the *process* of politics encourages the formation of parochial identities (which retain the tension of our contemporary inequalities) alongside those categories that offer the possibility of finding common ground that would allow us to abolish parochialism in favor of a complex universalism of the future. Such universal categories (of which "people of color" is one) might enable us to craft complex solidarities to struggle against the divisions among various communities.

The question of the position of South Asians within Asian America is not an abstract question posed for a Platonic solution. The question, in my opinion, is posed to allow us to tease out the contradictions within the question itself in order to bridge the "gap" through praxis. In order to open the contradictions of the question of the "gap," I want to explore the terms that are presumed to be sundered apart ("Asian America" and "South Asian America") and to see if these terms indeed belong to the same order of reality and can therefore be joined. This essay is then a meditation on categories as well as an argument for a particular category as the bridge between communities. In 1960, W.E.B. Du Bois heralded an acknowledgment of commonality between South Asians and blacks, which although premature in 1960, is important to repeat (and it is quoted below): the history of colonial oppression and the contemporary reality of capitalist exploitation links South Asians with other people of color and forces us to confront the question of linkages. The site of linkage, I argue, is already being mapped out by an urban youth culture that is notoriously radical and angry: in a revision of a Punjabi wedding song, Paaras sings the praises of "My Black Prince, My Black Sardar: Remove the Whites" (*Kala Shah Kala, Kala Shah Kala, mere kale hi Sardar, Gore aure dafa karo*). The lyrics' cultural roots provoke us to think about the antiracism of this youth statement as well as the ethnocentrism and masculinity of the Bhangra culture that it refers to (I will say more about the culture of Bhangra later, but for now it is enough to know it as the name that defines a cultural tradition originating in England among South Asians and heavily inflected by Punjabi and Caribbean traditions). The youth bear the hopes of the future, but they also carry with them avoidable components of our cultural history. This essay is an attempt to chart the structural location of South Asians in America as well as to argue that South Asians must craft a political category that is open to the formation of broad solidarities. In order to arrive at that point, I must first elaborate upon the central concept that governs the use of "South Asian American"—Asian American.

"ASIAN AMERICAN"

"Asian American" is a category with a series of meanings, each forged out of different political and historical contexts and projects. In his study of the Asian American Movement, William Wei offers us two dominant meanings: Asian American as a cultural identity, and Asian American as a sociopolitical movement.[1] In a remarkable oversight, Wei does not question the term "Asian American," which he uses in both senses simultaneously. In an important corrective to Wei's history of the movement and to his use of the term "Asian American," Glenn Omatsu historicizes the meaning of the term. Omatsu argues that the Asian American movement began as a sociopolitical movement that "embraced fundamental questions of oppression and power" only to be transformed in the 1980s into a movement "centered on the aura of racial identity" (Omatsu 21). The transformation of the category from a predominantly sociopolitical focus to a cultural (ethnic) focus occurred following a series of complex maneuvers exemplified by the rise of the New Right and the "new racism" that developed in the 1960s, but attained respectability two decades later.

"Asian American" emerged in the 1960s from a political movement provoked by a variety of issues, notably the autonomous control of institutions in ethnic enclaves (Chinatowns, Japantowns, Manilatowns) as well as in universities (Ethnic Studies). Activists fought for autonomy from the bureaucrats at city hall in order to fashion the space and texture of their own neighborhoods (which became the concrete manifestation of control over one's community). The political project around the term "Asian American" still endures among seasoned veterans of the movement and those who acknowledge its heritage. For historical reasons, the term Asian American largely refers to those who claim East Asian ancestry. West Asians (Iraqis, Israelis, Iranians, Syrians, etc.) operate under the rubric "Arab American" or "Jewish American," while there has not been a historically significant Central Asian migration (except Armenians, but their consciousness of "Asian" is rather limited). North Asians (Russians) are more likely to be seen as, and nominate themselves as, Slavic Americans or as European Americans. The only significant addition under the umbrella term "Asian American" has been from South Asians and that development begins in the late 1980s under pressure from South Asians in the academy. In the main, the term "Asian American" refers to East Asian Americans and this, I argue, has more to do with a racist ethnology than with the historical fact of the movement's origins.

The new racism of the 1960s, which fostered the ethnoracialization of terms such as "Asian American," has a simple logic: the Enlightenment's anthropology (written by Buffon, Cuvier, Gobineau, Maupertuis, et al.) is borrowed wholesale (particularly the typology of "races": Caucasoid, Mongoloid, Negroid) and transformed from a zoological classification to a statement about "culture." In one of the more confused gestures of modern logic, this transformation takes a theory saturated in blood and genetics and aims to make it tell us something of culture. The use of black (for Negroid) as an adjective is supposed to tell us something about the cultural system of blacks, for example. While "Asian American" becomes a "cultural" designation (from its origins as a political organizing category), it remains rooted in phenotypes (yellow skin and "slant" eyes). The liberal version of this racial hierarchy exists today in the guise of cultural or national differences, which rest on presumptions of racial division (European, Chinese, Indian, African, etc.). The new racism drew new boundaries for "Asian America" in terms of phenotypes. Culture and ethnicity, despite being understood as socially constructed, are grounded upon a zoological Chain of Being. That is, as a result of a historical homology between culture and race, cultural categories are based upon and governed by racial categories. The discourse of race, in other words, forms the bedrock upon which our categories of cultural groups rest.

Before moving ahead with a discussion of the new racism of the 1960s, I want to consider a formal problem with the term "Asian American." To hyphenate America with a place of origin prolongs the myth of America as a land of immigrants who each bring their continental ethnicity to enrich the new world: therefore, Europeans as European-Americans, Spanish-speakers as Hispanic-Americans, Africans as African-Americans, and Asians as Asian-Americans are given homologous histories and offered identical entry into the dialectic between assimilation and segregation (if we break these continental ethnicities into national ethnicities, such as Chinese-American or Italian-American, the point remains the same). The differences of power implied in the names are lost. The hyphen reinforces the celebration of ethnicity without a sharp political consciousness of the uneven development of the various peoples who are now under the American umbrella. Certainly, the continent of origin retains the *idea* of difference, but the *form* in which it is retained produces a tendency to assume a similarity in the experience of Americanization: that is, even though the content of different traditions is retained in the hyphenated names, the form of the practice serves to erase the differential histories of the various racialized communities. "Black," unlike "African-American," connotes the Black Power movement and symbolizes the history of structural disenfranchisement as well as the radical struggle for freedom; "Latino" and "Chicano," unlike "Hispanic-American," recall the invasion of the American Southwest, the Bracero program and the Chicano movement.

The erasure of differential histories and of relations of power implied by these terms reminds us of the shallow use of "equality" made by the New Right in order to revoke the gains of the civil rights, labor, and women's movements in this country. Equality, for a leftist agenda, cannot mean sameness, for then it loses its contradictory sense: as the need to produce an *equal* civilization from extant *inequality* that comes in myriad forms (Marx 9-10). To claim that all people are already equal obscures the inequalities that must be combated in order to produce equality. Equality is an instinct, and a simple gesture toward equalization of community names does not begin to address the structural gaps that divide people.

The "New Racism" of the 1960s

Alongside the efflorescence of the Asian American movement, the American state put forward its own agenda for "Asian America" in the form of the "model minority" stereotype. The stereotype emerges with special reference to East Asians, but its import is quickly grasped by new South Asian migrants who use the term to their own strategic advantage. When South Asians adopted the term from the 1970s onwards, they did so with a sense of pride and without an awareness of the racist history that produced that stereotype. The term "model minority" implies that Asians are a "model" for somebody and that the Asians are a "minority" in terms of a majority. These implications need to be elaborated. First, the issue of the "model." The "model minority" stereotype emerged in 1966 in the *New York Times Magazine* and in *US News & World Report*, which suggested that the Japanese and Chinese, respectively, are self-sufficient and their children are able to succeed because of family support. Why was it important to highlight these "successes," given that the Japanese and Chinese have historically been the victims of American racism? A statement by the *US News & World Report* makes the timing of these articles very clear: "At a time when it is being proposed that hundreds of billions be spent to uplift Negroes and other minorities, the nation's 300,000 Chinese-Americans are moving ahead on their own, with no help from anyone else" (quoted in Osajima 167). In the wake of the Black Liberation Movement launched in the 1950s, the ghetto rebellions of 1965, the Voting Rights Act of 1965 and the 1965 Moynihan Report on the "dysfunctionality" of the black family, the media created the stereotype as a weapon against blacks, as well as to ensure the growth of mutual suspicion between blacks and Asians. The Asians now represented all that the blacks were not and could not hope to be.

If the "Asian" was positioned as a "model" for blacks, in what sense was the "Asian" a "minority"? A "minority" of what? A "minority" must be counterposed to a "majority," but the history of attempts in the United States to find a legal definition for its natural citizens demonstrates its anxiety with regard to this question. The famous Ozawa-Thind cases in the early 1920s illustrate the depth of this racial anxiety. Unable to specify its tests for citizenship, the Supreme Court held that to be a U.S. citizen was to be white (skin color), which meant being European (culture). In the 1910 census, the state classified people from India as nonwhite because they represented "a civilization distinctly different from that of Europe" (Jensen 246-69). As Lavina Shankar's essay in this volume points out, "Asian Indians" have been confusedly named and renamed both as "whites" and as "minorities" throughout the twentieth century. Except for a period of three decades, the United States has seen the Asian Indians as nonwhite, hence their status as a minority. In real life, however, white Americans have been unable to decide how to identify Asian Indians in terms of race.[2]

The stereotype of the "model minority" had important effects within the East Asian community. Of course, it did not apply to *all* East Asians. In response to the Soviet launching of Sputnik in 1957, and other Cold War–related concerns, the United States revised the immigration laws (the

1965 Immigration and Naturalization Act) so that professional and technical workers could enter the country in large numbers. A large percentage of the South Asians who entered the United States after 1965 were professionals and graduate degree holders and established a demographically unusual community. Rather than attribute this unusualness to the nature of immigration law, American common sense and the South Asian migrant attributed it to a putative "Asian" culture of education. Asians, like Jews, are seen to have "family values" that encourage their children to study hard and succeed; others, it seems, do not share this heritage. An Asian who fails is a double failure—both as an Asian and as a human being. Working-class Asians (such as the Vietnamese and Hmong "boat-people," the Chinese American sweatshop workers, or the South Asian taxi drivers and kiosk workers) do not use the term "Asian American," which carries connotations of bourgeois status, to refer to themselves. The myth of Asian success excludes those outside the networks of cultural and mercantile capital from access to federal funding and special programs for the dispossessed (Crystal; Hu). Working-class Asians are marginalized from their "community" (which is unified only in the eyes of the American state). The emerging elites of the various Asian communities distance themselves from the working class, who are regarded as either failures or only potentially successful and only peripherally as members of the "community" (the "community" is not something one is born into, but something that one earns, much like the idea of "Society" in Victorian England).

The new racism of the 1960s is not a bipolar racism (black-white), but a racism that seeks to validate its zoological bipolarity on the basis of culture and "values" (in fact, on the intermediary "races" such as Asians). In the early decades of this century, Robert E. Park (who came to the University of Chicago after being Booker T. Washington's secretary) and the school of Franz Boas attacked the zoological notion of race: these arcadian Americans found the division by "race" contrary to the best instincts of humanity. Instead of a zoological understanding of "race," these sociologists and anthropologists argued that "races" are "ethnicities" that are socially formed. In the 1960s, such arguments supported the radical opposition to the naturalized notion of race. The American right used these arguments over the decades in a sinister manner to argue that Enlightenment racism is a paradigm superseded by that of capitalist merit (DeSouza). The right, in some versions, accepted the idea that race is a social construct and that cultures are real: once this was established, the hierarchy of races was simply transposed onto a hierarchy of cultures (which performed the functional role once accorded to race). This version of rightist discourse adheres to the belief that each culture (read race) has an indelible set of "cultural values" that are its own. Asians are all brain and no body; blacks are all body and no brain; and whites enjoy an Aristotelian medium of body and brain.[3] The cultural implications for this schema are that Asians are good at mental work and have tight family networks; blacks are good at sports and music and have no family networks; and whites enjoy a measured success in mental and manual work and have family networks that do not suffocate. The new racism allows Asians and whites to enjoy the privilege of some form of family network, although it is often said that the Asian family structure is too authoritarian (arranged marriages, etc.). This narrow construction of "values" underlies many stereotypes about Asian social life. For some upwardly mobile Asians, the stereotype is useful in supporting a new philosophy of mobility and empowerment. For professional South Asians, complicity with the new racism has short-term benefits, conferring a reputation as a hardworking and highly qualified group. Such racial typologies, however, also give rise to violence against Asians and the so-called glass ceiling; as such they are an obstacle to long-term gains.

Gary Okihiro has identified the powerful contradiction that strikes at the heart of the "model minority" stereotype. Alongside the notion of model minority, the idea of "yellow peril" sits, not "at apparent disjunction," but forming a "seamless continuum." "The very indices of Asian 'success' can imperil the good order of race relations when the margins lay claim to the privileges of the mainstream." As Asians begin to succeed in school and the professions, the media complain of an Asian takeover of America. Okihiro parses the stereotype accurately:

> "Model" Asians exhibit the same singleness of purpose, patience and endurance, cunning, fanaticism, and group loyalty characteristic of Marco Polo's Mongol soldiers, and Asian workers and students, maintaining themselves at little expense and almost robotlike, labor and study for hours on end without human needs for relaxation, fun, and pleasure, and M. I. T. becomes "Made in Taiwan," and "Stop the Yellow Hordes" appears as college campus graffiti, bumper stickers, and political slogans. (Okihiro 141)

The "model minority" image, therefore, embodies many contradictions whose elaboration encourages the proliferation of racism, elitism, and violence against succeeding generations, who are expected to measure up to the false standards set for and by the Asian community.

South Asians entered the United States in substantial numbers after the category "Asian American" had been narrowed from its political to its ethnoracial sense. Certain elements of the South Asian community, such as the Hindustani Ghadar Party, participated in the broad movement against racism and for internationalism in the 1960s and 1970s.[4] The bulk of the South Asian community, however, came to political consciousness as the "model minority," with no memory of the category's emergence and with no memory of the radical traditions offering contrary values. In our discussion of the South Asian community, this context is vital, or else we will fail to grasp the inconsistent use of the term "Asian American" among the various Asian groups in the United States.

SOUTH ASIAN AMERICA

> A Bangladeshi domestic worker who is active in Sakhi, New York City: "Sometimes I sense a difference between people in the [South Asian] community with regard to those who can hire and those who are hired. I don't feel everyone is the same. I feel some people have become established, say as doctors. They don't help other people—those who are taxi drivers or those who do not know English. How can we all feel part of a community?" (SAMAR Collective 15)

"South Asian American" is a very recent category, a rubric for a social movement that is still in its early stages. Social identities constructed outside social and political movements tend not to attract people, because they lack the historical traditions that elicit emotional loyalty from participants and beneficiaries of the social movement. Frustrated by the historical divisions between the peoples of the Subcontinent and anxious to forge a unity in this country, in the 1980s progressive activists began to deploy the term "South Asian" in the names of organizations in order to attract a diverse membership. These activists, united by the secular and democratic traditions of the anticolonial movements of South Asian history, are equally militant in the fight for justice and equality (not only among South Asians, but among all peoples). In the United States, progressive South Asian organizations evolved in the late 1980s after the realization that the Hindu Right (the Vishwa Hindu Parishad of America and the Overseas Friends of the BJP) finances much of its fascist work in India through front organizations in the United States (Mathew and Prashad).

Organizations committed to fighting religious bigotry, narrow regionalism, homophobia, and elitism used the term to unite progressive South Asians who share a common politics.[5] In a timely reminder, Naheed Islam has pointed out that in spite of the best of intentions, "the use of the term 'South Asia' has become interchangeable with the term 'India'" (Islam 244), but perhaps she draws the point too sharply. Although Indian activists and Indian concerns tend to overshadow South Asian organizations, many of the organizations are grappling with problems of definition and strategy, conscious of the pitfalls of tokenism. Recognizing that no category is flawless and no political project is without its limitations, there is a need to express the kinds of concerns put forward by Islam, just as there is a need to combat forces of oppression through political activism. We must pull together broad-based communities that are organizationally built on common ground. Race, for example, cannot be ignored; nor can it be the basis for an exclusionary politics.

Race, a social fact governing the way we interact in late imperial America, is not grounded in biology: as a social construction, the idea of "race" materialized into determinate practices and institutions that produced a dramatically racialized world. Recognizing race as a social principle, the state deploys race to shape social space and to reconfigure our various contested social compacts. This deployment is racist in two ways: first, in disseminating the ideology of race and, second, in the hierarchy of races (which promotes a form of white supremacy). Various activists mobilize race as a principle of organization against racism. When the organizational principle becomes a system of exclusion, "race" ceases to perform its progressive role. The Black Panther Party leader Fred Hampton (assassinated by the Chicago Police at the age of twenty-one on December 4, 1969), left a crowded Olivet Church in the days before his death with the following message:

> We've got to face the fact that some people say you fight fire best with fire, but we say you put fire out best with water. We say you don't fight racism with racism—we're gonna fight racism with solidarity. We say you don't fight capitalism with no black capitalism; you fight capitalism with socialism. (Hampton 9)[6]

An unalloyed notion of race (as a thing whose purity must be preserved) invariably falls prey to chauvinism and genocide. Politics on the basis of blood does not offer the potential for creating the benevolent community of the future. For this complex reason, I argue that there is a need to mobilize South Asians as South Asians (or as Indians, Pakistanis, Bangladeshis, et al.), and to organize according to a universal ethical agenda. Hence, begin with the narrow terms, but lead them dialectically to a broader community.

What are the parameters of this "community" called South Asian? South Asians are divided in three major ways: first, by religion, which is often but not always synonymous with nation (India/Hindu, Pakistan/Muslim, etc.); second, by language, which is often but not always synonymous with region and class (Tamil/Tamil Nadu, Hindi/Gangetic Plains, Gujarati/Gujarat, English/elites, etc.); and third, by class (professionals, taxi drivers, storekeepers, etc.). Given these internal fissures, what would a coherent South Asian agenda look like? Would many of the subcontinental folk refer to themselves as "Asian American" or even "South Asian

American"? Subcontinental people meet in our respective homes, in religious buildings, on college campuses, and at local ethnic enclaves, and our discussions center on "homeland" issues, some divisive (Kashmir, BJP, "liberalization"), others nostalgic (memorable personal or social events). Our sense of community manifests itself in many ways in everyday life, but there has been almost no attempt to explore the roots of this desire for community, which cuts across class, nation, region, caste, language and religion. Progressive South Asians do not use the term "South Asian" without sensing a need for such a term. What is that sentimental longing for unity and what are its implications?

At the most sentimental level, South Asians seek each other out to share commonalities based on a shared culture, history, and politics, and the shared experience of tokenism and marginalization in the overdeveloped nations. United by colonial institutions (such as schools, colleges, law courts) and institutions of society (such as caste identities; iconic figures from religion, politics, and film; jokes from college classmates; family and social relationships), the South Asian overseas has certain characteristics that make the desire for community a realizable goal. "It is only when we came here that we realized how much we have in common," a professional in California told me. "We learnt that we all had a thing for Amitabh and for Rekha [emblematic Hindi film stars], but also that we like the game of cricket perhaps more than we support our various national teams" (Shaliendra). Such common cause can be sought across the narrowly defined region, since many South Asians find that those Africans and Caribbeans who are raised in the aftermath of the British Empire share a similar culture.

The desire for community draws subcontinentals to socialize with each other and to seek solace from the rigors of corporate America in such gatherings and to share a common vision—to make enough money and then return to their respective homelands. Retirement in the homeland is viewed as liberation. Implicit in this narrative is a fundamental critique of the work ethic of corporatist America.[7] Work, central to accumulation of capital, is the evil that must be escaped by the South Asian economic migrant. Even for a community integrated into the networks of professionalism, the very foundation of the system (work) is anathema. The rigors of work and the travails of society are deemed worthwhile in return for the reward of a pension and a foreign-returned status in the homeland. This strand in subcontinental culture needs to be developed further for it provides us with a way to bridge a number of gaps: the antiwork ethos (idealized into the future) is in lived contradiction with a workaholic ethos (lived in the present). The social form of the consciousness of the South Asian migrant is structured around this contradiction. Retirement, however, is not chosen as often as it is discussed; as savings are reduced by increased consumption, particularly on college tuition, few can afford to retire.[8] A few South Asian migrants succeed, and the ethnic media accords them the status of "role model," which itself is not a generalizable condition. Retirement in the homeland gradually ceases to be a goal and becomes a dream. The feeling of social detachment from American life justifies a withdrawal from the social and political life of America. The most common place where the South Asian migrants enter American political discourse is to complain about the lack of individual economic growth (which will enable them to realize their retirement utopia). Herein lie the roots of the political conservatism of the South Asian migrants, and we will have cause to reflect upon the dangers of this element in South Asian America.

The American state reassures itself of the vitality of the South Asian community because of its high number of professional degree-holders. In the late 1970s, Maxine Fisher found, however, that despite their impressive degrees, "many Indians are unable to obtain work commensurate with their qualifications" (Fisher 20). In March 1995, the Federal Glass Ceiling Commission reported that despite their high qualifications, the bulk of Asians found that they were being held in technocratic rather than managerial positions (too much brain, not enough good sense). Unable to accumulate sufficient money to retire (and still ensure the best education for their children), subcontinental folk are altering their vision—to own a small business, the measure of success in contemporary America. Rather than ensure their disenchantment with a system that uses their skills for minimum rewards, the subcontinentals long for economic stability at the very least. Representing the retooled subcontinental, one entrepreneur explained that "you have to wait five years to vote, but you can be a capitalist the first day. I became a capitalist because I called myself a capitalist." With a master's degree in physics and many years experience working in the European electronics industry, this man is the owner of Action Instruments, which produces industrial products (India News Network). For progressive South Asians, retooled subcontinentals are not reliable allies for a project committed to social justice.

Is it possible, then, to craft solidarities that might include an entrepreneur, a taxi-driver, a domestic worker and a political activist? Is the only thing that unites them, their "ancestry," enough to forge a "community"? What would be the values in such a "community"? Is it worthwhile to deploy categories that include people whose political goals are irreconcilable? I am of the opinion that such categories are politically worthless because they fail to clarify the political differences within social communities. The current use of such categories (including South Asian American) is not at the level of the South Asian migrant, but at the level of their children and those who migrated to the United States at a young age. For the youth, a racialized notion of "community" has been inescapable, given the social milieu in which we live ("my people" is the operative self-designation of American minorities, whether this is used to indicate the black community or the Raza of the Chicanos). It is the young people who deploy categories such as South Asian American in order to create a space for themselves within this racialized social world; we need to offer a critique of such labeling in order to emphasize the political dangers inherent in such usage. The underlying point I have been trying to make is that we need not confuse our social and cultural longing for tradition and belonging with the need to fashion political solidarities. Before we try to close political gaps, we might check the ground underfoot.

YOU CAN'T FOOL THE YOUTH, BUT THE YOUTH CAN SURE FOOL YOU

Young people, in this age of mass production, seek to mark their bodies and minds with icons of difference in order to resist the relentless pressure of sameness. Over the years, corporate America has been able to absorb this desire for difference into its own universalist and imperialist dynamic, but the desire for difference remains an obsession with the young, who form subcultures to signal their retreat from the values of an overly acquisitive society. Often these markers of difference tend toward ethnoracial exclusivity (a kind of hypernationalism) rather than toward the creation of complex spaces that allow for the cultivation of common political ground. The hypernationalism of the young requires strong criticism precisely because they are closest to the project of complex universalism as well as to the project of ethnoracial exclusionism. Rather than set the former against the latter, I will try to explore the means by which the young people resolve the blatant contradictions between the two projects.

South Asians in the overdeveloped, or postindustrial, world have fashioned their cultural politics around many of the icons of a black diaspora culture, which itself seeks a way to keep from being culturally normalized at the same time that blacks are economically disenfranchised. A South Asian diasporic culture is being fashioned in this youth activity, but thus far it is largely parasitic on the culture originating in England.[9] The Bhangra and deejay sounds of Birmingham and Southall fill the headphones and the parties of the youth: the music of XLNC, Apna Sangeet, Apache Indian, Safari Boys, and the sounds of Bindushri and Bally Sagoo. Bhangra is a form of Punjabi music based on the beat of the dholak (a double-faced drum). In England, young urban children of Punjabi migrants used the beat and the songs of Bhangra alongside the dance hall sounds of Caribbean music and New York hip-hop to produce a vibrant sound unique to the complexities of inner-city England. This musical fusion allowed for a certain amount of social fusion, but one must not mistake the two. While inner-city South Asian, Caribbean, and white Britons forge cultures to combat the disenfranchisement of their localities, they also create ethnoracial subcultures that both enrich their lives and pit them against each other. One social group cannot be seen as more natural than another; what tends to happen is that "racial" groups are articulated in such a way as to appear to be more natural than class or neighborhood groups. This naturalness is constructed in accordance with the ideology of modernity (and of the vocabulary of the modern state, which judges people by race more than by class).

Youth culture, in its many manifestations, tries to negotiate the gaps between communities in everyday life, gaps such as the difficulties of living up to parental and societal utopias (most immigrant kids know that they can never be president and many realize that they might never have access to full-time employment). One must be wary of the easy expectation that these new cultural products will create a creolized youth. In December 1994, for example, a South Asian boy was beaten up by a group of white youths in Providence, Rhode Island, for playing a Bhangra tape (Hudson).[10] The sounds of music are not a passport into the New World. The music and its attendant cultures find their sustenance in communities of color (in Toronto, San Jose, and Queens) where the crisis of capitalism is starkly visible. But music and other cultural products implore us to listen to the youth's disenchantment with the false utopias of the past. As various class fragments of the subcontinental community meet, there is an appreciation of the failure of the parental utopia. When I write of various class fragments, I include the meeting of the Indo-Caribbeans and the subcontinentals in places such as Queens, New York, which has its own history of conflict and its own indices to show the shallowness of such myths as "model minority." With 42 percent of the taxi drivers in New York City being South Asian, the myth of Asian success is threatened and the utopia is at risk (Shankar; Bhattacharjee).

It is the duty of the South Asian political activists to inform the young people of South Asian America about the new world they are entering; we need to prepare this generation for the crisis that began after 1989. The parents of this generation entered the United States when the nation was in the midst of a Cold War struggle for technological dominance and was therefore expanding its educational and research institutions.

Since the fall of the Berlin Wall in 1989, education has become a low priority as the state shrinks its investment in training a workforce. Capital is keen to utilize the skills of those trained overseas, thereby transferring the work of nurturing and of the nursery, of training and of retirement, to countries with social-democratic welfare States (such as India, China, and Russia). During this extended crisis of capital, its managers use the profit-securing mechanism of contract labor in sweatshops, factories, and computer software firms (Prashad). Social costs are shifted overseas (where the value of labor is historically cheaper) or borne by the domestic working class itself (whose ill-developed traditions of proletarianism force it to focus on making ends meet rather than combating injustice). Steady at 4 percent in the 1950s, the official unemployment rate has moved to 11 percent in the 1990s. The nature of work has changed significantly:

> In the wake of the information revolution (now four decades old—the terms cybernetics and automation were coined in 1947), people are now working harder and longer (with compulsory overtime), under worsening working conditions with greater anxiety, stress and accidents, with less skills, less security, less autonomy, less power (individually and collectively), less benefits, less pay. Without question the technology has been developed and used to deskill and discipline the workforce in a global speed-up of unprecedented proportions. And those still working are the lucky ones. For the technology has been designed above all to displace. (Noble 50)

Weaned on dreams of a good life, our South Asian American brothers and sisters are going to be in for a major shock. The bedtime story used to be simple: go to college, study premed or engineering or prelaw or computer science, and success is ensured. Success, however, is no longer guaranteed. The burdens of the economic crisis are being laid at the door of working-class immigrants (particularly Mexican migrants). In order to differentiate between the "parasitic" migrant (the manual laborer) and the "productive" migrant (the professional), the South Asian migrant is inclined to support measures against working-class migration. This can be seen in the large South Asian support for Proposition 187 in California (to exclude all undocumented residents from state services, including education and medical care). The solidarities that must be crafted to combat our oppressive present must be alert to the desire among South Asian migrants to set themselves apart from the obvious targets of American racism (here the Latinos). The recent Welfare Reform Bill, which seeks to restrict the benefits to legal immigrants, demonstrates that the anti-immigrant dynamic knows no convenient boundaries, as is widely recognized even by South Asians within the Republican party (Potts). Asians cannot set themselves apart from other people of color in the United States, for at moments such as these, they are all lumped together by a powerful chauvinist movement (even when they join the movement as eager participants).

The story for the youth is slightly different. Much of their anxiety about the present is being organized into "gang" activity, whose radicalism is more than questionable. From Queens, New York (Malayali Hit Squad; Medina), to San Jose, California (Asian Indian Mob), to Toronto, Canada (Pangé Lane Wale), urban South Asian boys are forming "gangs" in order to protect their communities and to transmit the culture of the community to the next generation. As an "original gangsta" from the Asian Indian Mob put it, "we want to help the younger kids get involved in the community. We help them learn about their culture. They get to hang out with others like them" ("Gangsta', Gangsta'" 16). What is this "culture" that the "gangs" are transmitting and what is the notion of "protection" deployed by them with regard to the community? What kind of solidarity are these young gangs trying to craft?

To answer these questions, the experience of the Southall Youth Movement (SYM) and "gangs" such as Holy Smokes and Tooti Nung need to be shared on this side of the Atlantic. SYM was founded in memory of Gurinder Singh Chaggar, who was murdered in 1976, as a defensive mobilization against neofascist elements such as the National Front, the skinheads, and the British police. Tuku Mukherjee helps us understand the very specific context of SYM political activity: "The street has been appropriated by our youth and transformed into a political institution. It is for them at once the privileged space of confrontation with racism, and of a relative autonomy within their own community from which they can defend its existence" (Mukherjee 223). A convenient alliance was formed between the Asian commercial bourgeoisie (who did not want to lose control of their neighborhoods and marketplaces) and the local Asian lumpen-proletariat; the alliance was not radical, but defensive in order to protect the bourgeois aspirations of the community (Bains 237).

The "gangs" and SYM are fraught with an internal contradiction; they accept a rigid and racist notion of "culture" and they seek to protect this culture and its community against all odds. Part of this protection must be from internal elements who wish to transform the cultural practices in line with principles of justice and freedom. SYM accepts multiculturalism's racist dictum that each "culture" has a discrete logic that must not be tampered with. "Culture," however, is not a fixed set of practices that are determined without history and power. "Culture" is a field upon which some of the most important political battles are fought, such as questions of gender relations, the status of faith and of religious practice, the question of education and questions of elitism and prejudice. To close off these discussions is to narrow the rhetoric of freedom mobilized by the youth (and drawn, it must be added, from a moral universalism whose roots are as much in the pasts of the subcontinent as they are in Europe) (Sahgal).

The "culture" upheld by these "gang" formations is a specific Jat masculine culture (represented by the massive hit song *Jat De Dushmani* or "Animosity of the Jats" by Dippa) which has very detrimental effects. For instance, women are seen as the repositories of culture and as the showcases of the culture. Just as culture is to be preserved, so too are women. This means that women are denied moral equivalence with men and the capacity to make autonomous decisions. Women are more often the physical and psychological targets than the beneficiaries of this culturalism. Writing from the standpoint of the Southall Black Sisters (SBS), Pragna Patel speaks of the need to channel the male youth into radical activity alongside their sisters to produce "a culture in which violence and degradation do not exist" (Patel 46). SBS provides us with a model that is replicable and necessary; an organization of Asian and Afro-Caribbean women, SBS was founded in 1979 and has struggled against domestic violence, fundamentalism, Thatcherism, sexism, and racism. In the United States, there are many groups that do the kinds of work done by SBS, groups that find their hub in the Center for Third World Organizing in Oakland, California.[11] There is a need to write more about these groups that are drawing in young South Asians and training them to fight for social justice and not for narrow identity interests (which as the "model minority" stereotype shows often leads to antiblack politics). There is a need to formulate a theory of political work that will allow us to leave the language of political expediency behind. In the remaining space, short of such an analysis, I want to make a preliminary case for the revival of the class category "people of color" for the politics of South Asians and others in America.

PEOPLE OF COLOR

Peculiar circumstances have kept Indians and American Negroes far apart. The Indians naturally recoiled from being mistaken for Negroes and having to share their disabilities. The Negroes thought of Indians as people ashamed of their race and color so that the two seldom meet. My meeting with Tagore [in 1929] helped to change this attitude and today Negroes and Indians realize that both are fighting the same great battle against the assumption of superiority made so often by the white race.

—W.E.B. Du Bois, *Against Racism*

There can be no radical politics of South Asian America that does not deny the model minority stereotype and that does not ally itself with elements of the black and Latino Liberation Movement as well as with currents of American socialism. This is the minimum contribution that Asian communities must make to a political project against the racial formation that is embedded in capitalism. I propose that instead of trying to bridge the gap between South Asian America and Asian America, we put forward the call to renegotiate the category "people of color." The mobilizations around Jesse Jackson's candidacy for president in 1984 offer some indication of the widespread solidarities that can and must be crafted (Marable). In an age when the right is organized to destroy the last vestiges of the social democratic framework in America, the politics of identity plays firmly into its divisive hands. On the other hand, a voluntarist call like "Black and White Unite and Fight" will not provide the sorts of complex strategic and tactical analyses that will overcome the social divisions among those who are to continue the fight for social justice.

In the midst of identity politics, we are losing the politics of class. Identity politics is no more "natural" than class politics. Race, for instance, is a social construction of the eighteenth century. Class is a political construction of the nineteenth century that enables activists to forge solidarities against the political divisions of everyday life. Since "class," as a principle of self-conscious organization, is a place that welcomes people who share an opposition to the systematic exploitation of the proletariat and the oppression of women and racial minorities, the ruling class has sustained an attack on "class politics" by arguing that "class" is an unnatural bond. Saturated by racial sensibilities, American workers have been unable to adopt the language of class beyond its most economistic uses (Davis). When "people of color" was introduced to American politics, it provided a way for blacks to run a political campaign as a vanguard for the entire proletariat. That was the tenor of Jesse Jackson's campaign in 1984. In order to make a bid for power, the Rainbow Coalition fought to define the issues from the perspective of class (being very clear about inflections of race and gender). Such a socialist project enabled Asians to find room to struggle for social justice and equality alongside blacks, Latinos, and whites. To fight alongside another group politically is not to obliterate one's own community socially and culturally. The elision between the "cultural" and the "political" is the limitation of the political imagination of the votaries of identity politics and new social movements. To craft solidarity is not to undermine the basis for other forms of kinship and fellowship that often produce the means for us to live complex and rich lives. To craft solidarity is to negotiate across historically produced divides to combat congealed centers of power that benefit from political disunity.

The Jackson campaigns (in 1984 and 1988) did not grow from the vibrant political work being done by activists who were not organized on a national scale; the campaign simply brought these activists together for a momentary push for state power. Since these electoral campaigns, a wide array of political actors (labor unions, radical clergy and their congregations, community organizers, tenant rights activists, leftists intellectuals, left-wing political parties, and others) have attempted to negotiate a political future in opposition to the organized will of the right. Organizations such as the National Organizers Alliance (NOA, convened in 1991), the newly energized Young Communist League and the Communist Party, the newly militant AFL-CIO, the Labor Party, and the New Party are among the various groups engaged in crafting solidarities for a moral future.[12] Gihan Perera, trained by the AFL-CIO, at work in UNITE, offers a vision of the struggle:

> I desired to come together with all those great folks [in NOA] not only to affirm our commonalities, but also to be challenged by them, to challenge them, to venture toward the unfamiliar, to step on *un*common ground. I wanted to explore the gaps and contradictions in our own work, and take a bold leap into the unknown. (Perera 3)

Solidarity must be crafted on the basis of both commonalities and differences, on the basis of a theoretically aware translation of our mutual contradictions into political practice. Political struggle is the crucible of the future, and our political categories simply enable us to *enter* the crucible rather than telling us much about what will be produced in the process of the struggle. "Some things if you stretch it so far, it'll be another thing," Fred Hampton explains, "Did you ever cook something so long that it turns into something else? Ain't that right? That's what we're talking about with politics" (Hampton 10). In line with this definition of politics, we need to create spaces that allow for the discussion of contradictions just as we fight against the forces of reaction: Asian America (and South Asian America) are narrow spaces that, far from continuing a political dialogue across social divides, tend to perpetuate these divisions, along with the notion of the "model minority," which is the grain we must rub against.

ACKNOWLEDGMENTS

With thanks to Lisa Armstrong, Mark Tony, Sudhir Venkatesh, Nayan Shah, Biju Mathew, Naheed Islam, Rajini Srikanth, and Lavina Shankar.

NOTES

1. As cultural identity: "The concept *Asian American* implies that there can be a communal consciousness and a unique culture that is neither Asian nor American, but Asian American" (Wei 1). On sociopolitical movement: "In bringing Asian American activists together to participate in a common cause that transcended college campuses and Asian ethnic communities, the anti-war movement helped transform previously isolated instances of political activism into a social movement that was national in scope—the Asian American movement" (Wei 41).

2. In 1978, NORC survey no. 4269 asked a sample of Americans for the "race" of Indians: 11 percent said White, 15 percent said Black, 23 percent said Brown, 38 percent said Other, and 13 percent did not know how to classify them (Xenus, 2-3).

3. We are in the land of what has been called "Goldilocks-and-the-three-bears theory of racial culture and identity" (Gilroy, 89). The Social Darwinian side of the thesis has been recently revised in the spurious book by Herrenstein and Murray (which is based on graphs without scatter diagrams).

4. I have copies of *Chingari*, the monthly journal of the group which was published from Toronto, Canada, from 1968.

5. Using a geopolitical term was convenient, but the use of the term had little to do with the geopolitical farce known as the South Asian Association of Regional Cooperation (SAARC formed in Colombo in April 1981). SAARC's attempt to build bridges of peace and mutual understanding across the boundaries is foiled by the fifty year enmity between its constituent nations. There are, of course, some beneficial things done by the association, but by and large it fails its ultimate mission which is to encourage its member nations to pay more interest to each other than for each of them to be transfixed and manipulated by the advanced industrial nations, who operate under the hegemony of the United States.

6. Certainly, "race" has been mobilized in political battles against the modern multiracist States (battles in the United States, for instance, joined by the Black Panthers on *race* lines in order to combat *racism*). The Black Panther Party was aware of the problems of their use of "race." On Aug. 26, 1970, Huey Newton called a press conference to announce that the "the Black Panther Party does not subscribe to 'Black Power' as such. Not the 'Black Power' that has been defined by Stokley Carmichael and Nixon. They seem to agree upon the stipulated definition of 'Black Power,' which is no more than Black capitalism, which is reactionary and certainly not a philosophy that would meet the interest of the people" (Major 102).

7. I am basing these speculations on extensive interviews with South Asian Americans and with extended journeys through discussion groups on the Internet. I will present the evidence more scientifically in a later publication.

8. Interest rates in India for savings are generally much higher than such rates in the United States. The utopia of savings and retirement is classically Indian, where pensioners are not put in such economic straits as they are in the United States. In America, retirement is not economically viable for the salariat and small shopkeepers.

9. This has much to do with the generous funding unleashed by the state (in Britain and Canada) as part of the favorable contradictions of multiculturalism. On this see, Srinivas Krishna's film *Masala* which was funded by the multicultural ministry and yet pokes fun at the concept of such a ministry. As far as Bhangra music is concerned, the explosion has been encouraged by the commodification of world music as an hip genre (Bauman).

10. The most useful flyer was prepared by the South Asian Students Association, "It *Was* Racism" which offers some correctives to Hudson's university-friendly article (in my possession).

11. CTWO can be reached at (510) 533-7583 for more information.

12. Contact numbers for these organizations: NOA [202-543-6603], YCL [212-741-2016], CPUSA [212-989-4994], AFL-CIO Organizing Institute [202-639-6200], Labor Party [202-986-8700] and the New Party [510-654-2309].

WORKS CITED

Bains, Harwant S. "Southall Youth: An Old Fashioned Story." In *Multi-Racist Britain*, edited by Philip Cohen and Harwant S. Bains. London: Macmillan, 1988, 226–43.

Bauman, Gerd. *Contesting Culture: Discourses of Identity in Multi-Ethnic London*. Cambridge: Cambridge University Press, 1996.

Bhattacharjee, Anannya. "Yellow Cabs, Brown People." *South Asian Magazine for Action and Reflection* (Summer 1993): 61–63.

Crystal, David. "Asian Americans and the Myth of the Model Minority." *Social Casework* 70.7 (1989): 405–13.

Davis, Mike. *Prisoners of the American Dream*. London: Verso, 1986.

DeSouza, Dinesh. *The End of Racism*. New York: Free Press, 1995.

Du Bois, W.E.B. *Against Racism: Unpublished Essays, Papers and Addresses, 1887–1981*. Edited by Herbert Aptheker. Amherst: University of Massachusetts Press, 1985.

Fisher, Maxine P. *The Indians of New York City*. Columbia, Mo.: South Asia Books, 1980.

"Gangsta', Gangsta': an interview with South Asian gang members." *Hum* 1.2 (1994): 14–17.

Gilroy, Paul. *Small Acts*. London: Serpent's Tail Press, 1993.

Hampton, Fred. *You've Got to Make a Commitment!* Chicago: Black Panther Party, 1969.

Herrenstein, Richard J., and Charles Murray. *The Bell Curve: Intelligence and Class Structure in American Life*. New York: Free Press, 1994.

Hu, Arthur. "Asian Americans: Model Minority or Double Minority." *Amerasia* 15.1 (1989): 243–57.

Hudson, Lynn. "Racism Clouds Tranquil Brown University Campus." *India Abroad*, Feb. 24, 1995.

India News Network. "Digest." Feb. 6, 1995.

Islam, Naheed. "In the Belly of the Multicultural Beast I Am Named South Asian."

In *Our Feet Walk the Sky*, edited by the Women of South Asian Descent Collective. San Francisco: Aunt Lute Press, 1993, 242–45.

Jensen, Joan. *Passage from India. Asian Indian Immigrants in North America.* New Haven: Yale University Press, 1988.

Major, Reginald. *A Panther Is a Black Cat.* New York: William Morrow, 1971.

Marable, Manning. "Rainbow Rebellion: Jesse Jackson's Presidential Campaign and the Democratic Party." *Black American Politics from the Washington Marches to Jesse Jackson.* London: Verso, 1985. 247–305.

Marx, Karl. *Critique of the Gotha Programme.* New York: International Publishers, 1973.

Mathew, Biju, and Vijay Prashad. "The Saffron Dollar: Pehla Paisa, Phir Bhagwan." *Himal* 9. 7 (Kathmandu, Nepal: September 1996): 38–42.

Mukherjee, Tuku. "The Journey Back." In *Multi-Racist Britain,* edited by Philip Cohen and Harwant S. Bains. London: Macmillan, 1988, 211–25.

Noble, David. "The Truth about the Information Highway." *Monthly Review* 47 (1995): 47–52.

Okihiro, Gary. *Margins and Mainstreams. Asians in American History and Culture.* Seattle: University of Washington Press, 1994.

Omatsu, Glenn. "The 'Four Prisons' and the Movements of Liberation: Asian American Activism from the 1960s to the 1990s." In *The State of Asian America,* edited by Karin Aguilar-San Juan. Boston: South End Press, 1994, 19–69.

Osajima, Keith. "Asian Americans as the Model Minority: An Analysis of the Popular Press Image in the 1960s and 1980s." In *Reflections on Shattered Windows. Promises and Prospects for Asian American Studies,* edited by Gary Okihiro, et al. Pullman, Wash.: Washington State University Press, 1988, 165–74.

Paaras. "Kala Shah Kala." By Y. S. Pal. *Extra Hot 9.* Hayes, Middlesex, 1993.

Patel, Pragna. "Southall Boys." In *Against the Grain: A Celebration of Survival and Struggle,* edited by Southall Black Sisters. London: Southall Black Sisters, 1990, 43–54.

Perera, Gihan. "Heading Out to Deeper Waters." *The Ark: Membership Newsletter of the National Organizers Alliance* 7 (July 1996).

Potts, Michel W. "Welfare Bill Hits Legal Aliens: Indian Republicans Upset." *India West.* 9 August 1996.

Prashad, Vijay. "Contract Labor: the Latest Stage of Illiberal Capitalism." *Monthly Review* 46 (1994): 19–26.

Sahgal, Gita. "Secular Spaces: The Experience of Asian Women Organizing." *Refusing Holy Orders: Women and Fundamentalism in Britain.* Ed. Gita Sahgal and Nira Yuval-Davis. London: Virago, 1992. 163–97.

SAMAR Collective. "One Big Happy Community? Class Issues Within South Asian American Homes." *South Asian Magazine for Action and Reflection.* 4 (1994): 10–15.

Shankar, S. "Ambassadors of Goodwill: An Interview with Saleem Osman of Lease Drivers' Coalition." *South Asian Magazine for Action and Reflection* 3 (1994): 44–47.

Shaliendra, Manoj. Interview with the author, Aug. 12, 1993.

Wei, William. *The Asian American Movement*. Philadelphia: Temple University Press, 1993.

Westwood, Sallie. "Red Star over Leicester: Racism, the politics of identity, and black youth in Britain." In *Black and Ethnic Leaderships in Britain*, edited by Pnina Werbner and Muhammad Anwar. London: Routledge, 1991, 146–69.

Xenus, P., et al. *Asian Indians in the U.S.: A 1980 Census Profile*. Honolulu: East-West Center, 1989.

ANU GUPTA

6   At the Crossroads

College Activism and Its Impact
on Asian American Identity Formation

OVER THE last several years, I have become passionately interested in the influences on identity formation for South Asian Americans.
Specifically, I am intrigued as to why individuals choose certain identity
labels and reject others, and why some of them see themselves as "South
Asian," but not as "Asian American." From my experiences as a student,
counselor, and leader, I have observed that during college, most students have made some decisions as to how they will identify themselves.
Identity-based student groups play a significant role in helping students
clarify their feelings about their identity. However, it is not just the existence of these identity-based groups but the politics and interrelationships
among them that have the most significance in our ongoing discussion of
South Asian Americans and whether they are a part of or separate from
the notion of "Asian America," which is the critical question posed by this
collection of essays. An examination of the dynamics between the groups
representing these two communities at four different private universities
in the Northeast reveals three different patterns of Asian American and
South Asian American student interactions and offers insight into how the
gap in concentric identity formation may be widened or bridged.[1]

PERSPECTIVE

Before beginning the discussion, it is important to describe the perspective from which the essay is being written. The "formal" scholarship on
the topic of South Asian and Asian American campus groups is scarce.
What follows is not an academic sociological/anthropological account,
but a more personal view.[2]

Asian Americans are sometimes referred to as Asian Pacific Islanders
and Asian Pacific Americans. In this essay I use "Asian American" to refer
to individuals who trace their ancestry back to Asia and who also feel that
they have lived enough of their own lives in the United States to consider
themselves "American." It refers to all Asian ethnicities, including those
from the Subcontinent, and thus encompasses South Asian Americans. I

have chosen to use "Asian American" because on most college campuses this is the term used by students. These undergraduate organizations will be referred to as "Asian American groups." I will use the phrasing "other Asian" in discussing a situation that applies to Asian Americans other than South Asian Americans.

Similarly, I use "South Asian American" to refer to individuals who trace their ancestry back to the Subcontinent and who also consider themselves "American." Given the trends in immigration patterns, the majority of this community is comprised of second-generation individuals. Because many of these individuals refer to themselves as "South Asian," it can be difficult to determine by their self-identification as "South Asian" whether someone is "American" or an international student.[3] I will use "South Asian American," a relatively new identity, and one that I strongly identify with, when referring to the community, but in discussing the student groups at the schools I focus on, I will use the phrase "South Asian groups" when discussing organizational issues.[4]

GROWING UP

Many minority students come to college with a muddled sense of self that is largely shaped by both childhood and adolescent experiences and popular conceptions.[5] This confused sense of self stays with them during their first years at college when they are deciding which minority student groups to identify with and to belong to.

South Asian Americans, especially second-generation ones, can form organizations that reflect their identity on a number of levels, whether based on ethnicity and language (Bengali), religion (Sikh), nationality (Indian, Pakistani), region (South Asian), or geographical area (Asian), with the word "American" attached or assumed. As such, South Asian Americans might choose a specific identity (one based on ethnicity, such as Punjabi), interact with others who have chosen that identity, and therefore not see themselves as South Asian Americans or Asian Americans.

Many South Asian Americans become attuned to the nuances of identity formation at an early age, when they first identify as "Indian," an identity influenced strongly by their parents. Because Columbus misnamed the people of North America five hundred years ago, South Asian Americans find themselves correcting and clarifying their identity as "Indians." Although these individuals tend to have another more specific identity, whether it be "Punjabi" or "Sikh" or "Gujurati" or "Tamil," this is an identity based on home and family and not generally shared with society as a whole. Most South Asian Americans retain their identity of "Indian" or perhaps "Asian Indian" until they reach college, especially if they come from small suburban or rural, predominantly white communities where there are few South Asian American families. A few may identify themselves as "Asian," especially if there are other Asian American families in the neighborhood.

On the other hand, students who grow up in large communities with many South Asian Americans are more likely to identify strongly with their religious or subethnic identity, especially if it has been positively reinforced through socialization with other families of the same background. In fact, these South Asian Americans know not only what region of India they are from, but also what caste they belong to and what town their family emigrated from. Furthermore, they also have a strong sense of identity based on their visits to South Asia, which are frequent, since most of them still have family there. This early identity formation also applies to South Asian Americans from Sri Lanka (where there are two major ethnic groups with which to identify), Bangladesh, Pakistan (where a religious identity of being Muslim is extremely strong), and other South Asian countries. At the same time, it is important to recognize that there is a subset that chooses not to identify at all on any level with South Asian Americans; most of these individuals do not see themselves as people of color, having been assimilated into white mainstream culture.[6]

Complicating this identity formation are the popular conceptions regarding South Asian Americans, some of which are encountered in school. The most problematic, especially in the context of discussions of South Asian Americans as Asian Americans, is the scientific classification of South Asian Americans as "Caucasians." Almost every American high school student learns that there are "three" races, and that "Indians" are Caucasian and other groups from Asia are "Mongoloid."[7] Furthermore, Caucasian is widely used as a term interchangeable with "white." While most South Asian Americans realize that they are *not* white, they also feel that they are not Asian American because they are not Mongoloid. Otherwise, very little is taught in school about South Asian Americans, outside the context of Global/International Studies in which just a few weeks might be given to all of South Asia.

Reinforcing the scarcity of information taught in school is the invisibility of South Asian Americans in the media's homogenization of the Asian American image: someone with eyes without epicanthic folds, a flat nose, pin-straight black hair, and almost white skin. The racism that lumps Chinese Americans, Korean Americans, and Vietnamese Americans into one Asian image excludes South Asian Americans[8] and strongly dissuades them from identifying with Asian Americans as a group. Although South Asian Americans share the experience of immigration and resettlement with people from many ethnic groups, they have more in common with other Asian Americans than with other groups.[9] Nevertheless, differences in family and social structure, education, media images, and physical appearance tend to prevent South Asian Americans from seeing themselves as Asian American.

WHO ARE YOU?

On almost every college application they fill out, South Asian Americans must decide how to identify themselves. Though optional on most, there is a section that asks the applicant to describe him/herself. "Asian" or "Asian American" is always a choice and is sometimes followed by a list of the Asian ethnic groups underneath so that the applicants can specifically identify themselves. "Caucasian/White" is also an option, as is "Other." Most South Asian Americans tend to choose Asian/Asian American, especially when it is further broken down, because they see Indian/Pakistani on the list in that category. "Other" is also frequently chosen because it allows South Asian Americans to fill in the identity with which they feel most comfortable.[10] Finally there is a large segment of the community that does not fill out this section of the application for fear of discrimination during the admissions process.

During the first few weeks of school, college students are introduced to the various aspects of their lives as undergraduates, from academics to social life to extracurricular activities. Most schools have as part of their orientation an activity fair where different organizations each have a booth (usually a table and a few chairs) and recruit interested members by calling out to them, asking them to be on their mailing list, and distributing information about the group, while explaining to interested people what the organization has recently done and why they should join. Here students might see tables for a South Asian group as well as for an Asian American group and begin to understand that there are at least two communities to which they can belong. Whether they approach a table depends on their curiosity and interest, and a sense of shared interests with the group's representatives. These choices have a significant impact on identity formation, for it is within the context of the organization that identity is challenged and redefined by the other members of the group.[11] The most telling evidence of this is that many young South Asian Americans identify with the term "South Asian," which is almost never used by the older generation and seen only in academia or in journalism. This shift to what they regard as a more inclusive and empowering term directly results from participation in South Asian groups on college campuses.[12]

A group's membership, history, and leadership, and its relationship with the Asian American group are a major influence on whether South

Asian Americans will identify as Asian American. The most significant factor is the way in which the minority community is constructed on each campus. Each group's history, its goals, and its role within the university work to shape the relationship between Asian American and South Asian American student groups.[13] If there is a history of cooperation and partnership between the two organizations, then there is a sense that they are working together toward a common goal, and this commonality encourages South Asian Americans to identify as Asian American. On the other hand, if there is tension or lack of communication between the two groups, then there is a tendency to identify more strongly with one's own ethnic organization. This premise will be explored further through an analysis of the interrelationships between the South Asian and Asian American groups at four universities: Brown, Harvard, the University of Pennsylvania, and Yale.

OVERVIEW OF STUDENT MOVEMENTS ON COLLEGE CAMPUSES

During the 1950s, Japanese Americans were returning from internment camps to resettle and rebuild their communities. At the same time, exclusionary laws ended, allowing Chinese women to immigrate and enabling the growth of Chinese American communities. In time, students from these communities, along with a handful of other Asian Americans, were recruited through educational opportunity programs to a number of public universities across the country. Student activism related to the civil rights movement and the Vietnam War involved a broad spectrum of campus communities and highlighted questions of ethnicity and race in university programs and policy.

In the late 1960s student strikes at San Francisco State, the University of California at Berkeley, and Columbia University were mobilized in reaction to massive budget cuts that would have led to the closing of programs geared toward minority students. Asian American students participated in strikes with other students of color, as they made demands for educational access, relevancy, and support. For the first time, there was a critical mass of young adults who were Asian *American* and who wanted to develop social, personal, and professional ties with others who, though Asian by ancestry, had been raised in the United States. This pan-Asian activism in the context of a multiracial movement gave birth not only to a new ethnic identity, but also to student organizations that began tackling the issues of Asian American admissions and Asian American studies.[14]

One of their first tasks was to challenge the admissions policies of quota-based discriminatory ceilings placed on Asian Americans. The ultimate reversal of this policy resulted in a significant increase in the number of Asian American students on college campuses. This in turn led to the formation of numerous Asian student groups, because for the first time there were enough students to organize according to their various ethnicities, such as Chinese, Korean, or South Asian.[15] Given the isolation that many Asian Americans faced while growing up, these organizations offered a means of exploring and celebrating their specific cultures, their foods, and their holidays, which they would have been unable to do in a larger Asian American organization.

EFFORTS TO CLOSE THE GAP: ASIAN AMERICANS AT BROWN UNIVERSITY

At Brown University in Providence, Rhode Island, there is a strong history of activism among students of color. For the past twenty-five years, minority students at Brown have challenged the administration on various issues and have created a voice for themselves in every major area of the university, from admissions to student life and academic affairs. At Brown the number of groups representing the minority student body[16] has grown, as the number of minority students increased, from four to nearly fifty organizations, all housed in the Third World Center, which provides resources, administrative support, meeting space, office space, and a home base for the minority community at Brown.

The Asian American Students Association (AASA) at Brown has always been a cultural, social, and political organization. One of its main goals is to cultivate an Asian American identity among Asian American students. AASA holds bimonthly meetings with a variety of programs, ranging from strictly social events to workshops on how to deal with parental pressure. In addition, AASA, working with the Third World Center, sponsors Asian American History Month in November, when every day, for a month, there are speakers, workshops, events, cultural shows, and other events relating to the Asian American community.

AASA's most significant role, however, is political. Due to its history, AASA is one of the few groups that has representation on every major university committee and is regarded as the "voice" of Asian American students at Brown. AASA representatives sit on the president's advisory board, work closely with the alumni office, advise the deans of the college and the deans of student life, sit on universitywide committees concerned with minority issues, and participate in the admissions process through recruitment and reviewing of applications. No other Asian ethnic group is permitted this level of involvement. Therefore, AASA has the responsibility of accurately representing the views of not only the general Asian American student community, but also the various Asian ethnic groups. These representatives are elected by the general membership of AASA. Overall, AASA views itself as an organization of the Asian American community at Brown and holds itself ultimately accountable to this community.

Brown's South Asian Students Association (SASA), is a relatively young organization. Formed during the mid- to late 1980s, its primary goal was to serve as a social and cultural organization. The handful of students who first started it used SASA as a way to get funding for events such as dinners and dances. SASA's membership in 1989 was approximately fifty students; in 1995, there were close to three hundred active members. This tremendous increase was due largely to changes in the university's admissions policies. With 15 to 20 percent of each incoming class at Brown comprised of Asian Americans, it is not hard to account for such large increases in SASA's constituency. With more members came new ideas, and SASA started sponsoring additional events, including a cultural show and some workshops. Moreover, there was a need to become more involved with campus politics since there now existed a significant number of South Asian American students. SASA, like other Asian ethnic groups, accessed this arena through AASA and the Third World Center and quickly realized that in order to have representation in the university, they would need to work with AASA to that end, especially in the areas of admissions and student affairs.

The Asian American Students Association is the gatekeeper of universitywide representation but no longer sees itself as an umbrella organization for the other Asian ethnic groups. Meetings between the leaderships of AASA and the other Asian ethnic groups are infrequent. Many Asian ethnic leaders feel as though AASA is setting the Asian American agenda without adequate discussion with constituent groups; At the same time, not all Asian groups are equally concerned with campus politics, and this is a source of frustration to AASA, because it is the only group with a history of Asian American activism and, as such, has been following issues such as Asian American studies and admissions for a number of years.

Asian American History Month, however, brings the entire community together in a spirit of mutual cooperation, as the various Asian ethnic groups decide what they would like to contribute to the month-long celebration: AASA picks up the slack, scheduling events to fill in the holes. For example, SASA usually organizes its cultural show as its contribution to the month, but tends to shy away from workshops and discussion-oriented events. As such, AASA will research and sponsor a speaker to address some aspect of South Asian American student life. Since AASA is not an umbrella organization with formal representation from the various Asian ethnic groups (i.e., they do not send officers/members who "officially" represent that organization), the composition and diversity of its board is a determining factor in how the Asian groups, especially SASA, will interact with AASA.

Recognizing these shortcomings in organizational relations, SASA and AASA have cosponsored events to bring the two communities together. Because AASA has had two South Asian American presidents, both elected for their years of activism within the Asian American community, South Asian Americans have become more visible and more likely to join and participate in AASA. There is also a liaison who sits on the SASA board whose duties are to attend AASA meetings and serve as a communication link between the two groups. However, despite these inclusionary efforts, a segment of the South Asian American community still feels that the substantial differences (of religion, appearance, and experiences), between South Asian Americans and other Asian Americans and SASA's size and clout are reasons to insist on the organization's speaking as its own advocate.[17] They want SASA to work with other minority groups independent of AASA, thereby disrupting the role that AASA has historically played as the voice of the Asian American community and creating a more blatant gap than already exists.

The lack of direct access to many university committees has angered the leadership of the Asian ethnic groups, but they realize that AASA is more than willing to work with them as long as they commit to presenting their issues through AASA. At the same time, AASA realizes that the strength of the community comes from the Asian ethnic organizations. The dynamic of mutual cooperation depends on the people who occupy the leadership positions in all these groups and the perceptions they have of each other. When there are South Asian Americans on the board of AASA, there are stronger ties between the groups; at other times communication breaks down between them. It is not lack of effort, or lack of good intentions, but the organizational structure at Brown that precludes the gap from ever truly closing.

WHAT GAP? ASIAN AMERICANS AT HARVARD UNIVERSITY AND THE UNIVERSITY OF PENNSYLVANIA

Because the Asian American communities at Harvard University in Cambridge, Massachusetts, and the University of Pennsylvania in Philadelphia, Pennsylvania, are similar, I discuss them together. Both universities have one overall minority institution with a board comprised of student representatives. The Harvard Foundation's major role is to receive grant applications from minority groups and provide money to sponsor different events, most of which are cultural. Similarly, the Greenfield Inter-

Cultural Center at the University of Pennsylvania provides administrative support to students of color. At both schools, all minority groups have representatives that sit on boards affiliated with these centers, no matter how large or small the group.[18] As such, all groups are equally empowered.

According to Alex Cho, a past president, the Asian American Association (AAA) at Harvard has been active for over fifteen years and has waxed and waned in terms of its power on campus. Like Brown's group, AAA was founded as a support for Asian American students since there were no other resources at that time. Initially a political organization working toward faculty hiring and Asian American studies, AAA evolved into a more social group during the late 1980s but has come full circle, focusing renewed efforts toward pushing for ethnic studies and general campus awareness of other Asian American issues, such as Proposition 187/209. AAA also sponsors an annual intercollegiate conference, a film festival, and a month-long cultural celebration.

According to Srishti Gupta, copresident of the South Asian Association, the South Asian Association (SAA), formed in the late 1980s, has been growing steadily both in numbers and in power over the last few years. It was started primarily as a social organization; SAA was a mechanism through which social events (dances, dinners, parties) could be funded by the university. SAA, at that time, also had a large international student contingent. After a few years, there were many more South Asian Americans at Harvard, and SAA began to define its own goals. Nowadays, SAA holds its own political/educational as well as cultural events. SAA hosts both a fall and spring conference along with its annual cultural show, which is not only a huge success but also a community-affirming event. SAA has an active segment concerned with the lack of courses related to South Asia in the curriculum. Unlike Brown's SASA, SAA sends its own representatives to the Harvard Foundation and to the Minority Students Alliance.

Conversations with Gloria Lee, an undergraduate student active in the Asian American community, reveal that the situation is very similar at University of Pennsylvania, which, interestingly has two Asian American groups, the Asian American Students Union (AASU) and the Students for Asian Affairs (SAA). The former group is more cultural and social while the latter works with the administration, largely because the leadership of Students for Asian Affairs has a history of working on political issues on campus. For example, in the past, Students for Asian Affairs was quite active and played an important role in securing an Asian American counselor at the University Counseling Services and in the Asian American Studies Search Committee. Both these groups, however, are relatively impotent in comparison with the Asian ethnic groups. In fact, both AASU and SAA have failed to maintain regular representation on the United Minorities Council, which is the board affiliated with the Greenfield Inter-Cultural Center. SAA dissolved at the beginning of the 1994–1995 academic year, leaving the Asian American community voiceless in terms of the administration.[19]

The South Asian Society (SAS) is one of the largest and most powerful Asian ethnic groups at the University of Pennsylvania, according to Samir Shah, an alumnus and active member.[20] SAS has traditionally been a cultural and social organization only, and its events draw not only South Asian Americans from the campus but South Asian Americans from other colleges in the Philadelphia area as well. Their annual cultural show fills a two-thousand-seat auditorium. SAS works closely with the South Asia Regional Studies Department at the University of Pennsylvania to sponsor speakers and classes, mostly in language studies. The members of SAS seem concerned mostly with their large-scale events which take a great deal of time and people power. SAS tends to stay away from campus politics such as admissions and financial aid issues and the hiring and tenuring of professors. They did, however, organize a huge demonstration in response to the Dotbuster beating of a New Jersey physician and the subsequent verdict of the trial. "Dotbusters" was the self-proclaimed name of a group of white males who, during 1987 and 1988, terrorized Indian Americans in New Jersey. The group vowed to rid Jersey City of Indians. The "dot" in "Dotbuster" refers to the "dot," or red cultural mark, that some Indian women (typically Hindus) make on their foreheads to signify their married status.

At both institutions, the Asian American groups are de facto umbrella organizations, working with other Asian ethnic groups toward specific ends.[21] Intergroup cooperation no longer exists, largely because very few South Asian Americans are active in both organizations. Each organization works independently of the other, and most South Asian Americans see no connection with Asian Americans. Recently at Harvard, for instance, both AAA and SAA organized to protest the Personal Responsibility Act legislation during the House debates. Although both groups advertised to each other's constituencies, through e-mail lists, neither of them approached the other to work together. Both Cho and Gupta believe the lack of a history of working together along with lack of communication between individual board members in both organizations resulted in this situation; in other words, it was not enough for the presidents to know each other; the sense of community had to extend to all the board members so that those students in charge of this event could have collaborated directly with each other, rather than relying (or not, as in this case) on the organizational leaders. Thus, even though they recognized that there was significant overlap in terms of their concern for this issue, an opportunity for both groups to collaborate with one another toward a common goal was lost.[22] In fact, the Asian American groups at Harvard and University of Pennsylvania, while active and concerned about various campus political issues, lack the community in terms of membership numbers to convince the administration of the need to implement change. Moreover, the Asian American groups at both these schools emphasize their concern with an "American" identity, and as such, form stronger relationships with other groups of students of color such as African Americans instead of other Asian groups, which they view as Asia-oriented and Asia-focused. Thus, Asian American students at both of these schools are more concerned about connecting with other communities of color than with other Asian ethnic groups, including South Asian groups.

Both the South Asian Association (SAA) at Harvard and the South Asia Society (SAS) at University of Pennsylvania built their clout and credibility in the community by having strong cultural events that drew the community together. Using this foundation, each group was able to expand into other areas. Now both groups have the people power and resources to address not only the social and cultural needs of the community but the political ones as well. Even though they are powerful organizations with many active members, neither South Asian group (SAA or SAS) has a clear agenda or vision for its role on campus. At the University of Pennsylvania, SAS is content with the South Asia Regional Studies Department (which is primarily academic), but has been slow in advocating for student life issues of South Asian Americans. SAA is concerned with establishing a Harvard version of the South Asia Regional Studies Department. There is little discussion of admissions or South Asian American studies because South Asian groups are unfamiliar with these issues—they have never been involved with them in the past and they have only limited contact with the Asian American groups who are concerned about these issues.[23]

Part of the reason for the lack of cooperation is that at both schools the various minority groups have direct access to all university committees. South Asian groups can directly access the minority community and its financial resources and work independently from other Asian ethnic groups. Therefore, at both schools, the Asian American group and the other Asian ethnic groups see themselves as parallel organizations with no gaps to be bridged. The goal for all the groups is self-preservation; in pursuing that priority, working together goes by the wayside. With weak and struggling Asian American organizations and extremely strong South Asian groups, there is no group powerful enough to encourage coalition building among the Asian ethnic organizations. In other words, there is no perceived common agenda (socially, culturally, or politically), so there is no perceived need to come together.

CLOSURE OF THE GAP — YALE UNIVERSITY: AN OVERVIEW

A third way in which the Asian American and South Asian American communities have interacted is found at Yale University in New Haven, Connecticut. One thing that immediately separates Yale from the other three schools is the dynamics of the minority community. Yale does not have one big minority student union or center. On the contrary, there are four cultural centers, each with its own director, who is also a dean in the administration. These four centers encompass every member of the minority community. According to Mary Li Hsu, assistant dean and director of the Asian American Cultural Center, the two oldest centers were founded twenty-five years ago for the African American and Puerto Rican communities respectively, since they constituted the majority of the people of color at Yale during that time. There were small groups for the Asian American and Chicano students. During the early 1970s, the Asian American Students Association (AASA) was the only Asian American group on campus and was made up mostly of Japanese Americans and Filipino Americans. AASA became an active voice for the community and was instrumental in fighting for the establishment of the Asian American Cultural Center, which became a reality in 1981. The last cultural center, for Mexican American, or Chicano, students, was also founded around this time. AASA continued to push for, and finally obtained, an Asian American dean as well, during the mid-1980s. Now the Asian American Cultural Center has its own budget and director; any student group dealing with issues relating to Asians in the United States is affiliated with the center and can apply for money to fund events and use center resources.

AASA, which was a powerful group early on, encountered many problems as other Asian ethnic groups began to form at Yale. Its history during the past five years has been extremely tumultuous and complicated, as AASA grappled with the same issues that other schools face, namely how to be an umbrella organization and political voice for the community in the face of strong Asian ethnic organizations and how to maintain its credibility in the eyes of the administration and other major student groups on campus. During the 1992–1993 academic year, AASA at Yale was very similar to the AASA at Brown in that it was its own organization with its own members and it was also the main Asian organization. However, there was a great deal of sentiment on the part of the other Asian group leaders that AASA wasn't truly an umbrella organization, and as a result, many of these groups, including Yale's South Asian group, the South Asian Society (SAS), left the Asian American Cultural Center.[24]

AASA went through a painful restructuring during the 1993–1994 academic year, and a number of radical decisions were made at this time. First and foremost, each Asian ethnic group agreed to the concept of dual membership (which is not found on any of the other campuses discussed so far); simply, every member of an Asian ethnic group was automatically a member of AASA. This gave AASA the power and potential influence in terms of numbers that it needed to establish itself as a major organization at Yale. At the same time, AASA no longer needed to recruit members and compete with other Asian ethnic groups to that end. Second, AASA's old board was replaced with one comprised of the current head(s) of the various Asian ethnic groups. This new AASA board would elect a president who was either a former leader of an ethnic group or a leader of an AASA task group. AASA was to meet weekly to advise Dean Hsu, to represent Asian Americans to the administration, and to plan community-wide events that every group affiliated with AASA would support. The leaders of the various ethnic groups would then return to their members and inform them of AASA activities and events. AASA's meetings are open to the community, and in fact, many of the other board members of the Asian ethnic groups attend these meetings.

Even though this new AASA structure is very young, it has worked well. The first AASA president was a South Asian American woman, Vanita Gupta, who was simultaneously president of SAS (thus serving a dual role). Another AASA president was also South Asian American. There is diversity of representation at the events that AASA sponsors, since every Asian ethnic group participates in the heritage weeks (similar to the history months described earlier) by organizing an event. Thus, it seems as if, at least among the leadership, there is a feeling of Asian American unity at Yale University in which South Asian Americans are active participants. Moreover, all Asian groups, including the South Asian organization, have a voice in deciding what the position of the Asian American community will be on various campus issues. All Asian ethnic groups are equally empowered to set the Asian American agenda. Furthermore, all these leaders participate in AASA because they believe in a united political coalition. There are no "perks" to being part of AASA, especially monetary ones, because the center has such a small budget. Nor are the resources of the center large. In fact, most of the Asian ethnic groups do not even hold their meetings in the center because of lack of space. Therefore, every group participates with a common agenda in mind. It appears as though South Asian Americans have benefited the most from the new structure of AASA by having two of its leaders also hold leadership positions in AASA. As such, South Asian Americans finally have the visibility in the Asian American community and the equity with other Asian ethnic groups that the previous organizational structure prevented them from having.

The success of Yale's AASA structure is dependent on two things. One is the ability of the ethnic groups' leaders to mobilize their own respective communities. (But it is difficult to assess how much of SAS's membership understands and identifies with AASA's goals and issues.) The other is the ability of each ethnic group to elect a leadership that will continue to understand AASA's importance. There is a risk that new leaders will be elected by the community that do not want to participate in AASA for a number of reasons, including that they do not see themselves as Asian American, they feel that AASA is an ineffectual organization, or they do not wish to invest in building an Asian American coalition when their own organization needs so much support. These issues, however, can be addressed by former leaders' mentoring new ones. AASA is also facing a number of political issues on campus; these challenges give it a purpose and a goal. There are numerous areas in which Asian American students at Yale have few if any supports, creating a dire need for a strong united voice to advocate for Asian American student needs. Examples of areas in which Asian American students lack support include an insufficient number of ethnic counselors and inadequate space at the cultural center for meetings and other gatherings.

There are few conflicting agendas among the Asian American students at Yale. It is not as if one group is trying to fight for Asian American studies, while another wants a South Asian Studies department, while another fights for a Vietnamese tenured professor, while no one is keeping an eye on admissions of Asian Americans into the school. All groups decide what the priorities are and all groups work together toward achieving them, whether it be more money for Asian groups, administrative resources in the form of a center or a dean, or academic resources in the form of classes and professors. In addition, all groups are aware of what progress has been made, what needs to be done next, and what promises are yet to be delivered. There is no duplication of effort by groups from year to year. Therefore, the unique structure at Yale allows every Asian ethnic group to benefit because every group has participated in the fight, contributed the personal and organizational resources, and most importantly, agreed to the steps of action that need to be taken.

Yale's organizational restructuring significantly eliminated numerous gaps that exist at the other schools. By clearly defining membership, constituency, goals, and responsibilities, AASA has built solid bridges with all of the Asian ethnic groups, including SAS. Dissipating fears and insecurities, AASA has equally empowered every one of the members in its coalition. There is a mutual relationship in which Asian ethnic groups participate beyond token gestures in creating an Asian American community at Yale and, in return, receive a voice in the process. The pattern at Yale closes the organizational and institutional gaps with fundamental changes to the traditional Asian American/Asian ethnic group relationship, resulting in an effective coalition for both community spirit and political action.

IDENTITY FORMATION

Returning to the original discussion, what are the implications of these different political/organizational structures in terms of identity development? How do the complex relationships between Asian American and South Asian groups affect our ongoing discussion of South Asian Americans as Asian Americans? At Brown, Harvard, and the University of Pennsylvania, there exists one big minority community that has affiliated with it a center or foundation. Students of color can identify with a community and still feel part of the minority community at all three of these schools. Because of the organizational goals and structure, both the Asian American groups and the South Asian American groups are trying to create a sense of identity and community by actively soliciting members, holding meetings, and sponsoring events. The numerous activities of each group can become overwhelming. As such, there can be tension for the individual, especially if that person feels that he or she must choose between the two sets of identities or that the two cannot coexist. In deciding which group to join, South Asian Americans at all three schools are more likely to join the South Asian group. The acquisition of an Asian American identity takes place within the group, not in the classroom. The sense of a collective history and common issues and needs can be reinforced by the group, especially if its leadership is committed to maintaining a relationship with the Asian American group.[25]

At Brown, despite the political debates, there is a strong sense of both an Asian American identity and a South Asian American identity, largely due to the history of cooperation and goodwill between the two groups. But because so much of this relationship depends on the cooperation of group leaders, it is a somewhat fragile alliance. At Harvard and University of Pennsylvania, there is no relationship at all between the two groups, and identity formation ends with the South Asian group. South Asian American students at these two schools view themselves more as people of color or minorities than as Asian American.

The organizational structure of the Asian American and South Asian American communities at Yale resolves the identity issues that groups at

Brown, Harvard, and University of Pennsylvania face. Every Asian ethnic group, including South Asian American, feels a sense of ownership over the Asian American group and feels as if it belongs in the Asian American community; every Asian ethnic group, including the South Asian group, has a voice in the community because its members are Asian American.[26] At Yale, I believe, we see a glimpse of the future in which there is an acknowledgment of the limitations of the various identities and a rethinking of the many ways in which Asian American groups and Asian ethnic groups can best work together in social groups, community-based organizations, academic scholarship, and, most importantly, political activism.

NOTES

1. I realize that the choice of these four schools is problematic and biased. First, all four schools are Ivy League institutions on the East Coast and two of them are schools with which I have firsthand experiences. However, the dynamics within these four schools are so different from one another that an examination will paint three different pictures of the South Asian American and Asian American communities.

2. Having grown up in a community in Long Island, New York, that drastically changed from a neighborhood with few South Asian families to one with a plethora of South Asian faces, I became very active in both the South Asian American and Asian American communities as a student at Brown University in Rhode Island. I served as the secretary of the Asian American group and then became president of that same organization. I came to know intimately the issues faced by both South Asian and Asian American college groups through my experience in organizing cultural events, facilitating workshops, and rethinking the leadership structure and goals. I also spent three years as a resident counselor for incoming first-year students. During that time I studied the identity-formation process and the different factors that influence it. After graduation, I became copresident of the Asian American medical students group at Yale School of Medicine, in New Haven, Connecticut. This led to my election as president of the national Asian American medical students association. Over the years, I have informally interviewed many South Asian Americans on college campuses in the course of my interaction with them on a personal and professional level at school, meetings, conferences, and on the information superhighway. I am using this knowledge along with that gained from recent interviews with other leaders in the community as the mortar with which to construct this essay.

3. At some schools, this is a moot point because South Asian American students outnumber South Asian or international students. At other schools, however, numbers are more equal and this can become a serious concern. I feel another reason that the "American" aspect is not really emphasized is that the second generation is still trying to negotiate between "South Asian" and "South Asian American"; in other words, there is a cultural struggle that has yet to be resolved.

Interestingly, at the Massachusetts Institute of Technology (MIT) there are two organizations for the "South Asian" community: SAAS, or the South Asian American Society, and Sangam, comprised largely of international students. SAAS was created after a political rift when many South Asian Americans lost leadership positions in Sangam to South Asian students.

4. As other contributors to this volume have noted, "South Asian" is meant to be inclusive of all the countries and peoples in the Subcontinent but is often used as a synonym for "Indian." While I have tried to include examples involving other national groups, my attempts will most likely fall short, largely because most of my interactions, even in college, were with "Indian" Americans.

Only recently have more and more "non-Indian" South Asians been admitted to colleges and medical schools. I am not sure if that reflects immigration/baby boom trends, or an increased sensitivity to the fact that not everyone from South Asia is "Indian."

5. The many forces that shape how we see ourselves are complex and beyond the scope of this essay. Family, friends, school, and the media all play significant roles. I will focus on major issues relating to a student's culture and country of origin, in order to provide context for our discussion.

6. Interestingly, there is a fraction of the community that is identifying with other communities, especially with African Americans. In fact, in a recent issue of *Ebony*, there was an article about a young Pakistani Muslim girl from Harlem who identified herself as African American.

7. I realize that this a very antiquated (and probably racist) way of describing race, but unfortunately this is the paradigm that was taught to many college students when they were in elementary and junior high school and is still being taught in schools in the United States.

8. This concept of the "Asian" image is a very problematic one. Just look at the casting issues surrounding *Miss Saigon*, *The Joy Luck Club*, and *All-American Girl*. There are, of course, other Asian communities who are excluded by the Asian image (which is predominately an East Asian one), including Filipinos, Southeast Asians, and Pacific Islanders, as well as members of the East Asian community who defy the image (by being darker-skinned or having curly hair, etc.).

9. The discussion of similarities and differences is a topic unto itself and is addressed in other essays in this collection.

10. There is no evidence, other than anecdotes, to support the choices made by South Asian American college applicants. From my experience reviewing admissions folders, there is a significant segment of the population that identifies as Asian/Indian and an equally significant one that chooses not to identify. Those who select the "Other" option are either not Indian/Pakistani (i.e., they are Sri Lankan or Bangladeshi), or identify very strongly with some other identity. In fact, one young man on his application to Harvard, selected the "Other" box and wrote next to it—"Tamil, not Indian, not Asian—just Tamil."

11. I would like to acknowledge that there are a number of South Asian Americans who have a strong sense of being South Asian American who are not actively involved with the organization at their school for a number of reasons. These include personal differences with the leadership of the organization, feeling as

though the organizations goals are not in line with their own, feeling alienated from the group, feeling as though they are beyond the point of questioning their identity, and involvement in other interests such as public service, dance, or journalism. On the whole, though, the majority of the community does identify with and support the organization and it is in this larger context that identity formation is influenced by campus politics.

12. There are a number of schools that have multiple South Asian American groups based on country of origin, such as Cornell. Individuals at these schools probably do not see themselves as South Asian since there is no South Asian group at their school. They do, however, see themselves as Indian or Pakistani or Gujurati, based on the group with which they identify themselves.

13. One challenge of depicting and analyzing the experiences of student groups on college campuses is the lack of specific information regarding the inception and history of the various organizations. Despite numerous attempts, I was unable to identify when specifically each organization began, who its membership was, and how many actual members were involved over the years. Critical events in the evolution of the group seem to be the only historical evidence that is handed down from one leadership to the next. Most organizations recognize this lack of written records and have now started to document each year's experiences.

14. The presence of South Asian Americans in these movements during the late 1960s was limited, to say the least, largely because the same exclusionary immigration laws prevented the Sikh/Indian community from producing subsequent generations of South Asian Americans. In fact, Takaki discusses the near extinction of the South Asian American community. The 1965 Immigration Act allowed for South Asians to once again enter the United States in large numbers.

15. The pattern described in this paragraph holds true for many of the institutions of higher learning in the United States, including the other schools in this paper. A combination of "reversal" of admission quotas and an increase in the number of Asian Americans in high school (mostly children of that first wave of post-1965 immigrants) created a situation that allowed for the formation of ethnic groups. Prior to this, most schools had only one Asian American group because there were only a handful of students at each school. It is hard to create a Chinese Students Association if there are only ten Chinese Americans.

16. These minority groups were the Organization of United African Peoples (OUAP), the Latino American Students Organization (LASO), the Federation of Students from Puerto Rico (FEP), and the Asian American Students Association (AASA).

17. Discussions with these individuals revealed that they are extremely ignorant of the history and immigration patterns of both South Asian Americans and other Asian Americans. They expressed disbelief at the notion that there were settlers from India in the early 1900s. They feel that similarities with the immigration experience of other Asians are purely coincidental. Lastly, they feel that violence and discrimination against South Asian Americans more closely resembles that experienced by other minority groups than that by other Asians.

18. In this context, "minority groups" refers to any group that has a predomi-

nant minority constituency, including artistic groups (i.e. a cappella groups, performance groups, literary groups), religious groups, pan-ethnic groups, women's organizations, etc.

19. During the end of the academic year, the leaders of all the Asian groups met and decided to form a new coalition called the Asian Pacific Students Coalition (APSC) and elected an acting chair. At this time, little discussion has taken place as to the structures and goals of APSC.

20. In student organizational terms, the power of a group is measured by the number of events, the frequency of those events, the membership who participate in each event (dance, dinner, speaker), and the ability of the events to draw participants from other schools, especially when the event is not intercollegiate.

21. As an example, AAA and the other Asian ethnic groups have meetings to coordinate their calendars in order to avoid scheduling conflicts.

22. During the 1995–1996 academic year, AAA and SAA began cosponsoring events such as an Inter-Ethnic Community Service Day.

23. Most leaders from the South Asian American student community are unaware of the Asian American Admissions investigation by the Office of Civil Rights regarding ceiling caps/quotas on the number of students admitted each year. After a public appraisal of the admissions policies at Harvard University, Brown University, and the University of California at Berkeley, Asian American student organizations across the country took it upon themselves to monitor the numbers of students accepted and to work in partnership with their respective admissions offices to recruit underrepresented Asian Americans (such as Vietnamese, Hmong, Sri Lankans, etc.).

24. One of the reasons for SAS's decision to leave the Asian American Cultural Center was the East Asian focus of both the center and the Asian American organization (AASA).

25. I recently learned that at Stanford University, the South Asian student organization decided to leave the Asian American coalition because they were tired of trying to work together. It is important to note that Asian American students at Stanford are politically active and very involved in Asian American studies. On the other hand, the South Asian students continue to remain social and cultural. It is difficult to assess what the implications of this decision will be on the identity formation of South Asian Americans, especially since it was a decision made by one set of leaders and will affect subsequent classes of students.

26. A recent example is a voter registration drive that was sponsored by AASA. Each ethnic organization, including SAS, advertised it to its membership and committed at least three volunteers who would participate in the rally and voting drive.

SUMANTRA TITO SINHA

7   From Campus to Community Politics in Asian America

WHEN I was growing up and going to public schools in Queens, in the late 1970s through the late 1980s, my identity as an Asian American did not mean much to me. I imagine that to have been the case for most other South Asian young people at that time. It wasn't as if I didn't associate with other Asians. In fact, most of my friends were of one Asian background or another, and almost half of the students in my high school were Asian. I was Indian, and most of my friends happened to be Asian, but I thought of their backgrounds as being, for example, Chinese, Korean, or Pakistani, not primarily Asian, per se.

During those years, however, I was increasingly aware that the national media, universities, the Census Bureau, and other agencies interested in demographics were focusing on the emergence of Asian Americans and Asian immigrants and their impact on American society. Much of this discussion focused on Asian Americans, particularly Asian American students, professionals, and entrepreneurs, as a "model minority." Mostly, the discussion profiled the remarkable achievements of Chinese, Korean, and other East Asian groups. I don't remember seeing any South Asian groups being profiled as visibly in this discussion. If we were mentioned at all, we would be listed among the Asian groups in some statistical table or graph comparing our income or education levels, for example, with those of the other Asian American subgroups. Similarly, any group or organization that proclaimed to represent Asian Americans seemed to work for different East Asian communities on a variety of issues, such as anti-Asian violence, and the rights and concerns of immigrants. I remember noticing this and wondering why South Asian groups were not as central either to the discussion or to the work of the different organizations. This was strange to me not just because I had always learned, at least from home, that Indians, Pakistanis, Bangladeshis, and Sri Lankans came from Asia and were a significant part of Asian culture and civilization. But it was also strange, because the issues with which Asian Americans and Asian immigrants were being identified, such as the "model minority" myth, anti-Asian violence, and glass ceilings, were issues that also affected South

146

Asians in the United States. If South Asians shared these same concerns, they why did it seem we weren't being included in this picture?

Nothing at that time more forcefully proved to me that South Asians shared issues with other Asian groups than my experiences with my high school friends. We not only went to school together, we also hung out together, played ball together, talked about teenage stuff, ate at each other's houses, respected each other's traditions, and talked about our own families' struggles as first-generation immigrants. It was through my many experiences and discussions with them that I realized that my own confusions about being bicultural, bilingual, a first-generation immigrant, and the conflict I experienced living in a society that permitted much personal freedom while being raised in a traditionally conservative family were not unique. I saw that these tensions were common among many Asian immigrant homes, and centered on issues ranging from career choices and dating, to the pressure to study harder.

Consequently, while I could see that there was a gap between how East Asians and South Asians were identified by the society at large and also by how they identified themselves, my own experiences demonstrated that important connections between members of different Asian communities, and specifically between my friends and me, did exist. These connections centered around how we fit in with and were treated by the larger society, and how we negotiated the tensions between the expectations of our families, cultures, and communities and the expectations of the larger society. I don't recall these connections translating into any institutional form; that is, I don't remember any student clubs or community groups with pan-Asian membership. For the most part, student clubs and community groups represented individual ethnic constituencies. Even the groups that identified themselves as "Asian" had almost exclusively East Asian members. Yet in high school, this did not bother me in any profound way; just as there were East Asian groups, there were Indian and Pakistani clubs as well. What was more critical for me was the sense of belonging that I felt with friends who happened to be from a variety of ethnicities.

Most of my friends—both Asian and non-Asian—were raised with a strong sense of ethnic identity. Many of us, along with our families, participated in some kind of community or religious association. Of course, in New York with its many and large ethnic communities, having a strong ethnic and community identity is quite common. Yet, even though my friends and I were different ethnically and had a strong sense of our individual ethnic identities, I felt that we shared many common experiences and concerns. All of our parents worked hard and long hours. They sought to retain their cultural heritage and associations with others in their ethnic community. At the same time, our families tried to live peace-fully with people of different ethnicities, often in neighborhoods where we weren't really wanted. Our parents' struggles had powerfully colored our own experiences and worldview. So notwithstanding our different ethnic-ities, the fact that many of us were rooted with a strong sense of commu-nity and were influenced greatly by our parents' struggles enhanced our similar outlooks. Looking back, I feel these friendships provided an im-portant foundation for my later understanding that Asian Americans share many issues in common and my later desire to be active in coalition building in the Asian American community.

A New Context

It wasn't until I left New York City and went away to a small north-eastern liberal arts college in a suburban, upper-middle-class environment that I understood the significance of my Asian immigrant identity and be-came active in pan–Asian American politics. I never planned on becoming immersed in a pan–Asian American movement, but circumstances com-pelled me to do otherwise. While high school had offered an environment where most of the students were people of color and working-class and immigrant kids, college was a sea of upper-middle-class white faces. Even most of the students of color were children of privilege. In this new envi-ronment, I found that my most meaningful friendships were with people such as myself—mostly immigrant, mostly middle and working class, and mostly Asian American.

Prior to my first year of college, in 1989, most of the Asian American students at that college came from suburban upper-middle-class environ-ments. However, my class included more Asian American students from cities and from less privileged environments, as the college made greater efforts to diversify and more students from such backgrounds applied. Many of us had been raised amidst significant racial and economic diver-sity as well as with a strong sense of our respective ethnic communities. The elite culture of the school, with its coded racism, forced me and many of my close college friends to realize that the things we had in common were far stronger than any differences that may have divided us. That is, whether you were a Vietnamese immigrant from Seattle, a Filipino immi-grant from Los Angeles, or an Indian immigrant from New York, you felt a similar sense of alienation from the majority culture.

Some of us looked to the Asian American students' organization as a way to feel more at home. We hoped, first, that the organization might serve as a social forum where we would feel comfortable. Second, we hoped that the Asian students' organization would be an advocate for our concerns and needs as minority students. For example, we wondered why there were no classes concerning Asian Americans, such as Asian American history and literature. We also wondered why there were no support services for Asian American students, a counselor or appointed faculty member that we could turn to. Black students had an established support system in the form of a Black Cultural Center, with appointed faculty and staff associated with it, but there were no such resources for Asian American students.

Because of our interests in these and other issues, my friends and I began attending Asian student organization meetings. After a couple of meetings, we realized that the group would not meet our needs. The group's primary purpose at the time was to serve as a social forum, sponsoring events like pot-luck dinners, and it had no agenda of advocacy for Asian American students. The organization was run by Asian American students who were in many ways comfortable with the school's environment. Many of them had been raised in suburban upper-middle-class towns where there were few Asian Americans. Moreover, the organization consisted entirely of East Asian students, so its appeal as a social forum for me as a South Asian American was limited.

In spite of these limitations, my friends and I decided to become more involved in the organization's affairs. As the first year came to an end, we became regular members and were able to elect a president who shared our vision for the organization. The next year, the organization became a stronger advocate for Asian American issues, pressuring the administration for Asian American courses, Asian American faculty, Asian American support services, and recruitment of more Asian American students from disadvantaged and urban backgrounds. We also promoted public awareness of Asian American identities and history with exhibits, displays, and posters. In conjunction with this activism, others in my class began mobilizing student and faculty support for an Intercultural Center, which would provide space for minority groups on campus to meet and organize, and would also be an educational, cultural, and political resource for all students. Slowly, our Asian student group was becoming more of an advocate, and it began attracting more students as the new classes of students entered the school.

In the first couple of years, it often seemed as if I was the only South Asian American who was active in the group. Many of the South Asian American students were "apolitical," which was political in its own way. In all fairness, there were also many non–South Asian American students who were not interested in our group. The total student population at the college was approximately fifteen hundred, of whom roughly 12 percent were Asian American. In my first year at college, only ten to twelve Asian

Americans regularly attended the Asian student group meetings. Of this number, two were South Asian, including myself. In the following year, the number of Asian American "regulars" increased to thirty, and active South Asians numbered between three and six. In my final year at college, we established a separate South Asian American student organization with between ten and fifteen members. In any event, when a South Asian person joins an Asian organization and is the only South Asian person there, that person assumes an inherently political role because he or she may feel the added burden of having to represent "his or her people." This may be true to an extent for members of other Asian groups. But as a South Asian American, I have found this burden to be more apparent because I easily stood out as being South Asian—a racial distinction that I could not avoid.

Even though I was active in the Asian student organization, my presence did not necessarily attract other South Asian Americans. Many of the South Asian American students, like many of the other Asian American students, seemed to become friends, and mingle easily, with white, upper-middle-class students. Eventually I realized that although we had some things in common, in many ways I was different from the other South Asian students. It seemed that I was the only South Asian American student to have come from an urban environment, while other South Asian American students had grown up in mostly white suburbs with few people of color. For these students, the college environment was not that different from their home environments. That is not to say that these students didn't face their own feelings of isolation and alienation. But they did not feel compelled to join the Asian students' organization, with its mostly non–South Asian membership, to address those issues.

I had already seen how differences in economic and social backgrounds had created a gap between the members of the Asian student organization. Now, these same differences in class and social background were a critical factor in my gravitating toward the Asian students' organization as a forum where my concerns might be addressed, even though it was mostly non–South Asian. My upbringing had shown me the importance of working with other underrepresented students on campus, namely other students of color.

Eventually, other South Asian students and I founded a club for students of South Asian descent. We felt that there should be a forum where South Asian students could socialize and feel comfortable meeting one another. In discussing our group's relationship with the Asian American community, we agreed that the South Asian club would send representatives to the Asian organization. I felt that this was important, to demonstrate that South Asian students were not necessarily divorcing themselves from the Asian American community, but were creating a social forum for themselves, just as other students of another Asian ethnicity, such as Korean or Vietnamese, might. We hoped that South Asian students could enjoy the benefits of both being part of a South Asian community and participating in the activities of a larger Asian American community.

In the coming years, my activism, as well as the activism of my friends and the Asian students' organization expanded considerably. As this happened, we experienced a sense of solidarity based on friendship as well as struggle. More students became involved in our work, as the number of Asian American students increased to the point where Asian American students were the largest minority group on campus. We worked with other student groups in promoting a more multicultural curriculum and protesting racism on campus. We published our own newsletter. And we expanded our involvement to issues affecting Asian Americans off campus, such as working with young Southeast Asian inmates at a local prison who had limited English proficiency and were awaiting trial because they were involved in a fight started by a group of white teenagers which resulted in the death of one white. We also raised awareness of anti-Asian violence cases such as the trial of the attackers of Dr. Kaushal Sharan, an Indian medical student who had been severely beaten by three whites in New Jersey.

Underlying our activism was the awareness that despite our own differences, the struggle against racism was an important, unifying factor bonding many Asian American students together. On campus, racially motivated incidents and the struggle for a multicultural curriculum and greater diversity served to rally many Asian American students and allowed us to close the gaps between ourselves and other students of color. Off campus, our experiences with teenage Southeast Asian inmates who had been indiscriminately arrested after being picked up off the street corners and detained without adequate access to counsel opened our eyes to how their treatment paralleled the treatment of other defendants of color, especially when the victim is white. Similarly, the acquittal of Dr. Sharan's white attackers by an all-white federal jury reinforced the notion that race plays a role in the judicial system as well. These experiences combined to demonstrate that racism took many forms and inspired us to do what we could to fight it. Ultimately, this desire to fight racism and cultivate a diverse, tolerant, and just community played a major role in closing gaps within the Asian American and student of color populations.

My college experiences had given me a better appreciation of the importance of community work with people of color and people from lower-income, underrepresented, and disadvantaged backgrounds—all of whom struggled for representation and access to resources.

Looking for Work

During my senior year, I had applied to various foundations, nonprofit agencies, and programs for a public interest job. I applied for a grant at a noted civil rights foundation where I had expressed an interest in doing Asian American community work. During the interview, the subject of the Los Angeles riots came up. One of the interviewers asked me why we needed to hear Asian American voices. He said that Asian Americans weren't that significant a community, that we really didn't have problems or issues to deal with, that I wasn't Asian anyway, and even if I were, what did I, as an Indian American, have in common with East and Southeast Asians.

The interviewer's comments shocked me. They were made contemptuously, and not in the spirit of learning more about Asian American issues. Moreover, in light of how my college experiences had transformed me, I could not ignore how the comments affected me personally. I responded by saying that if the riots proved anything, they showed what can happen if the voices of all people are not heard and honored. And in any multicultural community, whether it is Los Angeles, New York, or the United States as a whole, if any of these voices, including Asian American voices, are ignored or disrespected, it fuels the fires of hate and violence. Furthermore, I noted that Korean store owners seemed to be targets of the rioting. Although the previous tensions between the black and Korean communities might explain these events, one can also look at the situation in the context of a long history of anti-immigrant and anti-Asian violence in California where, previously, disenchanted whites and, now, disenchanted blacks scapegoated Asian immigrants for their hardships. I also made it clear to him that I considered myself an Asian American, and that although there are differences among Asian Americans, in the context of this society, what we have in common—particularly, the Asian immigrant experience—far outweighed any differences that may separate us. Finally, I explained that Asian Americans are not a "model minority" and that we had problems and struggles like any community.

The interview was far from cordial, and I didn't get the position. It was revealing to me to see that there are people working in the civil rights field who have a very narrow understanding of race relations in this country. I am sure that there are a number of people in the civil rights field who continue to view American society only in terms of black and white. My experience also showed me that the traditional civil rights leadership may not be up to the task of dealing with our highly complex multicultural society. The civil rights movement needs to be reenergized by people who are themselves products of today's multicultural America. In this society, Asian Americans are well suited to exercise leadership because we know firsthand the complexities of multicultural, multiracial, multilingual, and economically diverse communities. Furthermore, South Asian Americans, in particular, are in a position to play significant roles because we, of all people, know from our own histories on the Subcontinent the difficulties and complexities of creating and preserving a multicultural democracy.

This incident was not the first time my Asian Americanness had been questioned, and I knew that it would not be the last. But having to justify my Asian American identity to someone else only reaffirmed my sense of being Asian American. Here were people who knew hardly anything about me other than where I had gone to school, what kind of work I wanted to pursue, and what I looked like; yet they had made assumptions about my identity. They knew nothing about my experiences in college or growing up in New York. The fact that they had challenged and attacked me from a position of ignorance only strengthened my belief in being Asian American. I was an Asian American not because someone had labeled me that way or because I had no other choice, but because of my experiences, I felt I was Asian American and I had a right to choose to identify as one.

RETURN TO NEW YORK CITY: WORKING WITH THE ASIAN AMERICAN LEGAL DEFENSE AND EDUCATION FUND

After graduation I accepted an internship position with the Asian American Legal Defense and Education Fund (AALDEF). I believe they were better able to appreciate my experience and activism in college than those agencies that did not specifically serve Asian Americans. I was the first South Asian American on staff at AALDEF. Since its founding in 1974, AALDEF has been involved in impact litigation, community education, and legal representation concerning anti-Asian violence, workers' rights, voting rights, immigrants' rights, police brutality, and other civil rights issues. Located in downtown Manhattan near Chinatown, AALDEF had primarily served the city's Chinese, Japanese, and, later, Korean communities. In the late 1980s, when episodes of racial violence against South Asian Americans were rising in New Jersey, AALDEF began working with South Asian American community groups and advocates to educate the community, monitor trials of the attackers, and raise support for a hate-crimes law in that state. Otherwise, AALDEF's contacts with South Asian American communities were limited to occasional South Asian American volunteers. In New York City, AALDEF had not worked on any substan-

tial projects in South Asian American communities, partly because no issue or incidents had compelled the community and AALDEF to come together in a way that was similar to what happened in New Jersey.

By the early 1990s, New York City's Asian American population was
changing both in size and in composition. Indians became the second-
largest Asian ethnic group in the city, after the Chinese. And a majority of
Asian New Yorkers now resided in the borough of Queens. In addition to
these changes, there were more Pakistanis, Bangladeshis, Guyanese, and
Southeast Asians—many of them living in new Asian neighborhoods in
the boroughs of Queens, Brooklyn, and the Bronx.[1] In this context I returned home from college and began a summer internship at AALDEF.

At the end of the summer, I was asked to continue full-time as a program associate of AALDEF's Voting Rights Project. My primary responsibilities involved policy work on issues affecting the entire Asian American community. For example, I was asked to analyze Asian American
voter participation in New York City elections, and I monitored voting
rights issues affecting Asian American communities. I also did some organizing, such as helping to coordinate exit poll surveys to monitor Asian
American voting patterns and organizing voter registration and education
drives to increase Asian American voter participation.

Through this work, I became familiar with many Asian Americans and
Asian American groups involved in grassroots organizing, voter education, and community organizing and was able to assess how the South
Asian community fared. For example, I found that almost every major
Asian community in New York City had an organization that was engaged in voter education and mobilization, except for the Indian community. Among the smaller Pakistani and Bangladeshi communities, there are
organizations which are beginning to engage in this work. Furthermore,
the Indo-Caribbean community seems to be better organized in this area
and has even had one of its own run for Congress from Queens. But
among the Asian Indian population, there did not seem to be any similar
services that were being provided for various reasons, some of which I will
later discuss. Thus, while the South Asian population is growing rapidly
and is a potentially powerful force in the city, many people in the community remain uninformed and uninvolved in the political process.

I was also involved in AALDEF's exit poll surveys of Asian American
voters. As a result of the voter surveys, we were able to get a glimpse of
how the Asian American community votes. AALDEF had traditionally
conducted these surveys in Chinatown and pan-Asian neighborhoods such
as Flushing, in Queens. In addition to helping coordinate the project in
these neighborhoods, I was also asked by AALDEF to help better target
South Asian American voters. I volunteered by expanding the survey to

my own neighborhood, where there was a significant South Asian American population. We found that in the 1993 mayoral election race between Rudolph Giuliani (Republican) and David Dinkins (Democrat) Asian Americans as a whole voted two to one for Giuliani. However, we observed that among South Asian American voters, Dinkins was favored 48 percent to 36 percent, while among the Chinese, Korean, and Filipino communities, Giuliani was the favored candidate. These results surprised me because I had always believed that the South Asian American community was generally conservative. Yet in examining the profiles of the South Asian American voters surveyed, we found that they were more likely to register as Democrats than other Asian American voters, and this was the most significant factor in explaining their voting patterns. Since then, AALDEF has conducted voter surveys each year when there are major elections. In the 1996 presidential elections, the surveys showed that 71 percent of Asian American New Yorkers supported President Bill Clinton with 21 percent supporting Bob Dole. And for the first time, a majority of Asian American New Yorkers polled—51 percent—are now registered as Democrats.[2] The results from the surveys conducted demonstrated to me that there was much to learn about the South Asian American community and its potential for political mobilization.

Along with this work at AALDEF, I was given opportunities to represent AALDEF at various meetings, conferences, panel discussions, and public hearings. As a result of my experiences in pan-Asian American community work, I felt I belonged to a broader Asian American community. Consequently, I saw that the gaps between South Asian Americans and other Asian Americans could begin to close in larger community work, not just at the college level.

My sense of belonging to a broader Asian American community was reinforced by my interactions with the staff at AALDEF. When I started work there, I was not sure how I, as the only South Asian American, would feel. I wondered if the same questions that underlay my college activism would reemerge: would I feel included in the group, or would I feel tokenized? But at AALDEF, my Asian Americanness was never questioned by anyone on the staff and I felt accepted as an Asian American. I worked on issues and projects affecting all Asian Americans, and at the same time served as a resource for staff members who needed advice on issues that concerned the South Asian American community. Also, while I was the only South Asian American on staff, I did not experience the same isolation I had in college because I was back at home reconnected with family, friends, and the larger South Asian American community. But perhaps more important, my sense of belonging to an Asian American community was reaffirmed by the guidance and mentorship I received under the supervision of AALDEF staff. This was significant because I received this support from non–South Asians who encouraged me to keep working on behalf of Asian American communities. Thus, I have seen that there are non-South Asians in the Asian American community who are interested in including South Asian Americans in Asian American organizations, and thereby wish to close the gaps dividing the Asian American community.

Aside from my voting rights work, I helped AALDEF conduct outreach to South Asian American communities. For example, we organized voter registration drives and information tables in Jackson Heights and at South Asian events, such as a Nusrat Fateh Ali Khan concert in Central Park and the India Day Parade. We sponsored a South Asian American community forum at Queens College in Flushing with speakers from different South Asian American community groups. In addition, I represented AALDEF at various meetings of South Asian American organizers. All of these efforts increased AALDEF's involvement and visibility in South Asian American communities. At the same time, more people in the South Asian community were approaching AALDEF to seek legal advice concerning issues dealing with discrimination, domestic violence, and immigration. Particularly, as incidents of anti-Asian and anti-immigrant sentiment increased, AALDEF has played a greater role in providing legal assistance to South Asian victims of bias attacks and discrimination.

In 1996, AALDEF assisted one of the first South Asian Americans to gain political office in New York City when it provided timely and critical legal representation to Sachi Dastidar by defending his election to a local district school board in northeastern Queens. Dastidar was one of four South Asian Americans across the city who ran in local school board elections in 1996. Two candidates, Dastidar, an Indian American, and Morshed Alam, a Bangladeshi American campaigning in a neighboring district, won their elections, thus becoming the first South Asians to gain elective office in New York City. Dastidar's campaign provides an interesting case study in the obstacles that South Asian Americans face in becoming involved in electoral politics, as well as lessons on how to overcome these obstacles.

I served as a volunteer coordinator for Dastidar, who campaigned for a seat in District 26 in northeastern Queens, which includes heavily South Asian areas such as Floral Park, Bellerose, and Glen Oaks. The campaign committee for Dastidar began meeting in January and consisted primarily of several first-generation middle-aged South Asian residents in the district. We were hoping to mobilize significant South Asian grassroots support for the May election because in New York City school board elections, noncitizens are permitted to vote if they have children in the local public elementary or middle schools. Our campaign held community forums, campaign committee meetings, and publicized the campaign through local media and through informal networks. Consequently, we gathered more than enough petitions to place Dastidar on the ballot and awaited the coming of election day.

In our district, where over 30 percent of the students in the public schools are Asian Americans, Dastidar was one of three Asian American candidates campaigning for nine seats. Since the school board elections employ a system of proportional representation, in which voters rank candidates according to their own preferences, it is critical for candidates to forge alliances with one another so they may benefit from each other's pool of voters. As a result, Dastidar sought to build alliances with the other Asian American candidates, who included a Korean American woman and a Chinese American man, both of whom had strong support from their own communities. We hoped for a similar show of support for Dastidar from the South Asian American community.

Unfortunately, the overall response from the South Asian community was disappointing. First, of the major Indian organizations in New York City, like the Federation of Indian Associations and the Association of Indians in America, not one responded to any request for assistance in terms of volunteers, technical support, donations, or other resources. In contrast, the few that did come forward to assist were people of limited income and moderate means. They were mostly middle-class Indian Americans and recent Bangladeshi immigrants who were willing to support Dastidar, a Bengali-speaking Indian. Furthermore, while some Indian media covered the campaign, it was the local mainstream and East Asian community media that paid serious attention to this "new ethnic group" joining the political process. Secondly, on election day, fewer than half of the people who signed the petition for Dastidar to be placed on the ballot actually went to the polls to vote. We knew this because over four hundred people signed the petitions—many of them South Asian American, yet the final election results showed that Dastidar received just over two hundred votes. These episodes demonstrate the level of apathy that continues to plague the South Asian American community.

While our campaign faced these obstacles from within our own community, we also faced obstacles from outside the community as well. On election day, a number of South Asian American voters were turned away from the polls by a combination of poll workers and police officers who denied noncitizens their lawful right to vote in school board elections. Many poll workers, who were mostly white, improperly asked the voters if they were citizens and then incorrectly told many of them that if they were not citizens, they could not vote. Many poll workers were rude and outright hostile to the South Asian Americans who came to vote. These tensions only reflected those of the larger community in which some white residents have resented large numbers of South Asian Americans moving into the area. In addition, there were several episodes of police intimidation of our volunteers who sought to distribute campaign literature near the polls in accordance with the election laws. This was the first time South Asian Americans were asserting themselves as a political force in our district, and we experienced a rude awakening as to the resistance we have to face when we challenge the status quo. We saw how the lack of organizational support or previous political activity had left us defenseless in these situations.

Despite the disappointing turnout, Dastidar still had enough votes to secure the ninth and final seat on the school board. But the tenth-place contestant, a white incumbent, subsequently challenged the results. After a recount, the Board of Elections announced that they had neglected to count some of the ballots and declared the incumbent the winner. At this point, Dastidar contacted AALDEF for assistance. AALDEF had been following the events in our district after newspapers had made public the instances of Asian American voters' being turned away. With the reversal of the outcome by the Board of Elections, AALDEF intervened and demanded another recount. After the second recount, during which AALDEF attorneys were present, the elections officials realized that there were even more ballots that had not been properly counted and, after counting them, declared Dastidar the winner by four votes. Finally, the white incumbent challenged the results in court. In defending Dastidar's election, AALDEF was able to uphold Dastidar's election. During the critical time when Dastidar's election was in balance or when reports of South Asian American voters being turned away became known, no South Asian group stepped forward to assist Dastidar. The only assistance we received from the South Asian American community during that critical time was from the volunteers of our own campaign who had already worked tirelessly for months.

The events surrounding Dastidar's campaign represented an important development in the process of closing the gaps between South Asian Americans and other Asian Americans in New York City. First, AALDEF, an established Asian American organization, was willing to reach out and assist in the development of a grassroots South Asian American political force when no other South Asian group was ready to do so. Second, the campaign demonstrated the importance of working with other Asian communities in our district. Third, the system of preferential voting and proportional representation in place for the school board elections facilitates the elections of minority candidates. Since that election, Asian Americans have been elected to school boards in a number of districts in New York City. All of these developments represent important steps toward greater grassroots coalition building between South Asian Americans and other Asian Americans.

Despite AALDEF's contribution to Dastidar's election, the use of AALDEF services by the South Asian American community is small compared to the number of South Asian Americans who could benefit from the service, and it is also small compared to the extent AALDEF is used by other Asian American communities. According to Anannya Bhattacharjee, who at the time of my interview was the executive director of the Committee Against Anti-Asian Violence (CAAAV), which seeks to organize Asian American communities in the New York City area to combat racism, bias-motivated violence, police brutality, and economic injustice, one reason why South Asian Americans and South Asian American community groups do not make use of services provided by pan-Asian American organizations such as AALDEF is that many South Asian Americans are not aware that these services are available.[3] For example, when Bhattacharjee served as the executive coordinator of SAKHI for South Asian Women before joining CAAAV, she recalled that SAKHI knew very little about AALDEF's services, interests, and agenda. (SAKHI, which is the Hindi word for *friend*, was started in 1989 to help battered South Asian women.) As a result, not many SAKHI clients took advantage of AALDEF services, such as its free legal clinic. If SAKHI had had more information about what AALDEF had to offer, it could have taken a more active role in building a working relationship. Thus, lack of knowledge and communication among pan-Asian organizations, South Asian community groups, and the South Asian community prevent South Asian Americans from better utilizing pan-Asian American services and resources.

Part of the problem is that many South Asian Americans do not perceive Asian American organizations as serving them. Similarly, many Asian American organizations do not reach out to South Asian American communities, informing them about their services. Bhattacharjee points out that "when one hears of an Asian organization, unless there is significant South Asian representation, one will assume that it does not serve South Asians. . . . As a result, Asian American organizations must continually do aggressive outreach to South Asians to ensure that they are being served."[4] Yet while Asian American organizations do their outreach, South Asian Americans must be willing to use these services.

An organization's ability to do aggressive outreach, however, is inevitably affected by a lack of time and resources, especially in a place like New York City, where Asian and immigrant communities are underserved and nonprofit groups are overworked. Margaret Fung, executive director of AALDEF, confirms that the presence of South Asian staff is essential to outreach efforts, and I have also observed that to be true.[5]

One South Asian American community organization that has had a working relationship with pan–Asian American groups is the Lease Drivers Coalition (LDC), which seeks to assist, organize, and educate South Asian taxi drivers in New York about their rights. LDC operates as a committee within CAAAV, and one of its community organizers at the time of my interview, Saleem Osman, was also CAAAV's program director. According to Osman, one reason why some Asian American groups have been reluctant to work with newer South Asian communities is the feeling of some, especially second- and third-generation Asian Americans, who have an established history of activism and struggle, that they have little in common with newer South Asian immigrants who seem to come mainly for economic reasons and adapt quickly to the society.[6] Thus, there is the perception among many Asian Americans that the South Asian American community does not face serious problems.

If Osman is correct, these perceptions of South Asian Americans by other Asian Americans are damaging because they attribute a "model minority" status to South Asian Americans within the Asian American population, which is already viewed as a "model minority" by the society at large. This dynamic is intriguing because it suggests that Asian Americans may have internalized the "model-minority" mythmaking of the society at large. According to Osman, "While the South Asian community may not share the extent of the problems faced by some Southeast Asian refugee communities, and while some of our community is affluent, to think that most South Asians are well-off and well-adjusted is a mistake. [Thus,] one of the most important goals in the Asian American community is to address our own misperceptions, biases, and racism toward one another. It's important to have a forum to address these issues."[7]

LDC has been instrumental in creating such forums. When I worked at AALDEF, LDC and CAAAV had organized a rally against police brutality toward taxi drivers, in response to a specific incident of racially motivated harassment and violence by members of the New York Police Department toward one South Asian taxi driver. This was not the first such incident. The rally consisted of about 75 to 150 people outside the city's main police headquarters. What struck me about the rally was that this was the first time I had seen East and Southeast Asians participate in significant numbers alongside South Asian activists, taxi drivers, and community people to show support for a South Asian victim of racial violence. (Although I had seen similarly composed groups showing support for East and Southeast Asian victims of racial violence, I was not sure whether such broad participation would be seen when the victim of racial violence was South Asian.) The rally opened my eyes to greater possibilities of coalition building when people of different Asian communities could recognize common problems and goals.

Nevertheless, Osman, who helped organize that rally, tempered his optimism:

> Demonstrations are a one-time thing. You need to have other programs which bring people together for the long term. For example, when we did our outreach to vendors in Chinatown [who were being harassed by the police as well], people in Chinatown were amazed to see Indian and Pakistani faces helping them. The vendors said they were glad to see us. So we decided to do more workshops and programs where we could talk more and discuss the issues we have in common. Similarly, we did a program with the National Congress for Puerto Rican Rights. And after we finished discussing some of the issues we have been facing, such as police brutality, they asked us, 'Are you sure you're not Puerto Rican?' So, through these programs and workshops, there is intermingling, and understanding develops. We need more of them because South Asians do share things in common with other Asians and other people of color.[8]

At the same time, Osman says, it is important for the various South Asian American communities to become more united and overcome nationalist tendencies and differences. During the 1995 India Day Parade, the Federation of Indian Associations (FIA) refused to allow several South Asian community groups to march, including the South Asian Lesbian and Gay Association, SAKHI, LDC, and South Asian Aids Action. The FIA contended that these groups were not exclusively Indian but broadly based South Asian in membership and so could not march in the parade. Much of the public controversy concerning the exclusion of the groups, however, focused on the exclusion of a gay and lesbian group. While acknowledging that homophobia in our community was a factor in the exclusion, Osman also pointed out that this was a clear example of how nationalist ideology is dividing our communities. The result is that South Asian groups are not considered to be Indian. "In this country, whether you are Pakistani or Bangladeshi, people group you with the Indians. We are seen as one. If this is the case, shouldn't we work with one another? . . . Furthermore, if they won't let Pakistanis participate, but I was born in India but had to move to Pakistan, who is to say whether I am Indian, or Pakistani, or both?"[9]

Thus, the notion of a South Asian or South Asian American identity is itself a conflicted one. There are internal obstacles preventing South Asians from coming together with any degree of unity, obstacles originating in regional, religious, caste, and language differences. Consequently, the impulse to bridge the gap with other Asian Americans may seem secondary or not even practical in the face of the divisions that exist within the South Asian American community itself. Osman believes that the South Asian community needs to be more united and mobilize around issues that affect us. At the same time, he says, larger and more established Asian American groups, such as AALDEF, that engage in broad policy matters, need to be able to share a common agenda, space, and power with smaller grassroots organizations in newer and less organized Asian American communities. One way of achieving this is for the staff of Asian American groups to be fully representative of the diversity of the Asian American population, thus helping them to be more sensitive to the concerns of all Asian Americans.

Conclusions

I draw three major lessons from my experiences in New York City about drawing together the South Asian American and other Asian American communities. First, Asian American organizations need to become more aware of serving the South Asian American community as well as other underrepresented segments of Asian America. This can be done by integrating issues concerning the South Asian American community within the general policy discussion of Asian American issues. This integration need not be difficult since many of the issues that South Asian Americans face are shared by other Asian Americans. For example, issues such as political mobilizing and the turning away of legitimate voters affect us all.

Asian American groups should also focus some of their program work on targeting the South Asian American community and engage in aggressive outreach to it. Some examples of focused program work include AALDEF's targeting the South Asian community for voter education, registration, and exit poll surveys, and CAAAV's Lease Drivers Coalition project focusing on South Asian taxi drivers. Asian American groups can take positive steps to make their services available to South Asian Americans, whether it be by providing information about their services to South Asian groups and media, distributing information at South Asian events, translating information brochures into South Asian languages, and doing presentations for community groups or student clubs.

Underlying these efforts, Asian American groups should have the broader mission of being representative of the diversity of Asian America. An important way for this to occur is to have South Asian Americans represented on their staff. Having a South Asian American staff member conveys the message that the Asian American organization also serves South Asian Americans. A truly pan-Asian American organization will be motivated by its unwavering commitment to inclusion, democratic diversity, and the empowerment of the underrepresented and less privileged among us.

Second, South Asian American communities need to further organize, mobilize, and unite around issues that affect our community. Traditionally, South Asian community organizations have primarily engaged in cultural, social, and religious activities. The occasional political activities have been limited to raising funds and awareness for issues on the subcontinent, or for organizing a fund-raiser for politicians whom they hope will support our causes on the Subcontinent. There has been little, if any, focus on social and political issues that affect our community's life in the United States. This agenda may be understood in the context that these organizations served South Asian communities that were predominantly economically secure and affluent, or with a high degree of education. Many South Asians in these communities may have felt that they were immune to many of the problems faced by the general population, and in particular, the problems of working-class people and other minorities. Thus, their community organizations did not focus on social and political issues, such as discrimination or domestic violence, which may have related to their experience in the United States.

The demographic changes in the South Asian American community, especially in urban areas such as New York City, are likely to continue. As it becomes increasingly economically diverse, with the majority of our population falling in the working-class and middle-income range,[10] it is becoming more vulnerable to issues of economic hardship and public policies that disproportionately affect working people, such as budget cuts, transit fare hikes, increasing health care costs, and fewer job opportunities. Whereas South Asian immigrants in the late 1960s through the 1970s came with credentials for academic and professional opportunities, those arriving from the early 1980s onward tend to have lower levels of education and find even fewer opportunities due to the declining economy. At present, there is great occupational diversity among South Asians, ranging from doctors and engineers to newsstand dealers, gas station attendants, teachers, social workers, nurses, cabdrivers, and domestic workers. Another change is in the increased proportion of second-generation South Asian American youth, and this results in a great need for youth support services and centers. For example, while South Asian American youth are often regarded as a "model minority" group, many of them need help with concerns about depression, sexuality, addiction, and dealing with parents, among many other issues.

Finally, the latest wave of South Asian immigration has reaffirmed that we have needs and issues common to other immigrant communities. Following the pioneering work of SAKHI for South Asian Women and the

Lease Drivers Coalition, various groups have emerged to address issues like substance abuse, family violence, mental health, AIDS, homophobia, and youth services. These groups provide much-needed services that are culturally sensitive. For example, in the New York City area, Nav Nirmaan Foundation serves South Asian families affected by substance abuse, family violence, and mental health issues. Another, South Asian Youth Action (SAYA!), promotes self-esteem, provides opportunities for growth and development, and builds cultural, social, and political awareness among South Asian youth. SAYA! has already begun offering program services and was started with the help of the Asian American Federation of New York. Culturally sensitive groups such as Nav Nirmaan and SAYA! provide a comfortable environment where South Asian Americans can freely discuss issues like addiction, substance abuse, and domestic violence, subjects that are often taboo in their families and communities.

In the political arena, after the elections of Sachi Dastidar and Morshed Alam to the school boards of neighboring districts in eastern Queens, local South Asian Americans formed the Indian/South Asian Community Organization of Eastern Queens (ISAC). ISAC's purpose is to serve South Asian Americans who are concerned about issues relating to education of their children, and their rights as parents, voters, and residents of eastern Queens. ISAC has also organized forums designed to educate the South Asian American community about these issues. The continuing problem for all such groups is the scarcity of resources and services, both in areas where work has begun and in the many areas where community-based services are lacking, such as health care, immigrant rights, language and educational skills, and employment and labor issues. Such groups do more than provide critical services; they keep South Asians informed about their rights and are a link to organizations in other communities.

As the demographics of the South Asian community in New York City and in the United States continue to change, our community organizations must address the concerns that affect us. For example, the new anti-immigrant legislation will restrict the rights of immigrants. Not only will undocumented immigrants suffer, but the new law will prevent legal immigrants and perhaps even some naturalized citizens from receiving certain social services. Similarly, most South Asian Americans in New York City have felt the impact of policy changes regarding budget cuts, fewer social services, transit fare hikes, increasing health care costs, and deteriorating schools. The community organizations must be active and vocal about these developments.

Furthermore, South Asian community groups, most of which follow specific regional, religious, national, language, and cultural bonds, need to cooperate for more effective advocacy. Exclusionary episodes and policies do not represent the sentiment of the majority of people in our community, but reflect the power struggles of so-called leaders. I believe most South Asian Americans would agree that people from all segments of our community need to become more involved in local politics, because they are the ones affected by crises and adverse public policies and increasingly do not enjoy the comforts of privilege. They must realize the importance of addressing many of the bread-and-butter issues faced by working people every day and neglected by our community leaders.

In fact, leadership on the various public policy and social service issues affecting our community needs to be addressed. In the traditional community organizations, the leadership tends to represent the South Asian elite who may not be attentive to such issues; consequently, we need to find other ways to cultivate responsible, visionary, and selfless leadership to address the spectrum of community needs. The composition of these new organizations is more likely to be economically diverse because they will address issues affecting working-class, middle-income, and poor people in our community. The issues affecting the South Asian American community are not unique to us, offering a basis for building coalitions with other Asian Americans—for example, racism; the "model minority" myth; anti-immigrant sentiment and immigration issues; community taboos on issues such as domestic violence, substance abuse, sexuality, and AIDS; the need for community organizing and political empowerment, in addition to issues that affect all working people, to name a few. South Asian Americans are making efforts in this regard, but we have a long way to go. As other contributors to this volume have noted, many Asians and non-Asians do not view us as being Asian American (partly because we seem to be racially distinct from other Asians) and, because we are not a monolithic community, we could use some coalition building within our own culturally diverse community.

Although the work of building coalitions is difficult and although some pan–Asian American groups may not appear to be inclusive, we as South Asian Americans have to take responsibility for ensuring that our concerns and our experiences are represented in all Asian American organizations and forums as well as any arena where our voices are not heard. This responsibility is especially important in the context of today's anti-immigrant sentiment, cutbacks in public services, attacks on civil rights, and fewer opportunities for working people and the poor.

Ultimately, South Asian Americans must respond to the issues that affect us personally. When we, individually and as a group, exercise our responsibility to address the issues we face, especially those faced by the disadvantaged and the more vulnerable among us, we take the first step toward finding those allies in the larger Asian American community and in all other communities with whom we can build successful coalitions. South Asian Americans can help redefine Asian America to represent what it already is—a community that is inherently multiracial, multiethnic, multilingual, multicultural, and multiclass. In this spirit, not only can South Asian Americans transform Asian American politics, but we can also have a positive impact on politics and life in a multicultural America.

ACKNOWLEDGMENTS

I would like to thank the following for their assistance on this essay: Anannya Bhattacharjee and Saleem Osman, both formerly of the Committee Against Anti-Asian Violence (CAAAV); Margaret Fung, Stan Mark, and Elizabeth OuYang from the Asian American Legal Defense and Education Fund (AALDEF); and Dr. Madhulika Khandelwal from the Asian/American Center of Queens College at City University of New York. Special thanks are due to Anu Gupta, Rajini Srikanth, and Lavina Shankar for their contributions to this essay.

NOTES

1. For example, according to the 1990 Census, of the more than 500,000 Asian Americans in New York City, Asian Indians totaled approximately 100,000, second to the Chinese population of about 240,000. In the borough of Queens, where 240,000 Asian Americans resided, Asian Indians totaled nearly 60,000, second only to the Chinese population of 90,000. As a result of increasing immigration and other demographic changes since 1990, the population figures for South Asians in particular and Asian Americans as a whole in New York City today are considerably higher, perhaps two or three times the 1990 figures. I saw these demographic changes firsthand in my own neighborhoods of Floral Park and Glen Oaks in Queens. In the late 1970s and early '80s, my family was one of a few South Asians living in this area of garden apartments and small one-family houses. But by the early 1990s, there had been a rapid rise in the number of South Asian families in these and other neighborhoods, many of them seeking to buy their first home or leave the more congested parts of the city. The population change is reflected in the local elementary school where around 35 to 40 percent of the students are now South Asian. As in many other places to where South Asians have moved, a number of Indo-Pak stores, restaurants, and services have sprung up. Thus, with the now familiar sight of South Asian faces, our area has in many ways become a South Asian neighborhood.

2. At this time, information about how specific Asian ethnic communities voted was not available. For more information, call or write the Asian American Legal Defense and Education Fund, 99 Hudson Street, 12th Floor, New York, NY 10013; phone: 212-966-5932.

3. Anannya Bhattacharjee, interviewed by the author, Nov. 1995.

4. Ibid.

5. Margaret Fung, interviewed by the author, Nov. 1995.

6. Saleem Osman, interviewed by the author, Dec. 1995.

7. Ibid.

8. Ibid.

9. Ibid.

10. For example, according to the 1993 Census Bureau report on the foreign-born population in the United States, the average per capita income for foreign-born Indians stood at $25,275 in 1989, a figure that compared well with the national average of $19,423 for all foreign-born citizens. But Indians who came between 1987 and 1990 have an average per capita income of $7,517. Similarly, while the poverty rate among foreign-born Indians in the United States stood at 5.1 percent, among Indian immigrants who came between 1987 and 1990, the poverty rate was 19 percent.

SANDIP ROY

8   The Call of Rice

(South) Asian American Queer Communities

FOR THE past decade or so, California has been home to *Trikone,*
a magazine for South Asian lesbians, bisexuals, and gay men all over the
world. I used to receive it when I was a student in India. In time I moved
to San Francisco, got involved with *Trikone,* and eventually became its
editor. San Francisco has a very strong Asian American gay community
with its own groups and newsletters and events, a community in which
we, as queer South Asians, are technically members. Yet even as we attended each other's banquets and fund-raisers and cosponsored dances,
nobody ever questioned why *Trikone* needed a separate identity, why it
could not be merged with the other Asian groups or newsletters. In the
spring of 1996, the Living Well Project, an Asian HIV/AIDS organization,
awarded me the Visibility Campaign Award for "outstanding contributions towards the Asian and Pacific Islander community awareness of
AIDS/HIV and sexual diversity." Although deeply honored, I was not
without mixed feelings. I wondered if *Trikone* served the "Asian and Pacific Islander community" in any way, outstanding or otherwise, for in
some ways I too was buying into the general equation of Asians with East
Asians in the perception of the American public. Was the award a gesture
of inclusion on the part of the larger Asian American community? Or was
it merely a token? Did they really think of *Trikone* as Asian? Did I really
think of *Trikone* as Asian? Or were we just trapped in the same box by
an accident of geography? This essay attempts to explore some of these
questions and dilemmas through my personal experience in working with
Trikone.
    In India I was Bengali. Our neighbors were Tamil and Punjabi and
Telegu. When the football teams, East Bengal and Mohan Bagan, clashed
on the field, even our Bengali identity split down the middle as we teamed
up as either "Bangals" (those who hailed from the erstwhile East Bengal
and supported the club of the same name) or "Ghotis" (from West Bengal)
who supported Mohan Bagan. Somewhere along the line we were vaguely
aware that we were Indian too—we were Indian when the prime minister
was being given a red-carpet welcome in some foreign country, we were
Indian when the cricket team won a match, and we were Indian when the

prime minister of some neighboring country accused India of meddling in its affairs. (But if the cricket team lost, we were quick to attribute it to too many Telegus or Maharashtrians or Punjabis on the team.)

But as soon as I left India, with every airplane that I boarded on my journey to the United States, it seemed my identity grew larger and larger, encompassing states and provinces and countries and, ultimately, continents, until one day, as I was filling out yet another government form, I realized that I had suddenly become an Asian, or at least that was the little box assigned to me on the form. I put my little cross in the box and, without thinking much about it, went on my way. Actually I was far too busy exploring my gay identity to worry about my place on a form. Once the initial euphoria (and shock) of exposure to American gay life—the bars, the groups, Castro Street in San Francisco—had worn off, I was forced to return to the question of my ethnic origin. That happened as a result of answering a personal ad in a gay paper. The person concerned was a Caucasian man who wanted to meet a GAM (gay Asian man) who liked the movies, reading, art, culture, and so forth. I replied to the voice mail number in the ad, and the next day the man called me back.

After a few minutes of pleasant chitchat, the man asked me where I was from. Playing coy, I asked him to guess.

"Thailand?" he ventured.

"Close, but not quite."

"Indonesia?"

"Wrong direction."

He seemed genuinely puzzled. For him the largest continent ended at the borders of Thailand. I finally told him I was from India.

He said, "Oh, I'm sorry. I, uh, meant, um . . . ," and then hung up.

The conversation left me feeling utterly rootless. In India, my Indian identity was a given, never a subject of dispute or doubt. In America, I suddenly felt that there was nowhere to place myself. According to the form, if I did not choose Asian, I would have to mark myself "Other." Yet as this man pointed out by hanging up, in the eyes of many, I was not really "Asian." I did not have the physical characteristics that this man thought of as Asian. I was crushed, not because I had not measured up to his image as an Asian, but because I did not know how else to label myself. In the abbreviated world of gay personals, I could see GW(hite)M, GB(lack)M, GL(atino)M and GA(sian)M. Where was I to hang my hat? Which body-type stereotype could I claim as my own? But it seemed that the definitions and parameters of what was Asian, what was Latino, had already been laid down. And there was no room anywhere for me. The labels were all taken.

Perhaps that is why, while there are gay Asian groups like GAPA (Gay

Asian Pacific Alliance) and APS (Asian Pacific Sisters), there are also gay and lesbian South Asian groups like Trikone and Shamakami, as if the Asian label was not one we could easily wear. That label had already been defined in terms of the countries of the Pacific Rim. In 1986, Arvind Kumar, an Indian engineer based in the San Francisco Bay area, founded a magazine and a support and social group for South Asian lesbians and gay men. He named it *Trikone,* from the Sanskrit word for triangle, a symbol that has been used in the West by various lesbian and gay groups.

He said, "It was tiring to try so hard to fit into other people's spaces. I wanted a space of my own. No one was looking at the South Asian community. It was as if South Asia didn't exist. In America's mental landscape, it still doesn't." He recollected that ten years ago "the only such [Asian] groups I was aware of were Pacific Friends and ALGA (Asian Lesbian Gay Association). Neither had any South Asian members, nor did they do any outreach to the South Asian community. Those groups were extremely East Asian– and Southeast Asian–identified. On the morning of Pride Parade in 1986, I saw some ALGA members setting up their booth. I went up to them and introduced myself and Trikone. At the least I expected some acknowledgment and encouragement from another Asian group. Perhaps they were busy setting up the booth, but I got a sense of 'Whatever—we have work to do.' Subsequently, we put them on our mailing list and left messages but we never got any response or feedback from them." [1] Kumar, however, asserted that GAPA, which was formed after the demise of ALGA, was much more proactive in doing outreach to Trikone and involving Trikone in Asian American affairs and thus helping to bridge the gap between the two communities.

Now Trikone marches alongside GAPA at the San Francisco Gay Pride Parade. Trikone members have marched with GAPA and APS in the Chinese New Year's Parade in San Francisco—perhaps the only other South Asians to take part in that parade. It all raises intriguing questions—when are we Asian American and when are we South Asian American? When it suits us? When it suits them? When we need the numbers?

THE NUMBERS GAME

In the United States we all have to stand up and be counted. That is one of the main reasons we have this whole concept of a South Asian American identity anyway. As a Hindu Bengali gay man growing up in Calcutta, my experience does not necessarily echo that of a Bangladeshi Muslim growing up in Sylhet. Or for that matter a Sikh youth growing up gay in an agrarian family in a small town in the heart of Punjab. We did not feel the need to identify as South Asian because there were narrower areas of greater commonality that we could identify with. And we had the numbers to make those narrow sectors of identification viable. But in America, if we each had our own little group, for example, a Punjabi gay group and a Bangali gay group and a Bangladeshi gay group, we would never get anywhere. So while in South Asia itself it may be all right to have an Indian group and a Bangladeshi group, in North America it makes more sense to come together to form one South Asian group if we are to make our voices heard and are to make our presence felt.

Why are the numbers so important? Because in America if you do not have the numbers, your views, however well-argued, remain the views of one person. Allocation of funds for specific interest groups depends on how many people in the community the money would serve. The mayor of San Francisco does not march in the Gay Pride Parade because in his heart he truly wants to identify with the lesbigay community. He is there because the community has the numbers and he needs to remain on good terms with it. When a minority gains critical mass in numbers, the majority is forced to listen to its voice. Daniel Bao, national programs director of the Living Well Project (LWP), formerly known as the GAPA Community HIV Project (GCHP), agreed: "At what level do you form a group? Some may say even South Asian is too broad and you need a gay male Pakistani group. So how far do you subdivide the pie? The fact is, we need smaller groups for the personal support and larger groups for the political muscle, because in the U.S. political scene the numbers that you represent are important." [2]

For homosexuals the problem is especially acute. They are in the unenviable position of being a minority within a minority, often faced with hostility and rejection within their parent South Asian communities on one hand and blithe indifference from the mainstream gay community on the other. South Asian American gay men, lesbians, and bisexuals often fear that they will lose the shelter of their parent communities if they come out. At the same time they are often ignored by the mainstream American gay community. But they often feel that regardless of what kind of treatment they get from the mainstream American community, they cannot turn to their parent South Asian American community for support and help either. And the lack of numbers becomes an even more pressing reason to find common platforms. That is why, while there is a Bangladeshi Cultural Association, there are no Bangladeshi gay and lesbian associations—not because there are no Bangladeshi gays and lesbians but because it makes much more sense for all gays and lesbians of South Asian heritage to come together under a common banner. Needless to say, this creates conflict, for India is almost always the big brother (or sister) in these groups, and all people of non-Indian heritage sometimes face an uphill struggle in trying to make their voices heard. But despite that fact, South Asian American gay men and lesbians have overlooked their differences in order to come together on a common platform of ethnicity and sexuality.

Of course, the numbers game works both ways. While joining forces with the Asian American lesbigay community enables us to cast a larger shadow, the Asian American community also benefits from our numbers. Yet the benefits we derive from each other are not the same. Before we analyze that, we need to see how our classification as Asian American manifests itself in the first place. The label applies in two ways—the first, when it is imposed upon us from outside, and, second, when we choose it for ourselves.

Imposed upon Us

This labeling is imposed upon us by the little boxes that demand to know our ethnicity on forms—where the only option is Asian, unless we choose to be "other." It is imposed upon us when the board of some organization, in an effort to be multicultural, appoints a Chinese American person to its board and feels it has now fairly represented an entire continent. It is imposed upon us when funds for a project like HIV education are allocated to the dominant (East) Asian HIV project in the hope that it will provide HIV education throughout the entire Asian community.

In 1990 Canadian filmmaker Richard Fung (of Chinese Trinidadian origin) made a "safer sex short" called *Steam Clean*, aimed at the Asian community for the New York Gay Men's Health Crisis (GMHC), a large grassroots organization involved in HIV/AIDS-related issues. This was part of a series of shorts made by GMHC like *Car Service, Current Flow*, and *Something Fierce*, all of which are particularly careful to include people of color, especially African Americans. But when it came to the Asian community, Fung admits "they (the video production coordinators for GMHC) approached me to produce the short for Asians, presumably because they knew and liked my work, but also because they could not locate an openly gay Asian videomaker in the United States who would undertake such a project." He also goes on to add that "although Asia encompasses a wide variety of peoples, from Turks to Japanese, the term 'Asian' is generally used in the United States (and to a lesser extent in Canada) to refer to East and Southeast Asians. In producing *Steam Clean*, I worked under the assumption that this was my primary target group."

Fung actually used a South Asian character in his film, but even in the sex scene between him and an East Asian man, the South Asian gay man's general invisibility in the Asian scene (which in effect eliminates him from the real target audience for the film) results in an interesting plot twist.

Generally, according to Fung, in pornographic films featuring anal sex between East Asian and Caucasian men, the Asian man is usually seen in the passive role. So Fung felt he could not perpetuate this stereotype by depicting the Chinese partner as the "passive" partner if he "wanted East Asian and Southeast Asian men—the target group—to relate to the tape. But what about the other man? Was it less problematic to show a South Asian getting fucked because, as a group, they are rarely represented sexually in North America?" Fung's compromise was to have the Chinese man do the penetration while the Indian man was sitting on top of him, in effect controlling the penetration in some fashion.[3]

Fung's "compromise" in some ways epitomizes the uneasy fit of the South Asian gay person in the East Asian gay society. Someone as politically aware as Fung cannot ignore the South Asian as part of the Asian community. But once he has accorded him a place within the community, he is stuck with the problem of what to do with him and where to place him. His candid explanation that he would give the South Asian man the passive role because as a "group they are rarely represented in North America" is telling. What Fung gambled on was that since the South Asian gay man was largely invisible at that time in America and not part of the short film's target East Asian American audience, his depiction in the film would not really perpetuate any damaging stereotypes. Not being considered a "real" Asian, the South Asian man was also presumably free from the Asian stereotypes. But on the other hand the invisibility of the South Asian American gay man also resulted in his having effectively no control over his depiction. In the end, despite sitting on top of his partner, he ended up not so much as an equal sexual partner in the give and take of pleasure but as a device employed by the filmmaker in breaking a stereotype about East Asians. So in effect even when the gap between South Asian American gay men is closing because of the progressive effects of many activists new complications have arisen. Because the issue then becomes where do we situate the South Asian American gay person in the Asian American gay community? What is his position there?

Choosing It for Ourselves

In the mainstream South Asian American community we don't encounter too many instances of South Asians who choose to identify themselves as Asian. That is because there are enough Indians and Pakistanis and Sri Lankans to form their own communities and cultural associations. They do not feel enough in common with Chinese and Vietnamese to stake their claim to being Asian too. But in lesbigay communities, which do not have the benefit of support from their parent South Asian American communities, the Asian American community is often the only community one can identify with. This is especially true outside the bigger cities like New York and San Francisco, where the visible members of the South Asian queer community can often be counted on one hand.

The reason for choosing to identify with the Asian community is not because of shared culture or heritage. Now there are South Asian gay and lesbian groups all over the country, from SALGA (South Asian Lesbian and Gay Association) in New York to Trikone, Los Angeles; and from Khush in Toronto to Trikone, Atlanta. But for the longest time most of the major cities had little or no organized South Asian American lesbigay activity. Queer groups were either centered on politics like ACT-UP or ethnicity like the African American or Latino groups. So if a South Asian wanted to join a group based on ethnicity rather than a specific political stance, he or she invariably ended up in Asian American groups. This was especially true when the person was not particularly activist in nature and had no desire to storm the Food and Drug Administration and confront government officials.

Since the Stonewall riots in the sixties, the focus of queer politics has moved way from the initial "coming out" stage to more national issues like gays in the military, right-wing religious fundamentalism, and AIDS policies. But for an Indian in the throes of coming out, the most important issues are closer to home—how do I tell my mother, and how do I stop my aunties from matchmaking? Because people from Asian American cultures are far more closely bound to the immediate and extended family than European American ones, issues of duty, family shame, and pressures to marry are far more likely to be discussed in ways that are more meaningful to gay South Asian Americans. Many members of the queer Asian groups are first-generation immigrants still struggling with a queer identity while their roots are in a culture bound by tradition and not overly homophilic. So unless they had a specific interest and joined the Gay Horticultural Association or the Lesbian Chorus, they would end up in the Asian American groups, which were usually broad social support groups with potlucks, outings, and rap sessions. When the Gay Asian Pacific Alliance and Asian Pacific Sisters decided to march in the Chinese New Year's Day Parade in San Francisco, their trepidation and concerns were similar to those experienced by the gay and lesbian South Asians when they decided to march in the India Day Parade. Both were in a sense staking a place within their communities and refusing to choose between their community and their sexuality.

But did they get here because the call of rice was irresistible? On the face of it, South Asians and East Asians seem to have little in common except that they both come from cultures that thrive on steamed rice. Even that connection starts breaking down as we go further west on the Indian subcontinent and wheat becomes the dietary staple. So the question remains—would South Asian lesbians and gay men have just as easily gone to a similar Latino group or black group, but felt that the Asian group was the only one they would be "allowed into"? After all, back in South Asia, a Korean or a Filipino was just as foreign as a Mexican or a Nigerian. Our only forays into East Asian culture were probably through Chinese food. We had never grown up with a sense of a pan-Asian identity. We were still struggling with a fragile South Asian identity. I think many of the South Asian gays and lesbians who went to Asian groups did so, not because of a shared sense of heritage and history, but more because it was a way to meet other gays and lesbians outside bar settings.

UNDER THE UMBRELLA

The success of South Asian American identification with Asian American groups depends on what we want to get out of that identification. If we are looking to nab a rice queen who is attracted to Asians we will probably be disappointed. The rice queen is probably not looking for us. We would need to find a curry queen!

If we are looking for a place where we can reconcile our Indianness or our Nepaleseness with our queer identity, an Asian American group may not be it. As queers, we always have a fractured sense of national identity. We have been bombarded with the message that there are no homosexuals in South Asia, that it is a Western perversion. Many South Asian homosexuals spend a lot of their energy in denying their South Asianness and embracing the Western (white) homosexual culture. I remember running into South Asian–looking men at bars and having them quickly look away from me. For them my recognition of their South Asianness was proof of the failure of their careful camouflage. It reminded them of Mummy making *chapatis* and Grandmother's *puja* room and the shame they feel as "the dirty, irresponsible, selfish" sons. It takes a lot of careful nurturing to strip away those layers of self-hate to realize we are not lesser people simply because we are homosexual people. And that is best achieved with other South Asians who have gone through that experience—the experience of a Chinese person may well be similarly shot through with shame and censure but it does not feel the same. We don't have enough experience with Chinese or Korean culture to identify with them deep down. We may bridge the gap between our cultures in some ways, but they are still distinct and we should not expect to be able to merge them into one.

Going to a gay Asian group to reaffirm one's national identity is a mistake. People in that group are as liable to mispronounce your name as any Caucasian. They will probably be as naive about your country as you are about theirs. Ashok Jethanandani of Trikone choreographed a Bharatanatyam piece for the GAPA Gay Men's Dance Company's 1994 concert. He recalled that "their interest in Bharatanatyam seemed to stem more from being dancers rather than from being Asian. My guess is that another dance company of white men or African American or Latino dancers may have had a similar interest in this dance."[4] Just because they were of Asian heritage, the dancers had no particular interest in, or understanding of, Indian classical dance. And it would be naive of us to expect it to be any other way—after all, we do not see throngs of Indian Americans at a Japanese Kabuki performance.

Just being under one umbrella does not automatically homogenize us. When Kenji Oshima, national programs coordinator of the Living Well Project, facilitated the Trikone board retreat in 1995, he was surprised at the vehemence with which board members argued with each other.[5] He was even more surprised when the board members informed him that in South Asia it is not culturally inappropriate to interrupt one another and is not really considered rude. In his experience East Asian groups tended to follow the wait-quietly-until-the-speaker-finishes model. Irrespective of which model is more conducive to meaningful dialog, it just demonstrated that whether all Asian Americans are grouped together or not, we all come from distinct cultural patterns and mores, none of which can be taken for granted, just because we are all Asian.

After all, even a South Asian identity is hardly monolithic and homogeneous. Shani Mootoo, Trinidadian-born writer of Indian ancestry, mentioned how at the South Asian Lesbian and Gay Conference in New York in June 1994 everyone was talking about India and how she found herself desperately trying to imagine India so as not to be excluded from the discussion. She admitted that "the truth is a gay Trinidadian of Chinese origin like Richard Fung, probably has more in common with me than most South Asian dykes outside of Trinidad."[6] So just as the gap exists between South Asian Americans and East Asian Americans, it also exists among South Asians themselves. Yet her stories like "Out of Main Street" and "Sushila's Bhakti" have unmistakably South Asian tones and colors, in their descriptions of *mehendi* and *burfis*. So the boundaries we draw around our South Asianness are at best only approximate. In the end we are pulled in many different directions by our histories, our cultures, and the places where we grew up in. No matter how hard we try to distill these various experiences into one cultural label we will always be confounded by someone who doesn't fit in.

MAKING ROOM

While we have discussed at length how far South Asian Americans "fit" under the Asian American umbrella and what they can really expect from it, it is interesting to see how Asian American groups have made room for South Asian Americans. For them it becomes a matter of wanting to extend the definition of Asian American (or at least rectify the popular perception of Asian). Many Asian American groups are interested in making South Asian Americans feel welcome, to shake their image as being concerned only with countries of the Pacific Rim. Voltaire Gungab, the dance director of the GAPA Gay Men's Dance Company, included a Bharatanatyam-based piece at their concert in November 1994 because he very much wanted to show that Asia included countries like India.[7] When he found out that Ashok Jethananadani of Trikone was a trained Bharatanatyam dancer, he approached him to choreograph a piece especially for the concert, using the dancers of the GAPA Men's Dance Company. Gungab also said that part of his motive in including the Bharatanatyam piece was to do outreach in the South Asian American community and get them to come to the concert as well. But it must be stressed that this did not happen in isolation—the dance collaboration was in many ways the result of a more general collaboration between Trikone and GAPA in other spheres over several years. The gap cannot be closed without active efforts on both sides.

Over the years the different queer Asian groups like GAPA, Trikone, Shamakami, and Asian Pacific Sisters have jointly organized benefit dances during Gay Pride Week. In 1993 Devesh Khatu, then one of Trikone's cochairs, became a member-at-large on the board of GAPA, which helped Trikone develop a good working relationship with GAPA. In 1994 Daniel Bao, the national programs director of the Living Well Project, informed Trikone that it could apply for a grant from the funds LWP receives from the Centers for Disease Control to disseminate to projects in the community. What worked here was that LWP recognized the need to connect with community-based organizations like Trikone instead of trying to be Indian and Chinese and Filipino all at once. It also recognized that Trikone was culturally in a better position to do outreach in the South Asian community. At the same time Trikone recognized the superior organizational ability of LWP and decided to tap into it instead of adopting an "if we can't do it ourselves we won't do it at all" mentality. LWP functioned in this case as the umbrella organization. It did not seek to supplant Trikone and thus ensured a good working relationship. And above all, it did not patronize, which is a real danger, because most Asian American groups are larger in number than South Asian American groups.

This has not always been the case. In many ways the Asian lesbigay community has had to learn to broaden its own horizons. Arvind Kumar recalls, "During a People of Color conference in LA in 1987, Ashok [Jethanandani] and I were the only South Asians who sat in on an Asian caucus of some forty people. When I tried to speak, I was cut off very rudely by someone who said they didn't have time and that they needed to move on to "Asian" topics; the moderator did not intervene. At that time, I didn't even know what hit me, and I was quiet for the rest of the caucus. But it became clear to me that we had to organize as South Asians in order to get the respect and space we deserve."[8]

Ultimately we will never have enough seats on every board to represent every conceivable community—East Asians, South Asians, Arabs, Africans, and what have you. Someone will have to speak for someone else. Like it or not, South Asians, East Asians, and Arabs are all lumped together. And while it may not be easy to find one person to speak for all these groups, it may often be unavoidable. But Arab groups and South Asian groups should be included so that board members do not always have to select an East Asian candidate.

WOMEN DO IT BETTER?

One of the most interesting things about Asian and South Asian groups is that there are often more South Asian lesbians involved with Asian lesbian groups than South Asian men with Asian men's groups. A casual look at queer Asian anthologies like *Witness Aloud* reveals input from South Asian women like Rini Das, Mrittika Datta, and Anu, but none from male authors. (Though of course it is entirely possible that South Asian women write more than their male counterparts do.) A possible and obvious reason for South Asian involvement in lesbian groups is that there are hardly any organized, consistently active South Asian queer women's groups. While most of the South Asian groups are co-gender in principle, in practice many of them are dominated by men, both in terms of organization and membership. Dipti Ghosh, who served as cochair of Trikone and has been actively involved with the Asian Pacific Lesbian Bisexual Network, agreed that that could be a valid reason, saying, "If South Asian women had the space and money to have their own organizations they might be less involved in the larger Asian groups. But to us being with women is just as important as being with South Asians. And so many South Asian lesbians might choose to be with other Asian women rather than in co-gender South Asian groups."[9] Coalitions occur along many lines—based on gender, sexual preference, ethnic origin, and so on. Sometimes these lines overlap. Sometimes they stay separate. But they occur along so many different continuums that there is no way to eliminate all the gaps.

As far as Ghosh is concerned, she affirms, "I have always felt very welcome (in Asian groups) though that may not always translate into actual things geared towards South Asians. We are always having to speak up. It's like having bisexual in the title of a group and then not really having any programs for bisexuals."

At the same time Ghosh acknowledges that there are many South Asian women who do not go to Asian groups because they feel they do not belong. Nusrat Retina, cofounder of the South Asian lesbian and bisexual women's group Shamakami, recounted one such experience in her essay "The Toughest Journey" in *A Lotus of Another Color*. She describes the excitement she felt when she went to attend the first-ever national conference for Asian lesbians in Santa Cruz in 1989. Then she recounts how left out she felt when at a slide show of images of Asian lesbians at the conference she saw no South Asian images. "Here, in the midst of a group of women who have often found themselves excluded from the mainstream lesbian movement, in an environment in which I had expected to feel safe and validated, I was feeling invisible. Some of my South Asian sisters, feeling the same sense of exclusion, walked out of the auditorium at various points. I sat and waited. And hoped. I hoped that the images I longed to see were still to come. I hoped that the betrayal I was feeling would prove to be unfounded." [10]

On the other hand, Minal Hajratwala, whose writing has appeared both in South Asian anthologies like *Our Feet Walk the Sky* and *Living in America*, as well as Asian anthologies like *The Very Inside*, attests that "I've had white people say, 'Oh, are Indians considered Asians?' to which my response is, 'Have you ever looked at a world map?'" but I have not had other Asians or Asian Americans question my inclusion; in fact I've found the opposite, a high level of interest and encouragement. I've always felt incredibly welcome as a South Asian in mainstream Asian American organizations and publications, whether straight or gay." [11]

NOT "REALLY" ASIAN

Sometimes the confusion between our Asian and our South Asian identities strands us between a rock and a hard place. This is most common when the outside world, on one hand, puts us in the Asian box but, on the other, claims we are not "really" Asian. When the National Asian American Telecommunications Association (NAATA) selected the South Asian feature film *Bhaji on the Beach* to be its opening-night film for the 1994

Asian American Film Festival, it provoked surprise in both communities. It was sometimes difficult to interest local Indian merchants in promoting the film and donating food and beverages because they felt that the Asian festival was not really something that Indians would be interested in. At the same time some members of the East Asian community were equally astonished that the festival director had veered away from the traditional Chinese/Japanese opening-night feature for something that was only "nominally" Asian.

Corey Tong, associate director of the festival that year, said that that year had been in many ways a turning point for NAATA. He said, "Our communities are changing very rapidly, and people, Asian or not, need to both reevaluate and expand their notion of who is included and why." [12] He cites the fact that in addition to opening with *Bhaji,* the film festival concluded with Arthur Dong's *Coming Out Under Fire,* a film about gay men and lesbians who served in World War II. Though made by an Asian American, it was not about Asian Americans at all and, thus in its own way, also broke out of the mold. As far as the board of NAATA was concerned, Tong said, "They knew we were pushing the status quo and we all knew that showing *Bhaji* meant we would have to do more outreach and research than usual. So we got *India Currents* [a San Francisco Bay Area–based monthly magazine] to copresent the screening and help us with outreach. It was an opportunity for us to work with communities we had wanted to." He maintained that after the screening the general response was overwhelmingly positive—from the film community as well as the South Asian and East Asian communities. "Interestingly," he said, "we could not enlist the help of the Indian consulate, but the British consulate helped to bring Gurinder [Chadha, the director who lives in London] to San Francisco."

There are several Asian and Friends groups that are primarily targeted at providing a social outlet where non-Asians (usually Caucasians) and eligible Asian men can meet. I attended one such gathering in San Francisco, and though everyone was polite and friendly, I immediately sensed that this was one place where I was not "really Asian." This was a social group with a fixed and narrow focus on the idealized Asian man as seen through Caucasian eyes. As a South Asian man I was a total outsider in that group. My kinship with other Asians came from a shared political identity, a shared sense of being outsiders in the mainstream gay culture, and a shared sense of being immigrants and newcomers. My kinship was not based on what I looked like.

This feeling of not *looking* Asian enough can translate in the political sphere into not *being* Asian enough. Nusrat Retina, cofounder of the South Asian lesbian and bisexual women's group Shamakami, recalled,

"In 1989, I was one of few South Asian women organizing and attending the first ever National Asian Lesbian Retreat in Santa Cruz, California. Despite my deep friendships with my East Asian women friends, we were very visibly omitted from the conference. I led a protest by South Asian dykes in that event." [13]

LOST IN THE SHADOWS

One of the fears of identifying with the larger Asian community in general has been that the South Asian community will lose its South Asianness, that we will never gain the confidence to stand on our own feet. That is a valid concern, though not necessarily a substantiated one. There are South Asian lesbigay groups all over the country, most of which have sprung up over the last few years. They are fully aware of the function they serve, and they also know that they are there because they fulfill needs that a larger Asian organization cannot.

The South Asian groups are based on culture and heritage. They may technically be a subset of the Asian groups, but they are a response to the simple reality that there is no cultural prism broad enough to encompass Iranian gays, Japanese lesbians, and Sri Lankan bisexuals and represent them all equally. That is not a deficiency of the Asian groups—that is merely an impractical expectation. And sooner or later any South Asian involved with an Asian group will realize that.

It is important for culture-specific groups like Trikone or Hasha (the Iranian group) to develop in order to address issues that emerge from their respective cultural traditions. If they are to ever stake a claim to a place in their own communities they must be organized around their cultures rather than being part of some nebulous Asian culture. At the 1994 India Day Parade in New York, the Federation of Indian Associations denied a permit to SALGA ostensibly because SALGA is a South Asian group, not an Indian one. [14] One can imagine their reaction if instead of SALGA, the Indian members of Asians and Friends had tried to march in the parade.

The development of South Asian groups is not about diminishing the importance of Asian groups. One can be part of both, and some of Trikone's board members have served on the boards of Asian groups as well. Prescott Chow, the national program HIV technical assistance and training coordinator for LWP, and publications cochair for GAPA, says, "It is necessary to form our own groups, and that is not a threat to pan-Asian groups. In fact, recently a thirty-five-and-older group formed out of GAPA, which we looked at as something positive rather than a threat. We believe at GAPA, we can't serve *all* the needs of *everyone*." [15] The importance of developing groups like Trikone is that it forces the outside world to acknowledge the size and diversity encompassed by "Asia." If someone is organizing an Asian film festival, or an Asian Queer Night, that person is more likely to involve non–East Asian groups as well. Through groups like Trikone, an Asian American group looking to work with South Asian groups will know where to begin outreach. While it may seem that such groups serve to highlight the differences between South Asian American groups and Asian American groups, they also serve as a bridge between the two in that they give South Asian gay men, lesbians, and bisexuals visibility and coherence.

Balancing Act

At first sight it may not be a bad thing for the South Asian gay movement to cut its Asian moorings and go free. The movement has been gathering steam lately and may be well on its way to becoming a full-fledged bloc in its own right—ready to fly out of the Asian nest, if it was ever in it in the first place. After all, we have argued that the umbilical cord to the Asian movement is really an artificial one and perhaps the South Asian movement has grown enough in numbers and energy to snap that tie.

But I feel that that tie is important. Even though it may be an artificial one, it has given us a common platform that would probably have never existed otherwise. Of all the population segments, it is in gay lesbian politics, that I see some of the greatest interaction between the Asian and South Asian populations. In the San Francisco Bay Area, which has large East Asian and South Asian population groups, there are many community organizations and activist groups. Few of them interact as much with the Asian groups as the gay/lesbian groups do.

The gay/lesbian groups do it not because they identify more with Asian groups but because they need all the support and expertise they can get. While an African American gay group might support us in one of our ventures, that support will have to be sought out. With the Asian groups, our Asianness, even if it is only geographical, gives us direct access to that support whether it is for a conference we are organizing or a signature campaign. This support and access are a valuable resource. By divorcing ourselves from our Asianness, we would squander this resource. That support is needed when gay and lesbian groups need to face some bigoted discrimination. That support becomes crucial when the mainstream gay community wittingly or unwittingly sidelines the minority communities— for example, a gay paper may be ignoring South Asian queer events. Pressure exerted from both South Asian and Asian groups is more effective than from a minority within a minority—volunteer-run and strained for resources. Sometimes we need to take up the cudgels for each other, sometimes we need to support each other, and if the fragile Asian identity gives us a ready-made starting point for building that base of support, then we would be foolish to spurn it.

The question remains, how South Asian can we be without losing our Asian identity? Nusrat Retina says her "strategy has been to work with pan-Asian groups and focus on South Asian specific groups or South Asian visibility in joint events and forums. My connections with the East Asian gay community are too strong (even today in the Washington, D.C., area) to completely sever the two families." [16] I think that the issue of needing to sever the two families need not arise, since the whole concept of an Asian identity is so amorphous and the points of conflict are really few. We can be as South Asian as we like but still remain Asian.

On the contrary, though, within a South Asian group the conflict between being Indian and being South Asian can be very real. Indocentrism can threaten a South Asian group in many ways—in terms of how the group is organized, in how the money is spent, in deciding which communities will receive outreach. India is the dominant partner in the group—the big sister as it were. In Asian groups the problem is a little different—there is no single dominant partner in all Asian groups. China, Japan, Vietnam, and Philippines, are all big sisters, some a little bigger than the others but all with enough representatives to keep each other in check. Also Asian groups have more members (compared to South Asian ones) who are second- or third-generation immigrants. Their loyalties often lie with America rather than their grandparents' countries. All of this means that Asian groups have had a little more experience in broadening their focus, in dealing with different communities, in not focusing on one country alone. South Asia has often been an euphemism for India. If Asia has been an euphemism, it has been for a group of countries—not just one. The Vietnam War, Imelda Marcos's shoes, Mao, and Sony have seen to that.

IN A FORTUNE COOKIE

At the end of the meal there must be a fortune cookie moral that neatly sums it all up. I don't know if the discussion above can be neatly summarized. The negotiation of identity between Asian and South Asian is ever-changing and under constant scrutiny and reevaluation. It depends upon the strength of the South Asian community, both numerical and organizational, in the area in question. Some areas like Houston may have large South Asian populations but lack organized South Asian lesbigay groups. Other cities with smaller South Asian populations have successfully organized South Asian queer groups.

However, when all is said and done, South Asian lesbigay groups seem to function better with their Asian counterparts than do many mainstream South Asian groups. The reason is possibly that the lesbian/gay identity is the strongest binding force there and the Asian connection reinforces that bond. For a mainstream group the area of commonality is the Asian identity, which is a rather tenuous point of connection in the first place. Until South Asian gay and lesbian groups enjoy unqualified support within their parent communities, they will need all the support they can muster, and Asian groups will continue to be a major resource for them. As South Asian groups grow stronger, the dynamics of that relationship may change, but hopefully the spirit of collaboration and cooperation will not. For South Asian or East Asian, we all inhabit a no-man's land between our traditional Asian communities and the larger (white) queer community. And we need each other's help to moor that no-man's land and define it and develop it so that neither community, Asian nor lesbian and gay, can pretend that we don't exist.

NOTES

1. Arvind Kumar, interviewed by the author, April 1995.
2. Daniel Bao, interviewed by the author, April 1995.
3. Richard Fung, "Shortcomings: Questions about Pornography as Pedagogy," in *Queer Looks, Perspectives on Lesbian and Gay Film and Video*, edited by Martha Gever et al.
4. Ashok Jethanandani, interviewed by the author, April 1995.
5. Kenji Oshima, interviewed by the author, April 1995.
6. *Baigan Aloo Tabanka Bachanal: Writer, Artist, Filmmaker Shani Mootoo in her own words* by Dipti Ghosh. Trikone, Oct. 1994.
7. Voltaire Gungab, interviewed by the author, April 1995.
8. See note 1.
9. Dipti Ghosh, interviewed by the author, April 1995.
10. Nusrat Retina, "The Toughest Journey," in *A Lotus of Another Color*, edited by Rakesh Ratti.
11. Minal Hajratwala, interviewed by the author, April 1995.
12. Corey Tong, interviewed by the author, July 1995.
13. Nusrat Retina, interviewed by the author, April 1995.
14. "SALGA Barred From NY Parade," by Sandip Roy-Chowdhury, *India Currents*, Sept. 1994.
15. Prescott Chow, interviewed by the author, April 1995.
16. Nusrat Retina, interviewed by the author, April 1995.

WORKS CITED

Gever, Martha, John Greyson, Pratibha Parmar Pratibha, eds. *Queer Looks: Perspectives on Lesbian and Gay Film and Video*. New York: Routledge, 1993.

Lim-Hing, Sharon, ed. *The Very Inside: An Anthology of Writing by Asian and Pacific Islander Lesbian and Bisexual Women*. Toronto: Sister Vision Press, 1994.

Mootoo, Shani. *Out on Main Street*. Vancouver: Press Gang Publishers, 1993.

Ratti, Rakesh, ed. *A Lotus of Another Color: An Unfolding of the South Asian Gay and Lesbian Experience*. Boston: Alyson Publications, 1993.

Tsang, Chi, ed. *Witness Aloud: Lesbian, Gay and Bisexual Asian/Pacific Writings Spring/Summer 1993*. New York: Asian American Writers' Workshop, 1993.

The Women of South Asian Descent Collective, ed. *Our Feet Walk the Sky: Women of the South Asian Diaspora*. San Francisco: aunt lute books, 1993.

RAJINI SRIKANTH

9   Ram Yoshino Uppuluri's Campaign

*The Implications for Panethnicity
in Asian America*

"I WANTED to write my own role because there wasn't one I could adopt, namely, that of an Indian/Japanese American politician." With these words Ram Yoshino Uppuluri comments on his bid for the U.S. House of Representatives in the 1994 Democratic primary in Tennessee's Third Congressional District. Uppuluri's father, the late K.R.R. Uppuluri, immigrated to the United States from India in 1957; in the same year his mother, Shigeko Yoshino, emigrated from Japan. Ram Uppuluri's combined Indian and Japanese heritage theoretically makes him a potential bridge between two Asian American subgroups that are usually considered to have relatively little shared history in the United States.[1] Uppuluri's candidacy could have brought these two groups together, but the alliance did not materialize and the gap between them persisted.

Consider this snapshot from the Uppuluri campaign. It is February 1994 and Uppuluri is in Washington, D.C., to introduce himself to potential donors. Jay Reddy, his point person in the capital, is organizing a "Meet-and-Greet-the-Candidate." With only a week's notice to pull together the event, Reddy gets on the phone and calls everyone he considers relevant in the Indian American community. Reddy, who has been working with Uppuluri's campaign coordinator, Baiju Shah, knows that Shah is interested in getting Japanese Americans involved in the campaign. So Reddy invites Leslie Hatamiya (who at the time worked in Senator Bradley's office) and Karen Narasaki (then of the Japanese American Citizens' League), currently director of the Asian Pacific American Legal Consortium (APALC), to the event. Hatamiya is unable to attend, but Narasaki arrives. When she gets there, she finds that there are about thirty South Asians in the room and she is the only non–South Asian. She listens to Uppuluri speak and then leaves. Reddy notices her brief appearance and quick departure. Neither Narasaki nor Reddy makes any further attempt to renew contact.

This particular incident, not the first gesture made by the Uppuluri campaign to involve the Japanese American community, stands as a watershed.

186

The sequence of events leading up to and away from the incident identify it as a moment of missed opportunity, a moment that was ripe with the promise of closing the gap between two Asian American subgroups. One might say with fairness that, following this event, Uppuluri's invisibility as a political candidate to the Japanese American community was virtually assured.

The central question this essay will address is why Uppuluri was unable to involve the Japanese American community in his campaign. At the outset, I wish to make clear that this article is not a political study. Rather, it is one illustration of the difficulties of closing the gap between two communities and realizing "Asian American panethnicity," a phrase popularized by Yen Le Espiritu in her book of the same title. In using Ram Uppuluri as a trope for Asian American panethnicity and his campaign as the site of potential panethnic coalition, I do not wish to suggest that the lessons learned from his campaign can be applied unaltered to all other efforts at coalition building. Yet, his candidacy reveals complicated scenarios that illuminate the obstacles to realizing intergroup cooperation in Asian America and the tremendous efforts that have to be made if the gaps among various subgroups are to be closed. What his campaign makes clear is that numerous psychological, sociological, historical, and political variables need to impinge on each other in significant ways before panethnicity in Asian America can become a reality. I do not mean to imply that panethnicity ought to be or is an unequivocally desired end in all situations. Clearly, there are some instances where panethnicity may be viewed as counterproductive to the interests of one or more group that is part of the potential coalition.[2] What I do suggest, however, is that, given the immense diversity of ethnic subgroups in Asian America, an understanding of the various factors that facilitate and inhibit panethnic coalition is a critical and necessary first step to strengthening the voice of Asians in the American sociopolitical landscape.

I have broken down the analysis of Uppuluri's campaign into three areas: Uppuluri's presentation of himself to the Japanese American community; the reception of his candidacy by the Japanese American community; and the candidate's sense of himself as a Japanese American and/or Indian American and/or Asian American. I have omitted from this paper a detailed examination of the Indian American community's response to the candidate primarily because it would entail analyses that are beyond the scope of this discussion.

My methodology is somewhat unorthodox in that it draws on techniques from diverse disciplines. I have relied heavily for my data on conversations and interviews with the following persons:

- Ram Yoshino Uppuluri, the candidate
- Key members of his campaign staff (Baiju Shah, Mahesh Ram, and Jay Reddy)
- Sherry Cable, a sociologist at the University of Tennessee at Knoxville who has interviewed 80 residents from Oak Ridge (the town in which Uppuluri grew up) and is currently in the process of transcribing the tapes
- Karen Narasaki, director of the Asian Pacific American Legal Consortium
- Editors of selected Japanese American and Asian American publications (Kazuo Inafuku, June Kawaguchi, Gerard Lim, Kimi Nakashima, Takeshi Nakayama, Richard Suenaga, Sandi Taniguchi, J. K. Yamamoto, Joy Yamauchi, and Paul Yempuku)

In addition, I examine the rhetoric of newspaper articles and other texts relating to Uppuluri's campaign so as to uncover unstated motivations and contexts. I touch upon scholarship in sociology and psychology to illustrate my arguments and findings. Finally, two brief visits to Uppuluri's district have given me a context within which to understand Uppuluri's representation of self both within and outside his constituency.

A note about my use of the terms "Indian American," "Japanese American," and "Asian American": the first two terms obviously refer to disparate subgroups that are connected only insofar as they appear under the same census category of "Asian and Pacific Islander." When I use "Asian American," I am invoking a panethnic sensibility, in which the imperatives of individual subgroups are subsumed within a broader identification of shared social and political conditions.

CANDIDATE UPPULURI INTRODUCES HIMSELF TO THE JAPANESE AMERICAN COMMUNITY

Baiju Shah, Uppuluri's first campaign coordinator and strategist,[3] made early efforts to involve the Japanese American community in the campaign. Shah, who readily admits to having limited knowledge of the Japanese American community, turned to Leslie Hatamiya and Karen Narasaki for help with selecting representative Japanese American publications to which he could send the introductory write-up about Uppuluri's candidacy. With their assistance, Shah identified twelve publications as possible vehicles for reaching the Japanese American and general Asian American community (the Indian American community was targeted through specific Indian American publications). I include a brief profile of each publication to show the breadth of Shah's outreach to the Japanese American community, both in the range of areas covered and the number and type of readers targeted:

1. *A Magazine* (general Asian American readership, 100,000 readers, largest distributed magazine in nation for Asian American affairs. Nationally distributed as a bimonthly. Last year was distributed as a quarterly. Considered to be an authoritative source for what's happening in Asian America. Median reader age, twenty-seven years old—60 percent female readership, 40 percent male; average household income of reader, $57,000.)

2. *AsianWeek* (San Francisco, largest nationally distributed pan-Asian newspaper, readership of 30,000)

3. *Chicago Shimpo* (5,000 readers, primarily Japanese American, in Chicago and the surrounding suburbs)

4. *Hawaii Hochi/Hawaii Herald* (8,000 Japanese American readers in Hawaii)

5. *Hokubei Mainichi* (Japanese American readership of 9,000 in Northern California)

6. *Nichi Bei Times* (San Francisco, 8,000 readers, Japanese American, with national circulation)

7. *The Northwest Nikkei* (Seattle, some circulation in Oregon and Idaho, 9,000 Japanese American readers)

8. *Pacific Citizen* (newspaper of the Japanese American Citizens' League; distributed nationally primarily to JACL members, with a readership of 20,000)

9. *Rafu Shimpo* (Los Angeles but with a national circulation of 21,000 Japanese American readers, in existence for ninety years)

10. *Rocky Mountain Jiho* (published in Denver)

11. *Southern Journal of Houston* (6,000 Japanese American readers, primarily in Texas, some in Georgia and Florida)

12. *Tozai Times* (a monthly newspaper serving the Los Angeles area with a readership of 10,000)

There are two ways of looking at Shah's outreach effort—as ambitious or as misguided. From the former perspective, one can see in the readership numbers and the distribution areas of the publications evidence of Shah's determination to reach as wide a Japanese American audience as possible. Alternatively, one could view the outreach as unfocused and not targeted to a specific type of Japanese American contributor or voter. Further, Shah could be accused of naiveté and lacking in historical knowledge. There is no historical data to indicate cooperation between Japanese and Indian immigrants in the United States (as discussed in detail later). Was Shah perhaps being too idealistic in expecting that the Japanese

Americans would respond to the "pull of blood," that they would see in Ram Uppuluri a Japanese son just as the Indian Americans had already responded to the candidate as an Indian son?[4]

There is no doubt of Shah's initial optimism in reaching out to the Japanese American community. He sent three separate press kits to the twelve publications—one in January 1994, shortly after Uppuluri's announcement of his candidacy; a midquarter update in February; and an April update, in which Shah included articles from the Tennessee press describing Uppuluri as the front runner in campaign contributions (by this time, Uppuluri had raised approximately $101,000). Thus, Shah sustained the initial contact through the early months of the campaign. He hoped by this effort, first, to generate interest in the Uppuluri campaign and, second, to stimulate potential donors to contribute.

Jay Reddy, who coordinated Uppuluri's campaign effort in Washington, D.C., tried to arrange for Uppuluri to meet two prominent Japanese American members of the House, Norman Mineta (the Democratic representative from San Jose) and Robert Matsui (who was then the Democratic representative from Sacramento but is now no longer in the House). The meeting with Mineta materialized. At the time, Mineta was in charge of the Democratic Congressional Campaign Committee.

Mahesh Ram, who managed Uppuluri's fundraising efforts in New York City, set up an interview for the candidate with *A Magazine*. The objective, says Mahesh Ram, was to present Uppuluri as an *Asian American* to the magazine's readership of young Asian American men and women. "Also," Mahesh Ram adds, "we had been talking primarily to the Indian American community. I felt that we should try to contact Japanese American political activists. I wanted to reach first-generation Japanese Americans through the second generation, and to energize the second generation to get behind the campaign."

It is evident that Shah, Reddy, and Ram made initial attempts to increase Uppuluri's visibility within the Japanese American community, to close the gap between the South Asian Americans and the Japanese American community. Their efforts were aimed at positioning Uppuluri as a candidate worthy of support, both with the press and with prominent Japanese American politicians.

RESPONSE FROM THE JAPANESE AMERICAN COMMUNITY
Press Coverage

Shah's efforts at publicity met with varying degrees of response from the Japanese American press. Reactions ranged from moderately interested to completely uninterested. Only *A Magazine*, *AsianWeek*, and *Rafu Shimpo* demonstrated some interest.

In *A Magazine,* "A Candidate for All People" (20) describes Uppuluri as having made a life of breaking "Asian American stereotypes" (20). The write-up exhibits a curious tension between describing Uppuluri with the panethnic term "Asian American" and the ethnic-specific term "Indian American." The "candidate for all people" appears, in the final analysis, to become a candidate for Indian Americans. The article presents Uppuluri as a candidate, who "marks a new stage in Indian American political activism" (78). Uppuluri himself speaks of the "maturation of the Indian political consciousness" (78). There is nothing objectionable per se in the article's Indian American–centered approach; after all, it illuminates the political awakening of one Asian American subgroup. However, the article misses one of Mahesh Ram's objectives of generating excitement for his campaign with second- and third-generation Japanese Americans.

I questioned Mahesh Ram about the focus of the article, and whether by this point in the campaign (Summer 1994) Uppuluri was beginning to see himself as an Indian American. Referring to Kamran Pasha, the author of the article for *A Magazine,* he said, "I think that Kamran's being a South Asian had everything to do with how Uppuluri was presented. Kamran was incredibly excited about what Uppuluri meant to the visibility of the South Asian American community, and he was eager to interview him and write about his campaign."

Pasha's ethnicity and its effect on the crafting of his article brings to the fore the complex issue of the press and its relation to the public. To what extent should *A Magazine* function as an agent of change within the Asian American community? Is the magazine's role merely to reflect the current dynamics within the Asian American community? Should the editor have sought out an Asian American of non South Asian background to write the article on Uppuluri? Would such a move have outraged South Asian American reporters? Should the editor have assigned a team, one Japanese American and one Indian American writer, to cover the candidate? Does such an editorial decision go beyond the domain of news reporting and begin to enter the realm of activism? That *A Magazine* is inclusive in its representation of all Asian American subgroups is evident from even a quick glimpse of its articles. However, inclusion can often take the form of a simplistic additive approach to enlarging Asian America. While I am not by any means suggesting that any publication should enter into the business of effecting structural changes in the relationships among the various Asian American subgroups, I would argue that inclusion must be accompanied by an understanding of its ramifications in political, economic, and social contexts. Given that the mainstream press is woefully reductionist and simplistic in its coverage of Asian American issues, it may fall to Asian American publications to be at all times cognizant of the complexities of intra–Asian American politics. Would it have been possible for Mahesh Ram to enlist the editor's help in achieving the campaign's objective of stimulating young Japanese American readers about the Uppuluri campaign and thereby closing the gap between the South Asian and Japanese American communities? The question remains: what role does the press play in the political sphere? [5]

Gerard Lim, who wrote the article for *AsianWeek* said, "We ran one introductory article in early February 1994, and we may have run a short notice when he lost the primary in August. Frankly, we don't have the time and resources to cover at length the campaigns of all Asian American candidates. We do, however, carry at least one story about every Asian American candidate who runs for political office, whether that person is in Oregon or California."

Lim's article is comprehensive in its presentation of the candidate's qualifications;[6] however, it does not position Uppuluri specifically as a Japanese American or even panethnic Asian American candidate; rather, it seeks to place Uppuluri within the context of rising political involvement by Indian Americans. Granted, *AsianWeek* does reach a pan Asian audience that includes Indian Americans, and this fact may have influenced the nature of Lim's write-up; but what is surprising is the paper's almost exclusive emphasis on the candidate's Indian American connection, with only a cursory treatment of the Japanese American connection. On page 1 of the paper, where the article begins, the text reads, "Uppuluri joins Neil Dhillon (of Maryland) and Peter Mathews (of Southern California) as young Indian Americans staking out their share of the political battleground."

The only clue on this front page of the candidate's Japanese American heritage appears in the second paragraph, in which he is referred to as "Ram *Yoshino* Uppuluri" (emphasis added). Later, on page 17, where the article continues, we find a photograph of Uppuluri and his parents and the first textual detail of the two Asian American cultures in which he has been raised. The final thrust of the article, however, is to align Uppuluri with other Indian American candidates running for political office and to describe him as "part of the new breed of Indian American politician." I would argue that such a representation of the candidate would lead a reader to characterize Uppuluri as an aspiring *Indian American* politician. One might see him secondarily as an Asian American politician, but it is extremely unlikely that a reader would view him as a Japanese American politician. Thus, in naming and positioning Uppuluri primarily as Indian

American, the article articulates a wide gap between the candidate and the Japanese American community. That the write-up on Uppuluri appears in *Asian Week* doesn't necessarily mean that all readers will consider Uppuluri a candidate with panethnic Asian American appeal.

Rafu Shimpo ran two articles on Uppuluri. This publication's editorial approach seeks to emphasize pan Asian coalition building over ethnic-specific political approaches.[7] While the Uppuluri reports do adhere in the main to this editorial perspective, both articles reinforce the impression that Uppuluri more readily turns for assistance to the Indian American than Japanese American community. Given that *Rafu Shimpo*'s primary readership is Japanese American, such a positioning of Uppuluri is not likely to go far in closing the gap between the two communities.

The first article, which appeared on February 1, 1994, prominently mentions Uppuluri's dual Indian and Japanese heritage in the headline and gives a detailed description of the candidate's stand on issues of importance to Asian America: hate crimes and immigration, in particular. Uppuluri is thus presented as an *Asian American* candidate. No extra coverage is accorded to his Japanese American heritage, and the general impression the article conveys is of a qualified panethnic Asian American candidate. However, one small but significant mention of his forthcoming fundraising trip to California has the effect of aligning him more closely with the Indian American community than with the general Asian American or Japanese American community. The text at this point reads, "Uppuluri . . . will also visit California in the near future to meet with members of the Indian community." The second article, which appeared on February 26, is headlined "Indian-Japanese American's Bid for Congress Gains Momentum." The write-up is brief; but here, as in the earlier article, there is a reminder of the contributions the candidate has received from the Indian American community. While *Rafu Shimpo* does not explicitly present the candidate as Indian American, the brief references to his fund-raising efforts among Indian Americans suggest to the reader that *this* is the community in which Uppuluri is seeking help. A Japanese American reader might conclude that the candidate did not feel the need to reach out to the Japanese American community for campaign contributions, and this reaction is evident in remarks by Karen Narasaki, director of APALC: "Of course, he didn't need the Japanese American community for money; he was getting enough of that from the Indian Americans." The reality was, however, that Uppuluri would have welcomed contributions—of time and money—from both communities. Narasaki's comment reveals the variance between Uppuluri's perceived allegiance and his actual desires.

Richard Suenaga, editor of the *Pacific Citizen*, said he "vaguely remember[ed]" receiving material from Uppuluri's campaign, but ultimately did not use it. Similarly, responses from other publications ranged from a "vague" recollection that they may perhaps have run one article (*Hokubei Mainichi*, the *Northwest Nikkei*), to a dim remembrance of his name but no knowledge of having run any article (*Tozai Times*, *Hawaii Herald*), and, to no recollection of having seen any material relating to his candidacy (*Southern Journal of Houston*, *Nichi Bei Times*). These responses would seem to indicate a lack of interest.

Given the sparse coverage of Uppuluri's candidacy by the Japanese American and general Asian American press, the campaign's attempted penetration of the Japanese American community yielded no significant results in terms of contributions. An analysis of FEC (Federal Election Commission) records reveals that of the 260 individuals who contributed $200 or more to the campaign, the majority—approximately 80 percent— were Indian American, 17 percent were non–Asian Americans (predominantly residents of Tennessee who knew the candidate personally), a mere 1.25 percent were Asian Americans who were neither Indian nor Japanese American, and only 1.25 percent were Japanese American contributors.[8] Of the 250 contributors who donated under $200, approximately 76 percent were Indian American, 23 percent were non–Asian American (again, overwhelmingly residents of Tennessee), and fewer than 1 percent were Japanese American. There were no contributors from any other Asian American subgroup.

According to Shah, it became evident early on in the campaign that the Japanese American community would not materialize as a source of support—financially, emotionally, or strategically. He recalls, "We tried getting in touch with fund-raisers in the Japanese American community in California, but there was absolutely no interest from them. So we decided to cut our losses and focus on where we knew we could get results." The gap between the candidate and the Japanese American community was seen as being too wide and closure was not viewed as a viable possibility. The extremely poor response of the Japanese American community led the Uppuluri campaign to turn increasingly to the Indian American community for money and for other types of campaign support. Ram Yoshino Uppuluri eventually "became" just Ram Uppuluri, with his Japanese middle name being dropped from campaign literature, and, outside Tennessee, Uppuluri's ties to the Indian American community were emphasized.

Mixed Perceptions

Karen Narasaki of the Asian Pacific American Legal Consortium attributes Uppuluri's failure to interest the Japanese American community in part to the campaign's insufficient emphasis of his Japanese American heritage. "I was surprised that they didn't seem to be playing up that aspect of his heritage, but then I thought it was perhaps because he identified more with being Indian American," she remarks. Campaign coordinator Baiju Shah, clearly surprised at her assessment (which I relayed to him), responds, "I don't see what more we could have done. Whenever we sent out material to the Japanese American or general Asian American press, Shigeko [Uppuluri's mother] was always mentioned very early on in the text and we always made sure to include his middle name, Yoshino." What makes Narasaki's and Shah's assessments significant is that their perceptions reveal how campaign strategies are often determined by personal reaction rather than researched data. In speaking with Narasaki, I got the impression that had she detected even the slightest interest from the Uppuluri campaign in highlighting the Japanese American connection, she would have become involved in furthering that link. However, from the point of view of Uppuluri's campaign staff, the initial gesture had been made and the response had been less than promising.

Let us return to the Washington, D.C., meet-and-greet. Karen Narasaki, in speaking of her appearance at the event, recalls that she was "one of the few if not the only non–South Asian there." Narasaki left a few minutes after hearing Uppuluri speak, not attempting to get to know the candidate better.

Uppuluri's Washington-area campaign organizer, Jay Reddy, who had invited Narasaki to the event, gave me his reasons for her quick departure: "The acoustics that evening weren't crisp and Uppuluri didn't have the same charismatic appeal that was typical of his other appearances. Maybe Karen Narasaki wasn't impressed. I noticed that she didn't stay around long." Reddy did not follow up with Narasaki, and Narasaki, feeling that as a Japanese American she was irrelevant to the campaign effort, made no attempt to stay connected with the campaign.

Her action, in conjunction with the poor response of the Japanese American press, perhaps further convinced Shah and Reddy of the futility of pursuing the Japanese American connection. One can only conjecture that Narasaki's assistance might have enabled the candidate to win greater name recognition in the Japanese American community. Whether that would have necessarily translated into successful fund-raising is questionable, however. The real benefit of Narasaki's entrance into the Uppuluri campaign might have been to get Indian American and Japanese American campaign workers to combine efforts and expertise, to begin to close the gap between these two Asian American subgroups.

Sumantra Tito Sinha, previously of the Asian American Legal Defense and Education Fund (and a contributor to this volume), says that coalition building within the Asian American community has to take place on two fronts: the dominant group has to invite minority groups to participate; at the same time, the minority groups have to feel empowered enough to demand representation and claim ownership in the issue or organization that presents itself as Asian American. Espiritu's recent work shows that in most pan Asian organizations, Chinese and Japanese Americans occupy positions of leadership and influence (see especially 83–106). Uppuluri's meet-and-greet, however, presents an interesting reversal of dominant and minority roles. At this event, Karen Narasaki was displaced from a usual position of prominence and dominance within the Asian American community to one of marginality. Perhaps in this instance, Reddy and Shah, as members of the "majority" group, should have made a more pointed effort to include Narasaki in the gathering and make her feel that her presence was valued in the service of closing the gap between the South Asian American candidate and the rest of Asian America.

A History of Gaps

Encounters between the Japanese and Indians in the United States have received scant attention, and the records describing these are, therefore, sparse. However, those documents that exist reveal significant dynamics between the two communities, that, because of their shared victimization under early-twentieth-century United States immigration and Land Law acts, ought to have joined in common cause but surprisingly did not. The two communities, although they lived side by side in California and were engaged in the same pursuit—farming—seem to have separated themselves from each other across a gap, the nature of which varied, depending on the situation.

Eiichiro Azuma's essay "Interethnic Conflict under Racial Subordination: Japanese Immigrants and Their Asian Neighbors in Walnut Grove, California, 1908–1941" cites "competition over limited resources" as one reason for the animosity between Japanese and "East Indian" fieldhands in the early decades of this century. The Indian laborers were willing to work for lower wages and so were more readily hired by the white and Japanese farmers to handle the asparagus crop in the area. Says Azuma, "Viewed from the Walnut Grove Japanese perspective, East Indians had became [sic] 'the greatest enemy' to their community. The Japanese association secretary argued that not only did East Indians take away Japanese jobs on the delta farms, but also attempted to steal farm leases from Japanese farmers" (35).

Focusing on the same historical period, Min Song's essay in this volume draws attention to yet another rift between the two communities in 1925 in the farming milieu of California's Imperial Valley. Alluding to the Alien Land Law of 1913 that prohibited individuals of Asian descent from owning land, Song makes the valid observation that "the existence of these commonalities does not mean that they [the Japanese and Indian farmers] immediately jumped to combine forces. What would have been the point of making alliances with people who were just as powerless under the law, perhaps more so, than oneself?" Thus, both the Japanese and the Indian farmers attempted to circumvent the law by making informal arrangements with white farmers, whom they saw as having more power than themselves. However, and this is where Song's essay is germane to my discussion, the Indian farmers were more adept than the Japanese in shaping a public image of themselves among the white population of Imperial Valley. They "were notorious for the frequency with which they appeared in court to sue not only whites but also each other. By turning to the judicial system to settle their disputes so often, something perhaps learned through the exigencies created by living under a British colonial administration, they became familiar to the court personnel." The familiarity appears to have garnered them support and friends among the local whites, gains perhaps not so easily made by the Japanese farmers whose contact with the power structures of the white community was not as extensive. Thus, in the eyes of the Japanese farmers, the Indians may have appeared to have had an advantage and, therefore, the gap between the two communities persisted despite their common victimization under the law.

Yet another gap becomes visible in the autobiography of Dilip Singh Saund, an Indian who in 1956 became the first American of Asian descent to be elected to the United States House of Representatives and be reelected for a second term. In listing some of his proudest moments as a U.S. congressman, Saund writes of

> a Japanese American who had not received his indemnity check for damages when he was incarcerated during the war. On misguided advice, he had failed to accept a check for ten thousand dollars offered him in settlement by the government, and not only that, he had failed to fill out the required forms within the prescribed time period. The statute of limitations had run out and he was left high and dry without his money, which he needed very badly to carry on his business.
>
> He wrote me, and I took the matter up with the proper agency. There had to be a special ruling in his case, but he got his money. (122)

This entry in Saund's autobiography makes visible the most significant gap between the two groups, a gap created by the "incarceration" and the different "fates" of two farming communities whose only dissimilarity is racial. One community had its lands seized, the other did not.

Against such a historical backdrop, what are the chances for closing the gap between the two communities? Post-1965 immigration of Indians has far surpassed that of Japanese, and the Indian professionals who came following the lifting of immigration restrictions had very little in common with the California Japanese and their history in the United States. Most post-1965 Indian immigrants came for economic or academic reasons, and the majority of them intended to return to India after a brief and economically successful sojourn in the United States. Anu Gupta, a contributor to this volume, points out that Indian American doctors are, even to this day, more committed to furthering medical causes in India than they are in lobbying for improvements in the delivery of health care services to low-income patients in the United States. Were Uppuluri, Shah, and Narasaki being impractical in their optimistic efforts to bring together the two Asian American subgroups? Do the realities of historical rifts run too deep to be bridged? Or, conversely, do the second and third generation of Asian Americans hold the key to interethnic coalition, because, being distanced from the historical gaps, they can focus on the imperatives of the present moment? Whatever expectations Uppuluri and his campaign staff might have had, their analyses of their "failure" to involve the Japanese American community demonstrate an appreciation of the complexities of closing the gaps between the Indian and Japanese American subgroups.

Shah's analysis of the campaign's lack of impact on the Japanese American community rests on the assumption that Japanese Americans might have had difficulty with Uppuluri in two areas: (1) perceiving him as a viable political candidate and (2) identifying him as one of their group. Shah explains his first point:

> Japanese Americans are politically sophisticated. They've been around longer, they understand the system. They probably looked at Uppuluri and assessed that he would have a hard time even making it through the primary. He was in a five-way race and running from a district in a conservative state. To them it may not have been a good use of their money to throw it on a candidate whose chances of winning were, in their opinion, practically non-existent.

As regards the second point, although Shah himself did not elaborate on it, Jay Reddy offered his views: "It's harder for Japanese Americans to identify with Uppuluri because he's only half Japanese; he looks more Indian than Japanese, and his name is Indian." At first glance, Reddy's analysis might seem overly simplistic in its underscoring of phenotype and name as dominant markers of ethnic identification. Yet research on mixed-race individuals bears out the validity of his line of thinking. For example, Cookie White Stephan found that "perceived physical resemblance to members of the group or . . . having a surname associated with the group" were among the reasons mixed-race respondents mentioned for their ethnic identities (56). Similarly, Paul Spickard observes that "one's choice of identity depend(s) on how one look(s)" (115) and "the way one looks has a powerful effect on the way one is treated and, ultimately, on the choice of identity one makes" (116).

Finally, Uppuluri, in offering reasons for his invisibility to the Japanese American community, points to three factors—his location, lack of shared experience with West Coast Japanese Americans, and sense of political contentment/fulfillment on the part of Japanese Americans:

> Most established and politically involved Japanese Americans live on the West Coast;[9] they have a long history in this country and have experienced a most severe form of discrimination and oppression. For such Japanese Americans, an East Coast part–Japanese American candidate will have little relevance. Many of the East Coast Japanese Americans, at least those in Tennessee, are not U.S. citizens. They're students and businessmen for the most part, many of whom either do or intend to return to Japan. Again, for this group of people, I am only of marginal relevance.
>
> Secondly, I do not have a shared experience with West Coast Japanese Americans. No one in my family was part of the internment, and, therefore, that whole very significant emotional tie to the Japanese within this country is not something I have [in a curious twist to this issue of shared experience, the Friendship Bell effort in which Uppuluri's family has been involved aligns Uppuluri more closely with the Japanese in Japan than with Japanese Americans. But more on this later].
>
> Thirdly, Japanese Americans already have powerful voices speaking for them in the House and Senate. There are Congressmen Bob Matsui and Norman Mineta, both of whom are very fine spokespersons for the community. So there's not a sense of urgency among the Japanese Americans that they need someone in the House. They appear content with whom they have. The Indian American community, on the other hand, needs visibility on Capitol Hill; so it's eager to support someone who appears to have a good chance of getting there.

Uppuluri's analysis of the indifference of the Japanese American community led him to concentrate his early campaign efforts on potential Indian American donors. At this point, I'd like to make clear that Uppuluri's attention to the Indian American community was, initially, only as a source of funding (the emotional ties developed later, as I will discuss). Within the state of Tennessee, Uppuluri strove hard to run an ethnic-free campaign, given the profile of his constituency (Asians constitute less than 1 percent of census figures within Uppuluri's district). Outside Tennessee, Uppuluri rarely overplayed his Indianness; if anything, he constantly reminded his Indian American audience how much of a Tennessean he was.

I asked Baiju Shah if at any point in the campaign he and Uppuluri had sat down to think about the benefits of hiring someone to "work" the Japanese American community specifically. Shah's response reveals the pressures of campaigning and illuminates the nature of the decision-making process that drives most campaigns these days: "The response was so poor, and the response from the Indian American community so encouraging, by contrast, that we decided to follow the path that made the most sense. There was so much to do, that Ram [Uppuluri] and I had very little time to reflect on the reasons for the poor response and what we could do to improve it. The money was tight and there was no way we could permit ourselves the luxury of hiring another staff member."

The Japanese American community was, therefore, after the initial penetration through press articles, abandoned as a possible source of funding. Further, Uppuluri's meeting with Mineta led the candidate to conclude, "I didn't get the sense from Mineta that he could get anything for me out of the Japanese American community." But, says Uppuluri, "It was still important for me to make that contact with Mineta because he is an important presence in the Asian American community."

Uppuluri's rationale for meeting with Mineta raises important questions about the extent to which Uppuluri identified himself as an Asian American candidate and how his perceived identity affected his campaign.

IDENTITY DEVELOPMENT AND ITS IMPACT ON CAMPAIGN STRATEGY

Uppuluri and his family moved to Oak Ridge in 1964 when Uppuluri was four years old. Since that time, Uppuluri spent all his schooling years in Oak Ridge, except during the 1976 academic year, when his father was at the University of California at Santa Barbara. After graduating from high school in Oak Ridge in 1979, Uppuluri did his undergraduate work at Princeton, then returned to Tennessee to work for a prestigious newspaper, the *Nashville Tennessean*. Until August 1995, therefore, Uppuluri lived most of his life in Oak Ridge and other parts of East Tennessee. In August 1995, he took a job with the Department of Energy, in Washington, D.C.

Uppuluri points to Oak Ridge as having been the dominant influence on his development of identity. The town was conceived as a secret military research site in 1942, and the famous Oak Ridge National Laboratory (ORNL) developed the enriched uranium that went into the atomic bomb that was dropped on Hiroshima. Oak Ridge began as a community of scientists, researchers, and the workers employed in nonscientific and nonresearch capacities at the various facilities. "There's a pioneer spirit in Oak Ridge," says Uppuluri. "Remember, people came here and built a town from nothing in the backwoods of the Appalachian mountains. My parents and those like them, who came to work at Oak Ridge National Labs, had the pride of pioneers and adventurers." Ethnic politics, claims Uppuluri, did not play a significant part in his upbringing. "If I had been growing up in California or New York City or New Jersey, places where ethnicity as a factor figures largely in the lives of children, perhaps I would have grown up with a keener sense of myself as an Asian American—as Japanese and Indian American."

The process by which Uppuluri turned eventually to the Indian American community and widened the gap between his candidacy and the Japanese American community had its beginnings in the kind of socializing influence that occurred at Oak Ridge.

Although Oak Ridge was built as a segregated town, it integrated with relative calm; this fact is surprising, considering that nearby Clinton responded to enforced integration by blowing up the high school. "Oak Ridge is anomalous in that it's politically liberal," says Sherry Cable, sociologist at the University of Tennessee at Knoxville.[10] An elderly resident of Clinton, speaking of the scientists who came to the area in the 1940s, told historians Charles Johnson and Charles Jackson in 1979 that there was a feeling in the county that Oak Ridgers were all "a bunch of Yankees," or at any rate "outsiders" (Johnson and Jackson, 194). In a phone conversation with me, Anand Raman, an Indian Jewish American who, like Uppuluri, grew up in Oak Ridge, described the town as "cosmopolitan." "There are people from all corners of the country, from all parts of the globe," he said. "People who live in Oak Ridge are very committed to the town. They choose to be here. Nobody would live here unless they really wanted to, because this is a town with a double tax structure—a city tax and a county tax. We're a very self-selecting community."

According to Cable, "Oak Ridge thinks of itself as having the largest number of Ph.D.'s of any community in the United States." She observes that Oak Ridgers think of themselves as unique: "The town was built as an isolated community, and it stayed isolated. The feelings of solidarity that grew out of the war effort persisted, and the town still sees itself in terms of us-versus-them. There's a very strong sense of an insider-outsider dichotomy."

Cable points to yet another characteristic of Oak Ridge that sets it apart from the sometimes fierce antifederal stance of southern communities:

There is a tremendous sense of economic dependence on the federal government in Oak Ridge. In fact, when the war was over and the government was considering cutting the strings and letting Oak Ridge off on its own, the town resisted incorporation because it didn't want to terminate economic dependence on the federal government. So, while the gates to Oak Ridge were thrown open in 1949, it wasn't until ten years later, in 1959, that Oak Ridge was incorporated as a township. And the residents agreed to this only after legislation was passed guaranteeing government subsidies to former military towns.

In a region of the country where one's race and ethnicity are markers of acceptability or rejection, Oak Ridge stands out as a place where these factors are less relevant than in other areas.

Uppuluri's candidacy was endorsed by the *Knoxville News-Sentinel*. The editorial underscores the uniqueness of Oak Ridge and Anderson County, of which the town is a part. Notice that the *Knoxville News-Sentinel* endorsement emphasizes Uppuluri's knowledge of and expertise on issues of concern to those who work in "high tech" Oak Ridge.

> Uppuluri is an especially appropriate candidate in the 3rd district. . . . Because the U.S. Department of Energy's facilities at Oak Ridge are in the district, [this] post has been the state's "high tech" seat in the House of Representatives.
>
> Uppuluri is fully qualified to deal with the scientific and technological issues that are a vital part of the 3rd district. In recent years, he has served as assistant director of the Joint Institute for Energy and Environment, an organization put together by the Tennessee Valley Authority, Oak Ridge National Laboratory, and the University of Tennessee. He also serves on the state's nine-member Science and Technology Advisory Council.

By contrast, the same paper commends Jeff Whorley, a candidate from the Fourth District, for his deep roots as a southerner, his familiarity with the social fabric of the county, and his solid membership in the community of illustrious families of the state:

> Jeff Whorley should represent 4th District Democrats ably. His political roots run deep in Tennessee. His great-grandfather was John Price Buchanan, state legislator and governor of the state from 1891 to 1893.
>
> A graduate of the Webb School in Bell Buckle and the University of the South at Sewanee, Whorley served in the 1978 gubernatorial campaign of Rep. Bob Clement and the congressional campaigns of Jim Cooper and Rep. Bart Gordon. . . .
>
> As a youth he worked in his father's furniture store in Shelbyville. He now teaches creative writing at the Bell Buckle school. (July 1, 1994)

Martha Wallace, chief assistant to Marilyn Lloyd, the representative from the Third District whose 1994 retirement from a twenty-year stint in the House opened up the seat, remarked that Uppuluri could not have run from any other district. It was Oak Ridge and Anderson County that created a climate hospitable to a candidate like him. The endorsement by the local paper, *The Oak Ridger*, points to "international flavor" as Uppuluri's asset (July 22, 1994).

Oak Ridge, then, offered an atypical environment for a person of Uppuluri's background: a setting in which neither race nor ethnic origins was overly emphasized and what was valued was one's contribution to the scientific effort that was the raison d'être for Oak Ridge's existence. It was in such a town that Uppuluri grew up and developed his first sense of identity.

He describes the effect of his heritage on his classmates:

> The fact that I was part Indian and part Japanese was a great conversational piece, good for show-and-tell times at school. Especially when I had come back from a visit to India or Japan, I could talk about my experiences on those trips. My classmates thought I was tremendously lucky to be able to go to such distant places; it made me feel special. But as cafeteria talk, my ethnicities didn't enter into the picture. With friends, outside the classroom, outside the structured time in which I spoke about my exciting trips, I was not conscious nor made to feel conscious of my difference. Perhaps there were several reasons for this.

The analysis Uppuluri offers is remarkably accurate in that he cites factors considered by researchers to be key influences in the shaping of identity—family, peer group, and larger community. "My parents never emphasized my dual ethnicity," says Uppuluri. While it is evident that the Uppuluri household quite comfortably blends Indian and Japanese cultural elements—in the food served and the furnishings, for example— what is also evident is that the candidate's parents are immensely proud of their son's ability to move smoothly through the culture of East Tennessee. "Maybe if my parents had called louder attention to the fact that I was Japanese or that I was Indian, I would have been more consciously aware of the way this double heritage was affecting my actions or my thoughts, but they didn't." Uppuluri insists that while both his cultural antecedents were and still are extremely relevant to him as a person, they were not presented to him with political overtones, as heritages that made him appear different in the eyes of those around him, or as attributes that would impede or hamper his ability to get ahead.

Oak Ridge, in the period of time that Uppuluri was growing up there, was not a town with a large Asian American population. Uppuluri's parents may have made a deliberate effort not to emphasize his Asian ethnicities because of the Southern milieu in which they lived. Research on Asian American communities in the South indicates that when these ethnic communities are very small, there is a greater tendency to assimilate and a corresponding reluctance to call attention to one's difference.[11] The small size of the Asian American population in Oak Ridge and the surrounding areas might have had a significant impact on why Uppuluri did not primarily see himself specifically as Indian American or Japanese American or as a panethnic Asian American. Paul Spickard's work calls attention to the differing levels of ethnic identification among Japanese Americans in various parts of the United States. He cites research to show that in areas of high Japanese American concentration, such as Hawaii and California, individuals are much more likely to identify as Japanese American, take greater pride in their ethnic heritage, and be more sensitive to assaults on their ethnic group than in areas where the numbers of the ethnic group are small (99–100).

Uppuluri reflects that there were no Indian American or other Asian Americans in his class throughout his high school years. "If I had grown up even in Knoxville, I would have had a larger group with which to identify. If I had been graduating high school in Knoxville today, I would have had peers with whom I could have felt a strong sense of ethnic similarity and identity." As it was, there was no peer network. Further complicating this "isolation" from ethnic influences is the fact that Uppuluri is an only child; so there were no siblings at home with whom he could begin to question and understand his racial heritage. Consequently, Uppuluri's socialization as Asian American (Indian or Japanese American) was minimal. Further, he was not politicized into thinking of himself as an "other," whose voice was denied opportunity to speak. Carole Uhlaner's research in the relationship between perceived discrimination and the creation of an ethnic self leads her to conclude that "the experience of prejudice reinforces a sense of ethnic identity. . . . Ethnic identity and perceived inequity come together in the concept of group consciousness" (341).[12] If anything, growing up in Oak Ridge provided Uppuluri with the chance to be vocal and visible. He was president of the student council and a leader in student affairs.

Two other factors likely played an important part in Uppuluri's minimal sense of an ethnic self: gender and class. I have argued elsewhere that women in immigrant and diasporic communities are seen as the repositories of cultural memory and are expected to preserve and reproduce ethnic traditions, while such expectations are not placed upon the male (151–161). Uppuluri's relative freedom from performing ethnic-specific roles can be clearly attributed to his gender.

Being the son of professionals, his father a scientist and his mother an educator, Uppuluri also enjoyed the benefit of class in avoiding the pressures of assuming an ethnic identity. Michael Omi's observation that "distinct class strata in the Asian American community experience a *differen-*

tial racialization" (207, Omi's emphasis) explains why Uppuluri was able to grow up feeling as if his ethnicities did not matter greatly to his sense of self. Had he been of working class background, the majority culture would have more quickly labeled him as "the other." Madhulika Khandelwal's study of Indians in New York City reinforces Omi's claim. She differentiates between those Indians who settled in Manhattan in the years before 1965, and those who arrived after 1965 and settled in Queens. The former were largely upper-middle class, Western-educated intellectuals who were viewed as cultural emissaries by the majority culture; the latter were of varying class backgrounds, including lower-middle and working class, and, therefore, less easily accepted by the majority culture and more inclined to separate themselves from mainstream living (181–84).

Thus, it comes as no surprise that before Uppuluri's departure to Princeton, his sense of ethnic identity was minimally developed. At Princeton, he had his first encounter with the politics of being Asian American. There he started receiving literature from the Asian American Students Association, and, as Uppuluri puts it, he was disturbed, because he was being courted for and because of his ethnicity. "I felt that I wasn't being valued for who I was as an individual, but for my ethnicity, the Asian American facet of myself. I was offended by the approach and what it implied." His sense of ethnic identity insufficiently developed as it was, Uppuluri did not see himself primarily as either Indian American or Japanese American. A panethnic Asian American consciousness was even further from his conception of self at this time. As a result, he held himself apart both from ethnic-specific and panethnic Asian American rhetoric on campus.

Uppuluri returned south to Nashville after his graduation to work as a reporter. Gradually, his sense of himself as a East Tennessean was being strengthened. In a 1994 interview with Rohit Vyas of TV Asia, when questioned about the richness of his dual heritage from two of the world's oldest civilizations, Uppuluri responded by saying, "And don't forget a third influence, that of East Tennessee." When asked to define himself, he most readily calls himself an Oak Ridger and then an East Tennessean.

Theresa Kay Williams, who has done research on Amerasian (Afroasian and Eurasian) children on U.S. military bases in Japan, demonstrates that a critical mass of mixed-race children is essential before these individuals develop a sense of themselves as a separate identity. "The 'haafu' label created by the Japanese media to refer primarily to Eurasians was used in interviews by both Eurasians and Afroasians [themselves] as a term of identification" (283). Williams contends that this label and the adoption of it by mixed-race children confirmed existence for this group of Amerasians; it signaled that they themselves acknowledged their existence as

a category of people (302), and it meant that they had successfully negotiated and manufactured an identity where none existed initially. In
Uppuluri's case, the lack of Asian American peers and similarly identified
others was perhaps instrumental in his identification largely with "regional" markers (in his case, being East Tennessean and an Oak Ridger)
rather than ethnic ones. Thus, before the start of the campaign, Uppuluri
stood at a distance from both the Indian American and Japanese American
communities.

Perhaps the most significant contribution of Williams's research is that
she shows how impossible it is to expect identity development to follow
predictable lines. For Uppuluri, the factors impinging on his sense of self
were numerous and complex in their interplay—his parents' different racial and cultural heritages, being an only child, growing up in a small
southern town, growing up in a predominantly scientific and atypically
liberal community, and lack of ethnically similar peers.

One thing, however, appears to be certain in regard to Uppuluri's development of identity: when he began his campaign, he largely thought
of himself as a product of his town, but as his campaign progressed, he
grew increasingly to reflect on his identity as an Indian American (both
Uppuluri and his campaign workers have spoken about this aspect of
the campaign). I would argue that at the start of the campaign Uppuluri
was neither emphatically Japanese American nor Indian American but emphatically Tennessean; either aspect of his ethnic self could have gained
the ascendancy during the campaign. It was the Indian American community's interest in Uppuluri that led to the Indianization of Uppuluri and
not what Narasaki believes to have been the case, which is that Uppuluri's
greater comfort and sense of identification with being Indian American led
him to turn to this community for help. As George Kitahara Kich points
out, the development of one's ethnic sense of self is closely linked to the
degree of acceptance by the ethnic groups in question (304). Interviews
with mixed-race African Japanese persons bears out Kich's conclusion.
Christine Iijima Hall found that many African Japanese individuals identify with the black community because they are more readily accepted by
blacks than by the Japanese (258–59).

There is an ironic twist in the narrative of Uppuluri's identity. Two
years before Uppuluri declared his candidacy, he became dramatically involved with his mother's antecedents: he assumed the position of coordinator of the International Friendship Bell project to mark the fiftieth anniversary of Oak Ridge as a town. The idea for the bell came from Shigeko
and K.R.R. Uppuluri in 1988 "to symbolize the new friendship between
Japan and Tennessee" (Siemens, *The Oak Ridger*, July 14, 1988:3).[13] In
1991, Oak Ridge adopted for its anniversary celebration the theme "Born

of War—Living for Peace—Growing Through Science" and saw the bell as serving to "memorialize those who died in World War II" and to "symbolize the fact that the enemity [*sic*] between nations can be healed and the people can work together toward peace and for the benefit of all citizens" (Carey, *The Oak Ridger*, July 17, 1991). The bell, which was designed and cast in Kyoto, Japan, is a Japanese temple bell. It is made of solid metal, is eight feet tall, and weighs approximately 8,250 pounds. Much controversy surrounded the inscriptions that are etched on the bell. Veterans' groups fiercely protested the project, claiming that the bell rewrites history "to make America appear to be the villain in World War II" (Kelly and Kelly, *The Oak Ridger*, Tuesday, August 17, 1993) and serves as an apology to Japan when none is needed or deserved.

I invoke the Friendship Bell for several reasons: to show Uppuluri's visibility in Oak Ridge, to remind readers that his written statements in support of the bell arguing against Veterans groups' denunciation of it could not have been missed by area Japanese and Japanese Americans, and to demonstrate that even as he spoke out about reaching to Japan he was also celebrating Oak Ridge and declaring his unequivocal allegiance to the town of his youth.

On August 31, 1993, Uppuluri wrote in *The Oak Ridger's* letters to the editor that "the International Friendship Bell is not an apology" and that "Oak Ridgers should feel proud of what was accomplished here during the war." The bell, writes Uppuluri, celebrates Oak Ridge, "[a] city on the frontiers of science . . . [n]estled away in the hills of Tennessee . . . [a] Secret City." Thus, shortly before the announcement of his candidacy, Uppuluri represented himself as a solid Oak Ridge resident.

In early 1994, when Uppuluri declared his candidacy, he did it in the midst of long-standing Oak Ridge residents, including his school teachers and the director of the ORNL. The site chosen for the announcement was the Alexander Inn, a historic landmark in Oak Ridge, where scientific celebrities such as Robert Oppenheimer had stayed. Uppuluri's campaign was decidedly drawing attention to itself as a local endeavor. It did not start out with even a trace of an Indian American or Japanese American perspective.

The manner in which the campaign became an object of interest to the Indian American community reveals the fortuitous and unplanned nature of that link. A fellow Oak Ridger, Anand Raman (junior to Uppuluri by several years in High school), heard through his parents about the announcement of Uppuluri's candidacy. Raman called Uppuluri from Yale, where he was studying at the time, and asked if Uppuluri had someone helping him. When Uppuluri indicated that he did not have a staff put together as yet, Raman informed him that he had just the person for him.

Raman put Uppuluri in touch with Subodh Chandra, and thus began Uppuluri's entry into the Indian American network. Baiju Shah, Mahesh Ram, Sejal Mehta, Neil Parekh, Jay Reddy, Jay Chaudhuri, and Meena Morey, who helped Uppuluri at various centers of his campaign, were all Indian American. As Uppuluri says, "My campaign attracted some of the brightest most committed second generation Indian Americans. In some ways that was what was so exciting about it for me."

One way of looking at Uppuluri's response is to see it as a serendipitous discovery of the ethnic peer group he was lacking in his years at high school. In other words, there was no grand plan to narrow the gap between Uppuluri, with his minimal sense of an Indian/Japanese/Asian American self, and Indian Americans. The embracing of his candidacy by the Indian American community was a transformative experience for Uppuluri. Uppuluri, Shah, and Chandra concur that the campaign was as much a run for political office as it was or became a journey in the search for self. Prior to the campaign, Uppuluri had conceived of himself as a Southerner, an East Tennessean who happened to have an unusual and mixed heritage. True, he had attended the TANA (Telugu Association of North America) conference in Atlanta in 1990 and visited the Nashville Ganesha temple (although his religious membership is with the Unitarian church in Oak Ridge). But the *campaign* drew Uppuluri down the emotional road of ethnic identification as an Indian American.

Exactly why his candidacy had such greater resonance for Indian Americans than for Japanese Americans is that Indian Americans have only recently become aware of their need to get politically visible and to place persons of their background in prominent positions of office.[14] Their sense of urgency regarding political involvement is much greater than that of Japanese Americans who, because of their longer residence in this country, have already entered the political system and occupy significant offices. In addition, Japanese Americans have established contacts with dominant-culture political groups, and so can rely for their support on non-Asian Americans. In fact, as Espiritu's book *Asian American Panethnicity* reveals, Japanese and Chinese Americans know how to work the system better than other more recently arrived Asian American subgroups, and can appeal to non-Asian American voters.[15]

One recent study further underscores this differing sense of urgency among various Asian American subgroups with regard to entering the political system. James Lai shows that in a three-way race involving a Japanese American, Korean American, and Filipina American candidate, the Japanese American candidate had the most contributions from non Asian Americans. The Korean and Filipina American candidates relied heavily on their ethnic groups for money (112–115).

The Japanese Americans' greater familiarity with the political system is further illustrated in Mark Takano's campaign. Like Uppuluri, Takano ran in the 1994 congressional primary. He stood from California's Forty-third District. Support for Takano came from several political action committees (PACs), whereas Uppuluri had virtually no PAC contributions.[16] His support was almost totally from individual contributors, showing that like the Korean and Filipino Americans of Lai's study, Indian Americans are still in the early stages of organizing as a political force and have yet to secure political influence among dominant-group voters.

THE REALITIES OF CLOSING THE GAP

Panethnic coalitions are still an ideal. They can be built only if one understands the complex dynamics at play. The ways in which Uppuluri's campaign failed to become a bridge between the Indian and Japanese American communities are instructive. While Baiju Shah initially hoped for a good response from the Japanese American community, his early attempts to reach the community, through newspapers and through fund-raising professionals, did not generate any tangible result. Shah, as a campaign professional concerned with effective use of resources, made the decision to concentrate efforts where they were most likely to yield returns. Uppuluri, on the other hand, began the campaign with minimal expectations of Japanese American community involvement and did not urge Shah to pursue it. Instead the campaign drew on the overwhelmingly positive response of the Indian American community for donations and emotional support.

Japanese Americans already have some political visibility and probably had less reason than the Indian American community to back the candidate. Had Uppuluri's ethnic heritage combined the Indian with one of the politically less represented subgroups of Asian Americans—Filipino or Vietnamese, for example—there might have been joint efforts to have him elected (as Lai's study suggests). It appears that no gap can be closed unless all the parties involved perceive a need to do so. Further, this initial perception of need must be followed by meaningful and often-repeated efforts to create spaces and contexts within which the separate groups can come together. Dominant groups may have to make several gestures of invitation to peripheral groups. The latter may have to assert themselves so as to establish a presence, continually challenging yet negotiating with groups at the center. Ultimately, all individuals and groups involved have to feel it is worthwhile to expend energy, fundamentally modify perspective, and commit time in the service of coalition building. In Uppuluri's campaign, that did not happen.

Notes

1. However, see Min Song's essay in this volume for a discussion of one sphere in which the lives of turn-of-the-century Japanese and Asian Indian immigrants intersected in a significant way.

2. See James Siu-Fong Lai's 1994 Master of Arts thesis, "At the Threshold of the Golden Door—Ethnic Politics and Pan–Asian Pacific American Coalition Building: A Case Study of the Special 1991 California 46th Assembly District Primary Election" (in the UCLA Asian American Studies library holdings) for the examination of a recent election involving three Asian American candidates—Japanese American, Korean American, and Filipina American—from the same district. The Korean American and Filipina American candidates were unwilling to negotiate with the Japanese American candidate to come up with a consensus candidate, because they saw the situation as an opportune moment to elect someone from their respective ethnic group to the State Assembly. The result was that the Asian American vote was split three ways, and a non–Asian American candidate won.

3. Baiju Shah was replaced in April 1994 by Sejal Mehta.

4. Subodh Chandra, who was instrumental in connecting Uppuluri with the Indian American community, remarks that "the Indian Americans saw in him the possibility that their sons, too, could one day run for political office."

5. For a discussion of the question of political activism by members of the Asian American media, see Diane Yen-Mei Wong, "Will the Real Asian American Please Stand Up?" in *The State of Asian America: A Public Policy Report. Policy Issues to the Year 2020* (LEAP Asian Pacific American Public Policy Institute and UCLA Asian American Studies Center, 1993), especially 270–277. Wong writes, "Some of the most difficult questions facing Asian Pacific American journalists are: Am I a journalist first or an Asian Pacific first? How does that affect work as a journalist? Do I advocate or do I remain totally neutral?" (275).

6. Both *AsianWeek* and *Rafu Shimpo* give valuable presentations of his qualifications as they related to the needs of his constituency.

7. In his study, James Lai compares the pan-Asian focus of *Rafu Shimpo* to the ethnic-specific coverage of Korean and Filipino American newspapers.

8. Contributors' ethnic groups were determined by their last names.

9. See Susan B. Gall and Timothy L. Gall, eds., *Statistical Record of Asian Americans* (Detroit, Washington, D.C.: Gale Research Inc., 1993), 647–53. According to 1990 census figures, the largest numbers of Japanese are found in Honolulu (195,149), Los Angeles–Long Beach (129,736), San Jose (26,516), San Francisco (23,682), and Seattle (22,835). New York is the only East Coast city with a significant Japanese American population (26,422). The corresponding numbers of Asian Indians for the same cities are Honolulu (864), Los Angeles–Long Beach (43,829), San Jose (20,164), San Francisco (8,531), Seattle (5,914), and New York City (106,270).

10. Cable, along with Thomas Shriver and Lachelle Norris, has interviewed eighty Oak Ridge residents. They plan to collect their interviews in a book tenta-

tively titled *The Vision Lives On: An Oral History of Work and Play in the Atomic City*. Two historians, Charles Johnson and Charles Jackson, also conducted interviews in writing their account of Oak Ridge.

11. Fred R. von der Mehden, writing of the Japanese in Houston, observes, "The small size of the Japanese population here meant greater interaction with other elements of the community, unlike their counterparts on the West Coast. In addition, the Japanese-Americans moving into the city did not congregate in one isolated residential area, but made their homes in various parts of metropolitan Houston. This . . . accelerated the process of assimilation." See his chapter "Japanese," in *The Ethnic Groups of Houston*, edited by Fred R. von der Mehden (Houston: Rice University Studies, 1984), 108–9. He attributes the high acculturation of the *sansei* and the *yonsei* in the Houston area partly to the "small and somewhat fragmented Japanese community" (111). James W. Loewen, in his study *The Mississippi Chinese* (Prospect Heights, Illinois: Waveland Press, 1988), explains that before 1940, "there were too few Chinese, spread too thinly throughout the Delta's sprawling area, to warrant a 'Chinatown' or cultural center for the group. If the Chinese community had been larger or more concentrated, its members could have reassured each other of their worth and dignity according to Chinese standards. As it was, the internalized values of the emigrants were not reinforced, and they found it hard to resist the challenges offered by the value system of white Mississippi" (71–72).

12. Werner Sollors, in *Beyond Ethnicity*, uses the term "ethnic" disingenuously, observing that the Yankee is also ethnic. He deliberately elides over the deployment of "ethnic" in the social and political spheres as "Other," "backward," "underprivileged," and "different and therefore less than the 'norm.'"

13. Some citations from *The Oak Ridger* are missing page numbers. The only access I had to past issues of the paper were photocopied sheets; several of these sheets, while they clearly specified the date of publication, did not indicate page numbers.

14. In 1994, three Indian Americans ran unsuccessfully for House seats in the United States Congress: Ram Upppuluri, Neil Dhillon from the Sixth Congressional District of Maryland, and Peter Mathews from the Thirty-eighth Congressional district of California. Since Dilip Singh Saund of California served between 1956 and 1960 in the United States House of Representatives, no Indian American has held an elected position at the national level. However, Indian Americans have held *appointed* positions of importance at the national and state level, as well as elected positions in State legislatures—for example, Nirmala McGonigley of the Wyoming State Legislature, and Kumar P. Barve of the Maryland House of Delegates. See *Statistical Record of Asian Americans*, 722–29, for a list of elected and appointed Indian American officials.

15. See Yen Le Espiritu, *Asian American Panethnicity: Bridging Institutions and Identities* (Philadelphia: Temple University Press, 1992), 75–79, 96–99. See also James Lai, "At The Threshold of the Golden Door": "The more developed Asian groups, such as the pre– World War II Chinese and Japanese Americans, who have been in the United States for more than two or more generations, tend

to become politically incorporated within the mainstream political networks and institutions" (109).

16. Data provided by the Federal Election Commission.

INTERVIEWS

Sherry Cable, sociologist, University of Tennessee, Knoxville, October 1995.

Gerard Lim, staff writer, *AsianWeek*, March 1995.

Karen Narasaki, director, Asian Pacific American Legal Consortium, October 1995.

Mahesh Ram, Uppuluri's campaign coordinator in New York City, October 1995.

Anand Raman, Uppuluri's friend, who grew up in Oak Ridge with the candidate, November 1995.

Jay Reddy, Uppuluri's campaign coordinator in Washington, D.C., October 1995.

Baiju Shah, Uppuluri's overall campaign strategist and coordinator between December 1993 and April 1994, interview, March 1995; phone conversation, October 1995.

Ram Yoshino Uppuluri: several interviews conducted between February 1995 and May 1995.

Rohit Vyas of TV Asia: television interview with Ram Uppuluri.

Martha Wallace, chief of staff for former congresswoman Marilyn Lloyd, for whose vacated seat Uppuluri was contending, February 1995.

Kazuo Inafuku, of the *Southern Journal of Houston;* June Kawaguchi of *Nichi Bei Times;* Kimi Nakashima of the *Chicago Shimpo;* Takeshi Nakayama of *Rafu Shimpo;* Richard Suenaga of *Pacific Citizen;* Sandi Taniguchi of the *Northwest Nikkei;* J. K. Yamamoto of *Hokubei Mainichi;* Joy Yamauchi of *Tozai Times;* and Paul Yempuku of *Hawaii Hochi/Hawaii Herald;* all in October 1995.

WORKS CITED

"Asian American Runs for Congress in Tennessee." *Rafu Shimpo* Feb. 1, 1994, 1.

Azuma, Eiichiro. "Interethnic Conflict Under Racial Subordination: Japanese Immigrants and Their Asian Neighbors in Walnut Grove, California, 1908–1941. *Amerasia Journal.* 20.2 (1994): 27–56.

Campbell, Jim. "Endorsing Third District candidates." Editorial. *The Oak Ridger,* July 22, 1994.

Carey, Ruth. "Friendship Bell to become permanent monument and attraction for tourists." *The Oak Ridger,* July 17, 1991.

Dockery, William. "Uppuluri, Whorley deserve support." Editorial. *Knoxville News-Sentinel,* July 1, 1994.

Espiritu, Yen Le. *Asian American Panethnicity: Bridging Institutions and Identities.* Philadelphia: Temple University Press, 1992.

Gall, Susan B., and Timothy L. Gall, eds. *Statistical Record of Asian Americans.* Detroit: Gale Research Inc., 1993.

Hall, Christine Iijima. "Please Choose One: Ethnic Identity Choices for Biracial Individuals." In *Racially Mixed People in America,* edited by Maria P. P. Root. Newbury Park, Calif.: Sage Publications, 1992, 250–64.

Johnson, Charles W., and Charles O. Jackson. *A City Behind a Fence: Oak Ridge, Tennessee 1942–1946.* Knoxville: University of Tennessee Press, 1981.

Kelly, Milton J., and Tommye F. Kelly. Letter to the Editor. *The Oak Ridger,* Aug.17, 1993.

Khandelwal, Madhulika S. "Indian Immigrants in Queens, New York City: Patterns of Spatial Concentration and Distribution, 1965–1990." In *Nation and Migration: The Politics of Space in South Asian Diaspora,* edited by Peter van der Veer. Philadelphia: University of Pennsylvania Press, 1995, 178–96.

Kich, Kitahara George. "The Developmental Process of Asserting a Biracial, Bicultural Identity." In *Racially Mixed People in America,* edited by Maria P. P. Root. Newbury Park, Calif.: Sage Publications, 1992, 304–17.

Lai, James, "At the Threshold of the Golden Door—Ethnic Politics and Pan-Asian Pacific American Coalition Building: A Case Study of the Special 1991 California 46th Assembly District Primary Election," master's thesis, University of California–Los Angeles, 1994.

Lim, Gerard. "Uppuluri Throws Hat in Congressional Ring." *AsianWeek: The English Language Journal for the National Asian American Community* 15.23 (Feb. 4, 1994): 1.

Omi, Michael. "Out of the Melting Pot and Into the Fire." In *The State of Asian Pacific America: A Public Policy Report. Policy Issues to the Year 2020.* Los Angeles: LEAP Asian Pacific American Public Policy Institute and UCLA Asian American Studies Center, 1993, 199–214.

Pasha, Kamran. "A Candidate for All People." *A Magazine* (Summer 1994): 20.

Saund, D. S. *Congressman from India.* New York: E. P. Dutton. 1960.

Siemens, Audrey. "Friendship Bell Is planned for Oak Ridge area." *The Oak Ridger,* July 14, 1988, 3.

Spickard, Paul R. *Mixed Blood: Intermarriage and Ethnic Identity in Twentieth-Century America.* Madison: University of Wisconsin Press, 1989.

Srikanth, Rajini. "Gender and the Images of Home in the Asian American Diaspora: A Socio-Literary Reading of Some Asian American Works." *Critical Mass: A Journal of Asian American Criticism* 2.1 (Winter 1994): 147–81.

Stephan, Cookie White. "Mixed-Heritage Individuals: Ethnic Identity and Trait Characteristics." In *Racially Mixed People in America.* edited by Maria P. P. Root. Newbury Park, Calif.: Sage Publications, 1992, 50–63.

Uhlaner, Carol. "Perceived Discrimination and Prejudice and the Coalition Prospects of Blacks, Latinos, and Asian Americans." In *Racial and Ethnic Politics in California,* edited by Bryan O. Jackson and Michael B. Preston. Berkeley, Calif.: IGS Press at University of California, 1991, 339–70.

Uppuluri, Ram Y. "The bell is not an apology." *The Oak Ridger,* Aug. 31, 1993.

Williams, Teresa Kay. "Prism Lives: Identity of Binational Amerasians." In *Ra-*

cially Mixed People in America. edited by Maria P. P. Root. Newbury Park, Calif.: Sage Publications, 1992, 280–303.

Wong, Diane Yen-Mei. "Will the Real Asian Pacific American Please Stand Up?" In *The State of Asian Pacific America: A Public Policy Report: Policy Issues to the Year 2020.* Los Angeles: LEAP Asian Pacific American Policy Institute and UCLA Asian American Studies Center, 1993, 263–81.

IV. LITERARY TEXTS AND DIASPORICS

RUTH YU HSIAO

10   A World Apart

A Reading of South Asian American Literature

THE HISTORICAL and cultural differences that separate South Asians from East Asians have also created divisions in academic discourse. The differences are real enough, and we would be deceiving ourselves to minimize their impact on literature. The mostly educated, middle-class South Asians who came to the United States after 1965 have roots in a subcontinent of such diverse linguistic, cultural, and religious traditions that the colonial legacy of bilingualism survives well into the present. This alone makes for an undeniable difference. Their linguistic bilingualism reflects a cultural bilingualism that equips them to see the world as multi-centered with fluid boundaries. A term as delimiting as Asian American, which also denotes political sensitivities and historical oppressions that post-1965 South Asian Americans do not share, understandably means little and is perhaps suspiciously patronizing.

In recent years the Association for Asian American Studies has issued repeated calls for an expanded vision for Asian America that would include all ethnic Asian people in the United States.[1] In the classroom, the increased diversity of students has forced many of us to expand our curricula and introduce a greater variety of ethnic authors of Asian origin. In 1987 I began including works by Bharati Mukherjee as part of a course on Asian American literature. The trend to expand the definition of "Asian America" continues as students demand the inclusion of works that speak to their particular ethnic identity.

The classroom merely mirrors the fracturing and rapid shifts in the global movement. It destabilizes our previous notions of identity based on mother tongue, static culture, and national boundary. Bilingualism, for example, is becoming increasingly common among other Asian immigrants in the latter part of this century. There is nothing very extraordinary about South Asians; they seem, on the contrary, very familiar. The global movement of remigration has brought increasing numbers of migrants to North America from lands that were formerly colonial possessions. Reflecting this trend, the meaning of "Diaspora," previously applied exclusively to the dispersal of the Jewish people, now takes a lowercase "d" and enjoys growing popularity as an academic topic for exploration. Many nationalities claim a diasporic component to their culture, and every ethnic group sees itself as part of an international movement. Asian Americans are no exception. The change in immigration patterns of Asians to the United States in the post-1965 and post–Vietnam War era brought growing numbers of Southeast Asians, Pacific Islanders, and South Asians to North America from ports other than their respective homelands, with a variety of hybrid cultural backgrounds.

Pedagogy and cultural history in this case have a theoretical analogue. Postmodernist thinking, as summarized by Linda Hutcheon, prepares us to see the disparate Asian ethnic groups united by "difference." As previous or current "ex-centrics," these groups challenge the center and force reconsideration of differences.[2] In defining minority discourse, Abdul R. JanMohamed and David Lloyd stress the need to articulate this discourse "in the singular" so that we can "describe and define the *common denominators* that link various minority cultures" because "cultures designated as minorities have certain shared experiences by virtue of their similar antagonistic relationship to the dominant culture" (1). From their different vantage points the literary and academic discourses of various Asian ethnic groups in America offer both a multiple reflection and a criticism of the center. Postmodernism has been thrust on them; they are united by difference, reinforcing commonality in diversity. The question of whether South Asians have anything in common with other Asian Americans merely signifies a passage in the politics of difference.

Like it or not, ethnocentrism and cultural specificity are giving way to a globalizing Pan-Asian sensibility, which is currently being debated on a theoretical level.[3] This passage in reconciling "multiplicity and difference" has the felicitous effect of stimulating literary output. The flowering of Asian American literature in recent years reflects the presence of new ethnic groups, as compared to the century before.[4] Literature by Asians in America shares an important commonality, which forms the basis for my reading of three works by South Asians.

The migratory experience produces disorientation and drastic changes that inevitably affect the immigrant's sense of identity. According to one study, the relatively high ratio of professionals and high levels of income may give South Asians the appearance of being different from other Asian groups. They are perceived to be free of the psychological disturbances experienced by other immigrant Asian groups, but, in fact, they are not.[5] A common thread that runs through all literary expressions of ethnic groups is the evolving self-identity of ethnic writers as reflected in their works. Whether in autobiography or in fiction, they write primarily to name themselves and to represent their experiences as they go through the various stages of encountering the dominant society. In his essay "Imagi-

nary Homelands," Salman Rushdie, himself a writer in diaspora, main-
tains that "to be an Indian writer in this [British] society is to face, every
day, problems of definition" (17) This is true not only for Asian Americans, East Asians, and South Asians, but for other American ethnic writers
as well.[6] In fact, this holds true for all minorities writing in the language
of the dominant culture. It is my intention to show that this ever changing and evolving identity manifests itself in different modes in each writer's work.

As with all nascent literature, South Asian and other Asian groups in
America have created a hybrid culture rooted both in what they have
brought with them and in the New World, which has become the "native
soil" that feeds the imagination. Even in the most hostile soil, as in the
conditions that greeted the early pioneers from China on the West Coast,
the seed germinated in the form of autobiographies and memoirs and
verses. However marginalized, a literature that both perceives itself, and
is perceived by the outside world, as being on the fringe displays a tenacity
in claiming a piece of the native ground. It is not accidental that the planting and growth metaphor has always been associated with American literature, which was for a long time Eurocentrically considered an offshoot
of European traditions.[7] Every ethnic literature repeats a similar cycle of
growth from seed to flowering; as James Clifford has noted, "Even the
harshest conditions of travel, the most exploitative regimes, do not entirely quell resistance or the emergence of diasporic and migrant cultures"
(108). Ethnic literature expresses this cycle of growth with its clusters
of themes marking the self-orientation of the writers on the migratory
journey.

This determination to preserve and reformulate identity makes its imprint on ethnic literatures in the United States, resulting in discernible and
definable modes of writing. These modes roughly echo the social and psychological stages migrants pass through in a new place away from their
ancestral land. Social scientists and psychologists have documented the
various stages of adjustment experienced by migratory and ethnic people.[8]
Not surprisingly, in her introduction to Asian American writings, Elaine
Kim categorizes them according to the self-identity they project; for example, "Ambassadors of Goodwill," "Chinatown Cowboys and Warrior
Women," or "Second-Generation Self-Portrait." These labels, I maintain,
are associated with the writers' own self-perceptions, whether as immigrants, immigrants' offspring, or native-born ethnic Americans.

My earlier writing argues that all ethnic writings, beginning with Jewish American literature, exhibit three modes of self-identity.[9] The first
mode is that of the emissary. Here the author explains his or her ethnic
identity and culture to a mainstream audience. In the second mode, there

is a declaration of the American self and a claiming of Americanness. The third mode is characterized by experimentation. In this stage, the author deconstructs fixed identities, explores the limits of the ethnic self, and reconstitutes notions of ethnicity. I will summarize here how these modes of expressing identity work. On the whole, Asian American literature reflects the writer's sense of identity as an ethnic minority in the majority culture. In examining the development of this literature, I have noticed three different modes of expression, based on the self-identity projected by the narrative voice. They conform to an evolutionary transformation according to changing external conditions. Historically these modes were shaped by external events and internal acculturation within the ethnic group. But the modes have persisted beyond the historical and social circumstances.

In the classroom this paradigm enables the students to better understand the literature by appreciating each work for its self-projecting voice that expresses its place in history. I am able to teach a variety of genres from autobiography to film, finding the four modes operating in every work of art. One mode, dominating an earlier era, is not more primitive or undeveloped than one that dominates a later or the contemporary literary scene. In fact, all three modes continue to exist side by side. In the works of many writers the modes may overlap and coexist. I am concerned only with the predominant voice or mode discernible in the writing.

In this essay I will focus on three works of South Asian writers, *My Own Country* by Abraham Verghese, *Coming through Slaughter* by Michael Ondaatje, and *The Holder of the World* by Bharati Mukherjee. Their biographies read like those of many recent South Asian immigrants to North America, showing a relative ease in crossing borders. All three writers have lived in, or immigrated to, Canada or the United States, or both. This short list necessarily excludes such important writers as V. S. Naipaul, Ved Mehta, Meena Alexander, Pico Iyer, and Sara Suleri, who also have intimate links to the Americas. I want to show how the authors I have chosen simultaneously exemplify in their writing the three modes of ethnic literature.

CAUGHT BETWEEN TWO WORLDS

From immigrant to American-born, the writers in this first mode project the voice of an explainer, one who has not yet regained a "homeland" after having lost an earlier one. We recognize that "between worlds" voice, a term used by Amy Ling to characterize female writers of Chinese descent, some of whom employ an apologetic, bridging-the-East-and-the-West tone and others who voice an angry protest for being outside of both worlds. Elaine Kim characterizes the former the "ambassadors of goodwill to the West" (24), and the latter as "Cowboys" and "Warrior Women" (173–213), with the two separated by a gulf created by the civil rights movement. This voice is by turns polite and caustic, humble and proud, patriotic and condemning. Jade Snow Wong's autobiography *Fifth Chinese Daughter* perfectly illustrates the apologetic posture. Its publication in 1950 came almost a century after the first shipload of Chinese laborers arrived in California in pursuit of their golden dream. To cast off the legacy of humiliation and misunderstanding and persecution meted out to the Chinese by a century of exclusion laws and racist practices, Wong's narrative centers around a "model" Chinatown family upholding positive values transplanted from China. Wong masked anger with a conciliatory and somewhat lighthearted tone. Her tone was dismissed by the next generation of Chinatown sons and daughters, who answered to the clarion call of 1960s protest.

Protest is merely the obverse of apology. The protesters, unlike apologists, dare to name the pain of exclusion, of being caught between two worlds. Saul Bellow's "dangling man" serves as a perfect metaphor of the frustration of the children of immigrants who feel left out. Genuine feelings of injury and frustration supplant the civility and accommodation that a more repressive era demanded of writers who sought approval in order to be published. In the decade of social and political radicalism in the thirties, for example, the voice of protest produced the "radical novel," the "proletarian novel," and "folk literature," all vying for a foothold in the American literary scene, and Jewish American writers, such as Michael Gold, used their pens to assail the establishment. Asian Americans vented their anger and expressed their social and political agenda through literature during the civil rights era. Emboldened and empowered by the Asian American movement, a new generation of Asians Americans with a heightened awareness of the historical injustices inflicted on their race came of age. They directed their indignation not only at the racist society but also at the ethnic traditions and values of the not-yet-assimilated world of home. The trouble is, in their hearts they could not distance themselves from the real and imagined ghetto in which their protagonists linger and dwell. Being perceived as "foreign" by mainstream society only compounded the anguish over the "between worlds" space they occupy.

The protest had the effect of exorcism and forged a new style, or voice, in this mode. As "Asian American" became a term of racial pride and a source of defiance toward the dominant culture, there emerged a nascent literary movement on the West Coast. Young Asian Americans organized poetry workshops and theater productions. The struggle went on internally, too, in gender politics that will likely continue for some years to come.[10]

The novels and plays by the generation that came of age in the civil rights era articulated a distinctly Asian American voice and self-defined identity. Defying the between-world marginalization, they elevated their own "folk" material and sought new ways to express themselves. A major spokesman from this group, Frank Chin, expressed the frustration of ethnic writers like him—with no language of their own—in the play *Chickencoop Chinaman*:

> I am the natural born ragmouth speaking the motherless bloody tongue. No real language of my own to make sense with, so out comes everybody else's trash that don't conceive. But the sound truth is that I AM THE NOTORIOUS ONE AND ONLY CHICKENCOOP CHINAMAN HIMSELF. . . . I speak nothing but the mother tongues bein' born to none of my own, I talk the talk of orphans. (7 and 8)

The militant stance, however, freed Asian American literature to develop its own tradition. The anger and protest paved the way for consolidation and growth.

Abraham Verghese's *My Own Country* (1994) is a good example of the first mode. On the surface, Verghese resembles his East Asian counterparts in the first stage of the "bridge" (cultural emissary) and the in-between-worlds writers. These writers derive much of their material from their own lives—Verghese's medical practice and family life—as a bridge between the ethnic world and the larger society. They unavoidably fall into the role of spokesperson and in part fulfill the responsibility of "explaining" and "bridging." Memoirs are a prevailing genre of this mode, and Verghese's book is an exemplary memoir of his experiences as an infectious disease specialist at the time the HIV epidemic first appeared in the bucolic hinterlands of Tennessee. The narrative voice of *My Own Country* also harks back to the theme of "rebirth" in America, frequently employed by immigrant novelists.

I could go on about the parallels between this book and the first mode of cultural emissary, but I will end here with one more observation. Verghese's book conforms with the first mode in its formal elements but less so in addressing the identity issues that were important to the earlier East Asian writers. Post-1965 America differs from the prewar America in important ways having to do with racial attitudes and public policy. For one thing, Verghese's narrative does not follow that of a journey toward fulfilling the American Dream. On the contrary, *My Own Country* reflects a built-in sojourner mentality and a state of inner exile. Verghese takes a rather dim view of success as measured by income or even professional satisfaction, since his efforts against the deadly virus are ultimately doomed; these feelings are exacerbated by the further frustrations of the limited resources allotted to him as a staff doctor and the social ostracism he encounters as a doctor treating patients with AIDS. Despite the possession of and identification with America implied by the title of the book, the narrator does not feel at home in his "own country" nor in his profession. He remains aloof from institutional medicine and its politics. Initiated into the politics of AIDS treatment, he learns that a hierarchy exists, with those specialties relying on high-tech invasive procedures on top and the lowly infectious disease and internists at the lower end: "On the playing field of medicine, with all its established positions and specialized players, I felt increasingly like the man from the moon, the man playing left-out (262). The journey is not about making it in the promised land, but a lonely journey of "playing left-out." He is equally alienated from his fellow Indian doctors in the Tri-Cities area. Their talk of "stock options and mutual funds and the benefits of incorporating" tires him (166). Not simply deracination and displacement, but the more basic alienation of living by principles and beliefs that go against the grain of a materialistic society, places him between two worlds.

The loneliness of belonging nowhere is the leitmotif of the narrative, which Verghese skillfully builds up. This journey into the heartland of America—the small-town culture—becomes a descent into wrenching pain and disillusionment. Most painful of all is the isolation he feels in his own home, in his marriage. His wife is fearful of his exposure to the deadly virus and complains about his frequent absence as a husband and a father to their young son. His sense of alienation echoes that of his HIV-positive patients, rather than that of the frustrated children of immigrants. Born in Africa of Indian parentage and educated in India, he admits to having a chameleonlike ability to adjust to any place he migrates to. In twentieth-century parlance that translates into being an isolate in his own home and his "own country," wherever it may be, not just America.

What lies behind the story is a desire to inscribe the reality of a special time and place in art. And literature is his medium. As a fitting ending to his narrative, Dr. Verghese leaves his practice in Tennessee to enroll in the Writers' Workshop in Iowa City.

Issues of ethnicity, though downplayed, do surface in the book. The HIV-positive sons who had fled their rural towns to live in faraway metropolises return home and are embraced by a compassionate doctor with dark skin and a foreign-sounding name. It is well known that Asian Americans have demonstrated high achievement in many professional and technical fields—hence the "model minority" sobriquet. It is also true that a large number of South Asians go into medical practice, but they are among the "invisible Americans," rarely heard from or written about.[11] Verghese's book becomes a social statement about the contribution to medicine of South Asian Americans.

EMBRACING THE AMERICAN TRADITION

In the works of ethnic writers who have received recognition and, in some cases, even acclaim, a self-assured American image emerges. The writings of Maxine Hong Kingston, David Henry Hwang, Amy Tan, Cynthia Kodohata, Gish Jen, Fae Myenne Ng, Bharati Mukherjee, and Chang-Rae Lee begin to make their way into college English courses, and they also receive wide notice. The literature reflects a degree of at-homeness. These writers feel comfortable, as it were, to satirize and criticize the apathetic assimilated "bananas" (that is, individuals who are Asian on the outside, in their appearance, but white on the inside), as well as the rampant racist stereotypes that are imposed on Asian Americans. But they speak with the security and ease of belonging, burdened by neither the self-hatred of angry sons nor the politeness of tour guides. Here, a distinction should be made between this and the earlier mode. The angry narrative voice of the between-worlds mode reveals the writers' inability to achieve distance. They have feelings of being trapped in limbo: ignored by the mainstream society and alienated by the ethnic community.

In this second mode, in which the writers forge an "American voice," the writing projects the confidence that comes from claiming America as home. Maxine Hong Kingston's *China Men* (1980) provides a perfect example of this confidence. She mythologizes the pioneering Chinese sugar plantation workers and railroad builders into folk heroes. These pioneering ancestors, she insists, have the right to start a new tradition and to "plant" their voices in American soil. She freely adapts Chinese and other myths to fit an American context and setting. Nor does she shy away from subverting canonical works in both Chinese and Western traditions. The combination of self-perceived at-homeness and a self-confident aesthetics confers on their works a boldness in claiming an American identity alongside their Asian heritage.

Bharati Mukherjee's *The Holder of the World* (1993) shows an ethnic writer's bold claim on the American literary tradition—the second mode. The novel adopts an American voice on the part of its narrator as she charts the journey of Hannah Easton from colonial Massachusetts to England, India, and back to Salem, the center of Puritan New England. The narrator, Beigh Master, is herself a descendant of the early Puritan settlers of Massachusetts and is now an asset hunter in the high-tech age of the late twentieth century. This blue-stocking Puritan lineage, however, is disrupted by East Indian influence. Hannah Easton's liaison with a Hindu raja produces a daughter, and the narrator relies on her Asian Indian computer scientist lover, Venn, to retrieve through cyberspace her remote ancestor's life in seventeenth-century Puritan America. Hannah Easton turns out to be the "historical" Salem BiBi on whom, according to Beigh, Hawthorne's Hester Prynne is modeled.

This novel, though written by an immigrant, claims the heart of American literary tradition by rewriting, reinterpreting, and subverting American canonical texts. First of all, the novel reverses the direction of migration from immigration to emigration. Both the contemporary character Beigh and the historical Hannah Easton are expatriates who spurn the security (also restraints) and the pretension of "continuity" of their own world. Beigh prefers Venn, a lover who "would seem alien to my family. A lover scornful of our habits of self-effacement and reasonableness, of our naive or desperate clinging to an imagined continuity" (31). Hannah's transplantation from the wilderness of Massachusetts to London, India, and back is transformative and enables her to come into her own. Likewise, Beigh sees security as "a kind of trap" (30).

Emigration ultimately implies leaving the center of cultural domination. The novel emphasizes repeatedly the richness of life on the periphery. What links the two characters is their shared predilection for living on the edge of "civilization" as defined by Puritan colonialists and contemporary American society. This place on the periphery of society gives them both access to other cultures and traditions. Born on the edge of civilization and orphaned at an early age, Hannah considers it a "privilege" to remain outside "family or society" (54). From Salem, the "capital of Puritan restraint," she would be liberated to experience such adventurous roles as the mistress of the Great Mughal while carrying the child of her Hindu raja.

Mukherjee's penetrating study of self-transformation in *Holder of the World* offers a new image of American woman. Instead of the Indian Jyoti, from the earlier work *Jasmine* (1989), who assumes a succession of American identities, this time it is a New World Puritan woman mapping a new life in India. The lives of contemporary Beigh Master and Puritan Hannah Easton become richer and freer as a result of their cross-cultural and interracial relationships with their Indian lovers.

Mukherjee further claims the American tradition by reinterpreting and revising the American texts. She accomplishes this by invoking three stories of captivity: *Narrative of the Captivity and Restoration of Mrs. Mary Rowlandson* (1682), the Indian epic of *Ramayana*, and *The Scarlet Letter*. From them she creates fables of freedom in captivity that blur the lines between Christian and heathen, civilization and savagery, and East and

West. Parallels are drawn between Mary Rowlandson's disdain for the savages who captured her and Rebecca Easton's willingness to fling herself into the arms of her Nimpuc lover. Mukherjee's reinterpretation implies that captivity leads to banishment from the center, geographically and mentally, freeing the women to love, to heal (Hannah is known for her medical skill in saving lives), to develop artistic talents (in the silent years she spends as a foster daughter, she becomes known for her exquisite embroidery), to brave hardships, and to stand up to the mogul in her effort to sue for peace. Mukherjee turns captivity on its head. It is Hannah's childhood in Salem that is a veritable imprisonment of the soul.

The liberation/captivity story grows in scope and variation as the heroine travels farther from the center of the Christian West. The American captivity story takes on new meaning when it is interpreted vis-à-vis *Ramayana*, the Indian epic. It clarifies for Hannah her own yearning, and its various endings of banishment and exile all have salutary effects on the captive woman.

The third and final story of captivity that the novelist-narrator invokes is *The Scarlet Letter* (1850). In this age of metafiction and postmodern, postcolonial deconstruction, what better way to better the master than by providing the missing, inner dimension of a work as canonical as *The Scarlet Letter,* or by boldly comparing her novel to that of an Anglo-American literary patriarch as revered as Nathaniel Hawthorne? Beigh Master produces "historical" data to prove that Hannah Easton lived in Salem during the tenure of the witchcraft judge John Hathorn, the great-grandfather of Nathaniel Hawthorne. According to "shipping and housing records," "the letters and journals and the Memoirs, and of course [from a source as reliable as] *The Scarlet Letter*," Hannah returned to Salem with her illegitimate, dark-skinned daughter. "Who can blame Nathaniel Hawthorne," mused the narrator, "for shying away from the real story of the brave Salem mother and her illegitimate daughter?" (284). Since Hawthorne shied away from telling the "true story," we have it now in *The Holder of the World* to understand the psychological inner dimension of Hannah's or Hester Prynne's life and experience of captivity. Whether or not we call this one-upmanship, in opening up a subject Hawthorne feared to probe, Bharati Mukherjee succeeds in writing a captivity narrative from outside the "White Circle" to convey the inner desires of a female character. Expatriation and captivity are relative terms for those who are oppressed by the center.

CREATING A BRAVE NEW VOICE

In the third mode ethnicity is subsumed by appropriation in the quest for an artistic model. The preoccupations of earlier Asian American writings—how to be accepted, how to assimilate and secure one's rights as an American—have lost some of their urgency in the third mode. In some cases it is fair to ask whether the label "ethnic" could still apply because of the non-ethnic content. But with their visible racial difference, Asian Americans never cease to be perceived as alien. The hallmark of this stage of development is the writer's sense of freedom to experiment. Ethnicity becomes a means of exploring limits.

Several elements characterize this third mode, which contains the most fluidity and slippage. It frequently transgresses geographic and cultural boundaries. If the ethnic neighborhood or milieu is evoked, its specificity expresses the writers' deepest desires in more than one language, not limited to the ethnic voice concerned with identity and survival in the American society. As a result, the novel in this mode challenges formal, geographic, or ideological boundaries, such as between history and literature, biography and fiction, or Eastern and Western, among others. The social and historical context (such as the exclusionary immigration laws or the internment of Japanese Americans during the Second World War) that was pivotal in interpreting the other two modes of self-expression in ethnic literature assumes a paradigmatic meaning and pattern for art and life in the modern world. Ethnic experience becomes a trope for global migrations, such as exile, diaspora, and various displacements.

Another characteristic of this mode is the transformation of the theme journey. In the first mode, for example, a journey is often associated with the birth of a new, American self—repeating the frequent typology of the Exodus story in American writings, as noted by Werner Sollors in *Beyond Ethnicity* (43); a journey in the third mode is often a quest for artistic models and inventions and seeks to embrace the state of exile to which we moderns are heirs. Being an exile or a deracinated outsider becomes an acceptable state of being, even a privileged position. It is a state of being that applies not only to Asians in diaspora Americans but to a vast number of people in our mobile world of shifting boundaries. The characters that inhabit the world created by these writers are at home nowhere and everywhere. The migratory journey is both a spiritual and physical condition to be embraced and celebrated even if it is fraught with pain.

A third characteristic is the tendency of this mode to appropriate all available models and traditions. Writers in this mode re-present cultural icons and canonized traditions from a variety of sources in a new language of bilingualism. The appropriation also stems from another impulse: the novelist as critic. The novelist deconstructs and pokes fun at earlier traditions and paradigms. The postmodern fiction turns metafiction. The self-reflexivity of the writers in this category knows no bounds in subverting, cannibalizing, satirizing, and transforming the old and established notions, forms, and ideas regarding race and ethnicity for their own artistic quest. Inversions abound; the traditional rebirth or from-slavery-to-the-Promised Land narrative as well as the in-between-world protest stories, and the claiming-America stance exemplified by previous modes are subverted in this third mode. Finally they even critique their own form and way of depicting the realities of being the Other in a society one calls "home." *Tripmaster Monkey* (1989) by Maxine Hong Kingston exemplifies this mode by its appropriation of traditional narratives, including the Chinese classic Journey to the West; its use of a chimeralike protagonist to challenge and subvert revered traditions; and the merciless debunking of cultural icons and practices held sacred by society, ethnic or mainstream. Increasingly writings by Asian Americans move away from themes associated with traditional Asian American milieux.

Ondaatje's *Coming through Slaughter*, published in 1972, illustrates the third and the most protean mode. Before writing this novel, Ondaatje had been practicing the postmodern poetics of mixing genres and appropriating historical documents. His long "documentary poem" *The Collected Works of Billy the Kid* already demonstrates his predilection for the Bakhtinian "heteroglossic" texts (Barbour 7). The Sri Lankan native, writing and teaching in Canada, found his material south of the border and in jazz: Buddy Bolden, a legendary cornet player in New Orleans. Ondaatje was intrigued by a line he accidentally read—"Buddy Bolden who became a legend when he went berserk in a parade"—and he became "obsessed" with this legendary but elusive black musician, saying he knew that he had "to face this character" (Barbour 3) He put aside a work in progress and began pursuing Bolden's life story. With what little information about Bolden he could glean from interviews, public records, and rumors, Ondaatje reconstructed Bolden's life by weaving a web of characters, scenes, conversations, and episodes. They cohere only as far as the multiple narrative viewpoints allow. The indeterminacy in the plot, the nonfictional eruptions, and the multiple perspectives all assert the artist's authority to defy generic definition and to discourage any attempt to read it as a "biography" of Bolden or to extract nuggets of ethnographic information from the novel.

Appropriation, a characteristic of the third mode, is given full play in this reassembled legendary, yet opaque, life. For *Coming through Slaughter*, appropriation implies borrowing from and assimilating the disparate views of characters who represent a community of castoffs in a little-known and hidden-from-tourists district with dilapidated houses and store fronts. The district has "little recorded history," and is "a mile or so from the streets made marble by jazz" (8). What little history there is has been handed down in the form of "fragments" of "tales" about the prodigious acts of notorious prostitutes who plied their trade in the district. The novel gives readers the distinct impression that these "fragments" and "tales" told by some truly misshapen, but entirely human, individuals come to us on the printed page unmediated by the pen of a novelist. Bolden's life is reconstructed with the multidimensional, gossipy reports supplied by Bolden's wife, Nora, the detective and friend Webb, fellow musicians, a pimp, a photographer, and an assortment of hangers-on. Like the gossips that go into the paper Bolden edited, fragments make up a composite, though incomplete, portrait of Bolden. Appropriation, in this case, means that the novelist departs from the ethnic world he is identified with and assumes the consciousness at the center of a black urban ghetto. It is rare for an immigrant writer to acquire, for his first novel, the milieu and language vastly different from his own. This feat of appropriation is plausible only coming from a writer who follows the desire to "start each new book with a new vocabulary, a new set of clothes" (Barbour 9).

The third mode of ethnic literature is also obsessed with the quest for new forms and new voices. Using appropriation as a form of remigration, the author creates a new self by assuming new identities. In *China Men*, for example, Maxine Hong Kingston appropriates and rewrites myths and Western canonical texts such as *Robinson Crusoe* to inscribe a new identity for her erstwhile Chinese characters. As noted by Patricia Linton: "The thematic threads which bind the various segments of the book together have in common the issue of appropriation. Typically men appropriate by marking the land, by building and planting; women appropriate by means of language, by naming and telling stories" (42). Appropriation grants the characters the transformative power to possess new land, new language, new narratives, or new identities. Similarly Ondaatje reaches into another ethnic tradition and another art form, the better to test his own power of creating a new language and a new voice. Furthermore, the enigma that is Bolden, a brilliant raconteur as well as a musician with mystical power, influenced the novelist to create a character possessed of the genius of creativity and self-destructive desires all at the same time. Ondaatje's use of language resembles the way Bolden could manipulate sound with his cornet. The novel is most effective when it captures with language the full range of surprises, betrayal, excruciating pain as well as exquisite joy in Bolden's music.

Writing the novel is finally a self-reflexive act. The author admits, as he addresses the character Bolden: "Why did my senses stop at you? There was the sentence, 'Buddy Bolden who became a legend when he went berserk in a parade . . .' What was there in that, before I knew your nation your colour your age, that made me push my arm forward and spill it through the front of your mirror and clutch myself" (134)? It reveals the novelist's quest for an image of himself the artist. In search of Bolden, he finds himself, in the clutch of creation. Nothing else matters, not one's ethnic or national identity, family or cultural heritage. The artistic vision overrides all else. The self-reflexivity in this telling image of the mirror shows two artists, widely separated by differences and by time, but one in spirit in their relationship to art. In smashing the mirror of traditional forms, Ondaatje also broadens our vision to new possibilities for the *ethnic* writer.

I have given a reading of South Asian writers' works as Asian American literature because these three novels fit the contours of Asian American literature. Although these three representative writers display considerable artistic virtuosity and stretch the boundaries of these modes, their works show a willingness to deal with all the themes, however adumbrated, that have preoccupied other Asian American writers. As a function of the more hospitable historical and political forces that greeted their arrival in North America, the apologist and protest voices are absent in their work. Added to that function is their own background of re-migration and acquaintance with the cosmopolitanism conferred on them by the British Commonwealth. Because South Asians do not share the same historical experience of some of the early East Asian pioneers, the social and psychological conflicts of earlier times simply do not possess the same emotional urgency and importance in their fiction. By no means have the realities of racial and ethnic conflict vanished from the canvas of their works, but at this point South Asian American literature, like all Asian American writings in our time, exhibits the self-regarding aspects of postmodernism. The need for literature to address literary and social concerns like breaking silence, searching for identity, countering stereotypes, appropriation, and claiming the American texts, will no doubt continue to occupy Asian American students and writers. Most of all, issues of identity will continue to preoccupy Asian American students who read the literature. At this point, the literature is redefining and stretching its boundaries by challenging the critical standards based on the "great literature" of the dominant Western world. It is also resisting conventional ideas about the role of ethnic writings. If nothing else, East and South Asian writers share these goals. They have too much in common not to be considered together. Therefore, with no apology, this essay situates South Asian American writers squarely within the conventions derived from the writings of earlier Asian American writers. Both South Asian and East Asian American writings belong to the "minority discourse" that challenges the center. The gap in this case is therefore negligible.

Notes

1. In the proceedings of its 1995 annual conference, entitled *ReViewing Asian America: Locating Diversity*, the Association for Asian American Studies called

for revising Asian American curriculum to accommodate new groups. Contributors express the need to shift from the California model, which tilts teaching and research toward the Chinese, Japanese, and other early arrivals in this country. The editors hold up as noteworthy the symposium held in 1991, "East of California: New Perspectives in Asian American Studies," which called for the need to expand our curriculum and our vision of what constitutes Asian America: "There are more 'new' Asian Americans east of California, pointing to the need for courses and readings that address their interests and needs, and many of those Asian immigrants and refugees come from different parts of the world. Asian Indians east of California, for instance, could as likely have immigrated from Africa and the Caribbean as from India" (11).

2. Linda Hutcheon reasons thus: "Difference operates *within* each of these challenging cultures, as well as against the dominant. Blacks and feminists, ethnics and gays, native and 'Third World' cultures, do not form monolithic movements, but constitute a multiplicity of responses to a commonly perceived situation of marginality and ex-centricity. And there have been liberating effects of moving from the language of alienation (otherness) to that of decentering (difference), because the center used to function as the pivot between binary opposites which always privileged one half: white/black, male/female, . . . objectivity/subjectivity. . . . But if the center is seen as a construct, a fiction, not a fixed and unchangeable reality, the 'old either-or begins to break down,' as Susan Griffin put it . . . the new and-also [as distinct from 'the old either-or'] of multiplicity and difference opens up new possibilities (62).

3. *Amerasia Journal* devoted a double issue, volume 21, numbers 1 and 2, to formulating new theories for Asian American studies. Most notably, in the article "Asiacentrism and Asian American Studies?" Paul Wang, Meera Manvi, and Takeo Hirota Wong raise the provocative possibility "to conceive of Asiacentrism as an important foundation for theory-building and theoretical analysis of phenomena," and to use it as an antidote to Western-dominated perspectives in theory-building" (139). Learning from "Afrocentricity," which is grounded in the worldview conceived and validated by people of African descent, the authors suggest that Asian American Studies might explore an "Asianness" existing in the "deep structure of culture that could be used as a "unifying principle, transcending fragmentation" (140–41).

In the same issue, Kent A. Ono's essay "Re/signing 'Asian American': Rhetorical Problematics of Nation," both concedes that the term Asian American is no longer useful as "a term of collective identification" and suggests that we may want to refigure the term to allow for slippage, dissent, and multiplicity. In his discussion he evokes the theoretical positions of like-minded scholars, such as Lisa Lowe in "Heterogeneity, Hybridity, Multiplicity: Marking Asian American Differences," Karin Aguilar-San Juan in *The State of Asian America: Activism and Resistance in the 1900's*, and R. Radhakrishnan in "Is the Ethnic 'Authentic' in the Diaspora?" (67–78).

4. For the range of publications both by Asian American writers and critics see the "Introduction" to *Reading Asian American Literature* by Sau-ling Cynthia Wong (3).

5. See the latest study on Indo-Americans, "Invisible Americans," in *Amerasia Journal* (Winter 1995–1996). The researchers note: "While on overall measures of socioeconomic status Indo-Americans appear to be relatively affluent, our data show that they also suffer from psychosocial stressors primarily due to issues around identity and assimilation, intergenerational conflicts, gender-role conflicts and concerns about interracial conflicts" (Shehendu B. Kar et al., 37).

6. The self-exploration of identity is used throughout my writing as the organizing principle of ethnic, and in particular Asian American, literature, while I am not averse to applying many of the contemporary theories, such as tricksterism, nomadology, deterritorialization/reterritorialization, and a number of other postcolonial and postmodern theories in interpreting "minority" literatures. I based my paradigm of reading Asian American literature as applied to the writings of Chinese Americans on a comparative study with Jewish American writing. When I was finishing my dissertation on this subject in the early eighties, I was happy to note that my reading concurred with the focus of Elaine Kim's pioneering work *Asian American Literature: An Introduction to the Writings and Their Social Context* (1982). In the preface she declares that "I have focused on the evolution of Asian American consciousness and self-image as expressed in the literature" (xi). While she uses "the evolution of Asian American consciousness and self-image as expressed in the literature" as the general thrust of her study, she does not delineate the stages of this evolution and how they directly influence the form and content of their literature. My dissertation does precisely the latter and derives these stages from Jewish American literature, one of the richest ethnic literatures in the twentieth century. The fact that some of the major American novelists are Jewish and retain their ethnic identity led me to see this particular ethnic literature as containing the stages that parallel the development of Chinese American literature or any other ethnic literature of the United States.

The critics I drew on, such as Lionel Trilling, Robert Alter, Allen Guttmann, Irving Malin, Irving Howe, Leslie Fiedler, Alfred Kazin, and Marcus Klein, among others, may sound like names from a distant past, but their astute observations, especially in regard to Jewish writings, have stood the test of time. Few would refute the claims made by these critics that Jewish writers share with other modern Jews the need to define themselves in the tension between Jewish and non-Jewish or between minority and majority and to rediscover their identity within a common cultural heritage, Jewish and American.

7. For example, the literary historian Robert Spiller uses the growth metaphor in the titles of three of his major books that span his long career: *Roots of American Culture* (1933), *The Cycle of American Literature* (1955), and *Late Harvest* (1981). His books trace the organic and evolutionary process of creating an American national character and giving it expression in literature. Each cycle begins with the impact on an old culture by the new environment. The horizontal movement of migration corresponds to the literary movement from seed to flowering.

8. Psychoanalysts Leon Grinberg and Rebecca Grinberg have documented the psychological impact of migration in their enlightening and comprehensive study *Psychoanalytic Perspectives on Migration and Exile*, trans. Nancy Festinger (New

Haven: Yale University Press, 1984). The Grinbergs' study confirms several features central to my model of ethnic literature: the "continuous becoming" that migration requires (176) of an immigrant, the impact of migration on the children of immigrants, and migration as a metaphor of human growth.

Even more relevant to my model is L. Ling-Chi Wang's patterns of Chinese migration to the United States and types of Chinese American identity. They clearly correspond to the historical experiences of the Chinese in America, which reflect the internal politics of China as well as the Sino-American relations.

9. This is an abbreviated version of my doctoral dissertation, "The Stages of Development in American Ethnic Literature: Jewish and Chinese American Literatures," Tufts University, 1986.

10. For a fuller treatment of the gender debate, read the "Introduction" to *Aiiieeeee*, in which the editors insist that Asian American manhood has been vitiated by American devaluation of Asian males. Read also critic Amy Ling's discussion of the mutual parodying by Chin and Kingston in their works (*Between Worlds*, 150). Finally, for an analysis of this debate, see "The Woman Warrior versus the China Pacific" by King-Kok Cheung.

11. Kar, Campbell, Jimenez, and Gupta's study in *Amerasia Journal* shows that compared with the general population, a significantly large proportion of the Indo-American population go into professional and academic fields and that "among all recent immigrant physicians of Asian origin, over 50 percent are Indo-Americans" (21.3, p.27).

WORKS CITED

Barbour, Douglas. *Michael Ondaatje*. New York: Twayne Publishers, 1993.

Cheung, King-Kok. "The Woman Warrior versus the Chinaman Pacific: Must a Chinese American Critic Choose between Feminism and Heroism?" In *Conflicts in Feminism*, edited by Marianne Hirsch and Evelyn Fox Keller. New York: Routledge, 1990, 234–51.

Chan, Jeffery Paul, Frank Chin, Lawson Fusao Inada, and Shawn Hsu Wong, eds. *Aiiieeeee!* Washington, D.C.: Howard University Press, 1974

Chin, Frank. *The Chickencoop Chinaman and The Year of the Dragon: Two Plays*. Seattle: University of Washington Press, 1981.

Clifford, James. "Traveling Cultures." In *Cultural Studies*, edited by Lawrence Grossberg, Cary Nelson, and Paula Treichler. New York: Routledge, 1992, 96–116.

Hsiao, Ruth Yu. "The Stages of Development in American Ethnic Literature: Jewish and Chinese American Literatures. Ph.D. diss. Tufts University, 1986.

Hutcheon, Linda. *A Poetics of Postmodernism: History, Theory, Fiction*. New York: Routledge, 1988.

JanMKohamed, Abdul R., and David Lloyd. *The Nature and Context of Minority Discourse*. New York: Oxford University Press, 1990.

Kar, Snehendu B., Kevin Campbell, Armando Jimenez, and Sangeeta R. Gupta. "Invisible Americans: An Exploration of Indo-American Quality of Life." *Amerasia Journal* 21.3 (Winter 1995–1996): 25–52.

Kim, Elaine H. *Asian American Literature: An Introduction to the Writings and Their Social Context*. Philadelphia: Temple University Press, 1982.

Kingston, Maxine Hong. *China Men*. New York: Alfred Knopf, 1980.

Lim, Shirley Geok-lin, and Amy Ling, eds. *Reading the Literatures of Asian America*. Philadelphia: Temple University Press, 1992.

Ling, Amy. *Between Worlds: Women Writers of Chinese Ancestry*. New York: Pergamon Press, 1990.

Linton, Patricia. "What Stories the Wind Would Tell": Representation and Appropriation in Maxine Hong Kingston's *China Men*." *MELUS* 19.4 (Winter 1994): 37–48.

Mukherjee, Bharati. *The Holder of the World*. New York: Fawcett Columbine, 1993.

Ng, Wendy, Soo-Young Chin, James S. Moy, and Gary Y. Okihiro, eds. *ReViewing Asian America: Locating Diversity*. Pullman, Wash.: Washington State University Press, 1995.

Ondaatje, Michael. *Coming Through Slaughter*. New York: Penguin Books, 1976.

Ono, Kent A. "Asian American": Rhetorical Problematics of Nation." *Amerasia Journal*. 21.1 and 21.2 (1995): 67–78.

Rushdie, Salman. *Imaginary Homelands: Essays and Criticism 1981–1991*. London: Penguin Granta Books, 1991.

Sollors, Werner. *Beyond Ethnicity: Consent and Descent in American Culture*. New York: Oxford University Press, 1986.

Spiller, Robert. *Late Harvest: Essays and addresses in American Literature and Culture*. Westport, Conn.: Greenwood Press, 1981.

Wang, Paul, Meera Manvi, and Takeo Hirota Wong. "Asiacentrism and Asian American Studies?" *Amerasia Journal*. 21.1 and 21.2 (1995): 137–47.

Wong, Jade Snow. *Fifth Chinese Daughter*. New York: Harper, 1945.

Wong, Sau-ling Cynthia. *Reading Asian American Literature*. Princeton, N.J.: Princeton University Press, 1993.

Verghese, Abraham. *My Own Country: A Doctor's Story*. New York: Simon & Schuster, 1994.

SAMIR DAYAL

11 Min(d)ing the Gap
South Asian Americans and Diaspora

> I am the one
> who always goes
> away with my home
> which can only live inside,
> in my blood—my home which does not
> > fit
> > > with any geography.

> —Sujata Bhatt, "The One Who Goes Away"

IN RESPONSE to the central question of this collection of essays, I would say straightforwardly that "Asian-America" is a category into which "South Asian America" does not and should not seek to "fit." I examine the slippage between the category "Asian-American" and the apparent subcategory of "South Asian American"—a category that hybridizes "Asian-America" from within, and in the second part of this essay, I consider a memoir of one prominent South Asian American: Meena Alexander's *Fault Lines*. This memoir captures, in its substance as well as in its title, a sense of the troubling of identifications, the lack of "fit," that is the focus of my essay.

At a very general level, I would argue that the very rhetoric of the inclusivity of "hyphenation" obscures the fact that whiteness is by implication invested with normativity. Hyphenated citizenship is itself a sign constructed differentially, in logical opposition to that spectral authenticity that does not bear the mark—"stigma" may be too strong a synonym— of hyphenatedness, namely real and unqualified Americanness.[1] This spectral ideal Other is by definition a condition of the othering for many "ethnic" groups, though less so for white ethnic groups (such as Irish or Italian Americans). It is important to recognize this difference, this gap, in the current atmosphere of legislation discriminating against even legal immigrants or resident aliens. But South Asian Americans experience a further gap, a gap at another level, whether consciously thinking of themselves as

American citizens or as diasporics or something in between. That gap is what this essay addresses.

There is a productive parallel, both structural and logical, between the articulation of minority culture with Euro-American culture and that of South Asian American culture with what is usually understood as "Asian-America," in official, academic, and popular representations (that is, for example, in television, or in the realm of employment statistics). My argument is that it is precisely at the cusp between the (fashionably multiculturalist) category of Asian-America and the (tenuous and unfashionable) subcategory of South Asian America that South Asian Americans should situate themselves—both minding the gap (observing and theorizing it), as well as mining it as internal fissure, as potentially destabilizing fault line, for the interstitial perspective it affords on the sites of culture and on the prospects for a more civil society. A civil society assumes that an ongoing civil discourse is encouraged and enabled between minorities and majority groups within the nation-state, and within and among minority groups. It is only if such a dialogical notion of civility is guaranteed that (civic) justice can be said to exist—indeed, as Mark Kingwell argues more generally, "vigorous public debate, if we can ever find it, is all the political meaning that the vexed word 'justice' should have for us" (vii).[2]

Only recently have South Asian Americans become a significant presence on the American cultural and political landscape. Until a few years ago they were not recognized as having legal minority status—nor could they fill affirmative action quotas. Situated on the threshold of inclusion, as it were, they now present an exemplary case of the dilemma between assimilation and the preservation of a diasporic, liminal sensibility. But why, one might ask, do they find it difficult, or why are they reluctant, to assimilate unproblematically? It may be because of the fairly significant cultural distances between Eastern and Western cultures, or because deep emotional, family, cultural, and other ties (such as economic) bind South Asians to the ancestral homeland and therefore to a diasporic sensibility. It is possible that they perceive or imagine advantages to accrue from a calculated self-positioning as diasporic. Or it may be that they feel they must remain in between the home they left behind and another that will never truly allow them to feel at home.

South Asian Americans may also feel they cannot help living their "difference," because what W.E.B. Du Bois might have called "color lines"— race or ethnicity—prevent ethnic groups from being able to forget their differences. One might even say that South Asian Americans inhabit the image of a diasporic rather than an unproblematically "American" identity whether they want to or not. Some prominent members of this group find the presumption of difficulty in becoming "American" to be the prick against which they kick, witness Bharati Mukherjee when she abrasively insists on her Americanness in an interview with a *Newsweek* reporter: "You don't routinely say of John Updike or Russell Banks that they are European-American writers. How dare you insist on categorizing me as an Asian-American?" (Griffiths 34). And clearly, many migrants and diasporics, particularly those who flee real poverty or political oppression, may want nothing more than to overcome their sense of exclusion from unproblematic belonging to a nation-state.

In Meena Alexander's case, diaspora precludes any simple reading of national belonging, of "nationality." When she says, "In my dreams, I am haunted by thoughts of a homeland I will never find. So I have tuned my lines to a different aesthetic, one that I build up out of all the stuff around me, improvising as I go along" (27), or when she asks rhetorically, "Is America this terrible multiplicity at the heart?" (201) she is saying that she cannot be simply Indian again, just as she does not identify herself as simply a U.S. citizen. What is interesting about an approach like Alexander's is that the diasporic self is situated on fault lines (in the plural, let us note); this is neither, then, a nostalgic construction of diaspora as a longing for a home left behind, nor a crude exceptionalism in the host country.[3] Something of this complexity is captured in her self-reflexive account of the time when her son Adam was asked whether he was American:

> "No," said my son very boldly.
> "Indian then. You Indian, child?"
> Adam shifted his weight "No." . . . What did my first-born wish for himself? Some nothingness, some transitory zone where dreams roamed, a border country without passport or language? . . . "Jedi, I'm a Jedi knight" . . . His head filled with . . . planets of lost origins, Adam knew exactly what he was talking about. (172–73)

It is such a postnational, passportless ideal that Alexander herself wants to explore in this memoir, connecting diaspora to the details of living in the dailiness of India or Somalia or the United States. Does all this mean, however, that

> faced with the multiple anchorages that ethnicity provides, learning from Japanese Americans, Chinese Americans, Filippino [*sic*] Americans, Mexican Americans, Jewish Americans, African Americans, Native Americans, and yes, Indian Americans, I can juggle and toss and shift and slide, words, thoughts, actions, symbols . . . Can I become just what I want? . . . .

> I can make myself up and this is the enticement, the exhilaration, the com-
> pulsive energy of America. *But only up to a point. And the point, the stick-*
> *ing point, is my dark female body.* (202; emphasis added)

In this essay I explore both the metaphoric and labile identities implied
by "becoming just what I want," and, across the overdetermined gap of
gendered, raced, deterritorialized spaces, the ontic limit of "my dark female body."

By keeping open the fracture within the category of Asian-America, we
can explore the complex conflicts or allegiances that obtain among differently situated Americans who are somehow linked with Asian cultural
spaces (if not "ancestral homelands"), as well as exposing complicities
among Asian-Americans and majoritarian groups that are a source of tension among Asian-Americans and African-Americans or Chicanos, for
instance. This interstitiality can be seen as disturbing received notions of
minorities as a homogenized and monolithic target of anti–affirmative
action, anti-preferential rhetoric, but it is also a problematization of the
categories of nation, class, and gender. These categories are too often
displaced within an exclusively ethnicized minority discourse, so the address of coalitional politics obscures rather than acknowledges cultural
difference. The irony here is that on the basis of that very difference, coalition, cooperation, and united fronts are urged onto the more "fringe"
elements of "Asian-America." The South Asians' marginal position within
the rather more reassuringly minoritized grouping referred to as "Asian-
American" is not simply a threshold to cross or a gap to close. Such a
liminality enables a crucial and "critical" agency (to reactivate the linking
etymology from *krinein*, which invokes the idea of crisis, as well as of
critical judgment), and a refusal or a reluctance to be comfortably assimilated, in preference for a wider and more differentiated public sphere of
negotiation. This is, at least, one way to encourage the ongoing negotiation, based on cultural difference, that enlivens civil society. To put it
baldly, the gap may be left productively open.

Perhaps this sounds like a recommendation for a radical separatism or
factionalism. It is not. The South Asian American diaspora's liminal positioning highlights, but also adds a wrinkle to, what Frederick Buell calls
the "startling paradox of the era of the melting pot—simultaneous inclusion and exclusion, assimilation and segmentation, nationalizing Americanization and colonial exploitation" (148). The paradox is complicated
by the fact that diasporic groups have a different perspective from those
who considered themselves unproblematically Asian-American: the South
Asian diaspora at any rate is not included and excluded, or assimilated
and segmented, in equal measures compared with other minority groups.

This diaspora's location on the outer edge of the multicultural discourse repunctuates the complacent chic of "hyphenation" and its classification of minorities into a structure of simultaneous inclusion and exclusion—a discursive structure that is not often open to analysis, possibly because of its potential for revealing some embarrassing inequalities. After all, some minorities are more equal than others. Isabella Furth seems correct in a general sense when she writes that

> The hyphen, the mark that simultaneously conjoins and separates, is a central trope of multicultural theory, yet it is seldom more central than it is in the discussion of Asian-American writers. It adheres to Asian immigrants with particular tenacity, for one; whereas for most European immigrants the hyphen drops out after a generation, it remains with citizens of Asian extraction like Kingston's hero Wittman Ah Sing even unto the fifth generation born on U.S. soil, a mark of Otherness and of the persistent failure to inscribe the Asian-American fully within the limits of American discourse. (34)

But Furth's discussion also illustrates that when an observer of multicultural literature, even when she is not a partisan with a special allegiance to a particular Asian-American group, refers to "Asian-American writers," she means primarily Chinese- or Japanese-American writers. (Furth, I presume, is not a member of a minority U.S. group herself, although I would not want to be misunderstood as endorsing a "credentializing" of such critique in any sense.) It is rarely noted that the hyphenated category "Asian-American" subtly, if not always deliberately, elides the presence of some other Asian Americans. This elision may be effected precisely within the academic version of the rhetoric of "inclusion," where one might expect more discernment from the cognoscenti.[4]

It is precisely such a double-edged language of "inclusion" that sometimes excludes (by subsumption) a minority within a minority; for this reason calls to "put aside our differences" and to assimilate into either the Asian-American collectivity or into the American mainstream ought to be viewed with something less than total credulity, while of course leaving open every possible opportunity for meaningful solidarity. This would be true even if it meant risking being labeled unfairly and irrelevantly as un-American and perhaps facing the considerable violence directed at aliens, as if under the reign of a new McCarthyism. The risk is particularly acute for those who are most easily discriminated from white America by phenotype (physiological type)—skin color, "ethnic" dress, religious affiliation, or "alien" customs. And it is not too hard to find academic discussions in which at least the more prominent South Asian academics are viewed with something close to skepticism or resentment.[5] Alexander's memoir dramatizes some of these tensions.

The history of South Asians in this country suggests that the machinery of their exclusion has not been subtle. Taking the case of California (among the states historically most popular with immigrants from Asia), Gary R. Hess points out that "studies of Asian-Americans and of California 's racial history have given scant, if any, attention to the East Indians" (158). Thousands of Sikhs came to work in railway gangs around 1900 and ended up within a decade or so as farmers in California, only to encounter the same social obstacles as other immigrants: antimiscegenation laws, prohibitions against land ownership, and exclusionary immigration policy; the 2,545 Indians were classified as "Other," even if "pure-blood" Hindus managed to have themselves considered "Caucasian," because they came from "a civilization distinctly different from that of Europe" (cited in Jensen 252). Hess points out that the 1909 Immigration Commission investigation of East Indians described them as the "least assimilative of any immigrant group" (165). The "barred zone" language of the 1917 immigration law denied that East Indians were suitable immigrants, on the basis that they were not white, and the 1923 Supreme Court ruling in *United States v. Bhagat Singh Thind* was that Indians were not eligible for naturalization—the ruling was used even to annul prior naturalizations of East Indians. No doubt partly as a consequence of the public attitude represented by this ruling, between 1920 and 1940, three thousand Indians returned to India, most of their own volition, although some were deported; an equal number, however, entered the country illegally (Hess 171). The Immigration Restriction Act of 1924 ended all legal Asian immigration; by 1940 there were only about two thousand Indians left in the country, mainly in California.

Punctuating a thirty-year ban, in 1946 Congress passed legislation establishing a quota of one hundred, and made Indians eligible for naturalization; and the 1965 Immigration Act removed the quota system, thus encouraging a great increase in immigration. Between 1965 and 1970, writes Hess, immigrants from India "showed a higher percentage increase than newcomers from any other country" (176). "Asian Indians" were acknowledged officially as an ethnic group in the 1980 census, which counted 361,531 Asian Indians; in the 1990 census there were 815,447. But even now, the retention of "native" customs and dress, historically speaking, has worked to keep those East Indians who wished assimilation from being fully accepted as Americans, and their "acculturation" has been "limited" (Hess 165, 175). From the perspective of this essay, published in 1976, this group of Asian-Americans has a history of being constituted—or disarticulated—as a "forgotten" community. While in 1982 the National Association of Americans of Asian Indian Descent applied for recognition as a minority constituency, the Indian League of America

opposed the move, fearing a backlash from "the truly disadvantaged minorities" (Varma 35; Takaki *Strangers* 446–47, cited in Sharpe 194).

In response to Hess's view, the argument can be made that more recently things have changed, and that there is no longer an elision of South
Asian America under the sign of Asian-America. But even a cursory glance
at the explosion of studies in Asian-American literature and culture belies
this objection. As an example, a recent essay by Wen H. Kuo cites both
scholarly and popular news sources that suggest that Asian-Americans
face a rising number of hate crimes and general resentment in retaliation
for perceived economic competition from them or from Asian countries in
the global market (109). While this is no doubt true, it is also interesting
for the purposes of my argument that the focus of his essay is on Chinese,
Filipino, Japanese, and Korean Americans. Subcontinental Indians are not
even mentioned. This is not just a random instance of those other Asians'
being overlooked, but it is symptomatic of a more pervasive tendency.
While it would be unfair to expect any study of Asian-Americans to offer
a comprehensive coverage of all Asian-American groups, studies such as
Kuo's seem to "cover" over or simply overlook the magnitude of the violence, oppression, and exclusion that the South Asians in the country face,
as witnessed by a range of recent examples, from the terrorism of the Jersey City Dotbusters[6] to the fact that the 1980 census suggests, according
to Sucheta Mazumdar, that along with Filipinos, even U.S.-born Asian
Indians "experienced higher levels of unemployment than non-Hispanic
whites and other Asian groups"—to the tune of unemployment rates five
times higher than that of Japanese- and Chinese-Americans; not surprisingly, poverty rates among Asian Indians are also five times that of
Japanese- and Chinese-Americans (32–34). All of this points to unequal
degrees of access to social power, political representation, and education,
and to very different levels of general cultural respect within what is called
Asian-America.

What I would stress, however, is an examination of the available strategies of response to the situation South Asians face.[7] This essay is emphatically not advocating special treatment for South Asians in America.
I do not maintain the absurdly parochial view that there is something
unique about the minority politics of South Asian Americans. Nor can
this group of diversely constituted individuals be said to have a single unifying agenda or a rigorous and fully theorized program, any more than
can other diverse collectivities. I would not even classify South Asian
American literature as constituting what Leslie Fiedler and others have
termed, more or less condescendingly, "regional" literature, that is to say
"writing intended to represent the values and interests of a group which
feels penalized, even threatened, by the disregard of the larger commu-

nity" (Fiedler 74; quoted in Ferraro 2). Indeed, I find most unhelpful the crude expectation of minority literature that it "represent the values and interests of a group" because this is to impose a programmatic and formulaic intentionality that may be inimical to even a minimal principle of the literary work's aesthetic autotelism or to the logic of narrative as such. South Asian American writing, then, should not be read simply for its representative verisimilitude. Sara Suleri, Bharati Mukherjee, and Meena Alexander may have much in common with someone like Zulfikar Ghose. But such a level of representativeness can hardly be said to have much promise as a basis for analysis.

Even so, South Asian Americans are situated at a border from which it is possible to rethink issues involved in the culture wars—political, ethical, and aesthetic issues, and issues of cultural value and meaning. Not the least of the aesthetic issues (for my current purposes) is the valuation of cultural production as art—although of course there are those who would seek to dismiss "regional" literatures as "parochial, transient, and delusive simultaneously: self-congratulation and public relations masquerading, just barely, as literary art" (see Ferraro 2). The border is not just a neat bifurcation between "us" and "them," as it is sometimes represented as being. Rather, the border runs in a rhizomatic network like the root structure of grass or like the network of cracks in glass. Border conditions may manifest themselves in the American workplace, but they may equally appear as social taboos, such as those against interethnic or interracial social and sexual contact, that persist alongside the rhetoric of multicultural diversity. They may manifest themselves as factional ethnic tensions in the academy and elsewhere. The tensions between Japanese- or Chinese-Americans and South Asian Americans, for instance, constitute evidence of a turf war. And a cold war it is—much of it is conducted sub rosa, under the aegis of a fragrantly multicultural public discourse.

Such tensions also drive the rhetoric of "deserving minority" groups: groups that have earned their place on the totem pole by virtue of the degree of suffering their people have endured—slavery, the sad oppression of Native Americans, the Japanese internment following Pearl Harbor, and so on. Thus even when people with such fully developed political positions as Cornel West and Michael Lerner speak about the prospect of a coalition between African-American and Jewish-American groups (as they did in a recent interview on NPR), they point out that each of these communities inevitably asks whether the other community has suffered as long or as intensely. In the arena of this kind of competition, a group such as the South Asian diaspora risks being seen as an interloper unqualified to claim an equal place at the table with those bona fide minorities in the West-Lerner debate—or at least as having too many advantages, as a minority, to complain. For even though South Asian diasporics may have endured the indignities of colonization, they have also reaped certain portable institutional advantages from the infrastructure of education put in place by the colonizers, not to mention the so-called "blessing in disguise" of the English language—all of which has an implied "payoff" in the U.S. academy. And even considered as displaced persons, as migrants, they may be seen, for instance, as not having suffered the utter brutality of slavery, so they cannot be considered to have equal claim to the same cultural space as blacks, or indeed, without due deference and self-deferral, to the category "diaspora," for that sign somehow belongs in the first instance to Jewish history, in which "a people" have collectively suffered the unspeakable inhumanity of the Holocaust.

Nobody would deny that harmony among the various ethnic groups and between minority and majority groups would be a desirable goal or that discrete groups have discrete histories or experiences of suffering; indeed one ought to regard with respect and see as instructive such histories as are represented by what Paul Gilroy calls the "Black Atlantic." But one can hardly endorse a glossing over the asymmetries of the strange hierarchy of deserving minorities. Nor on the other hand can one expect great enthusiasm about responding to the expressed desires of those other, less "entitled"—and less organized—minorities in most public debate about contemporary U.S. race relations or about needed reform in immigration policy. Their ongoing stories and emergent identities also deserve telling.

I am not suggesting that the subsumption of South Asian America within the category of Asian-America is evidence of some dark calculus initiated by the many Asian groups that largely constitute Asian-America. The effect, in any case, is that South Asian Americans can be accommodated and domesticated as already constructed, politically neutralized subjects or objects (even as other categories are naturalized in their hegemonic cultural locations). In this sense they are denied full agency, by which I mean unmediated access to the processes of civil society and to the fruits of the material opportunities and intellectual and cultural resources that attract so many migrants to American shores. I am suggesting that such exclusions are already evident in the culture at large, and that sometimes these exclusions are abetted by other Asian-Americans in an implicit denial to the more recent, diasporic groups of full status even as Asian-Americans. They are observable in academic as well as non-academic hiring.[8] Similar marginalizations of South Asian Americans are at least implicit in the awarding of contracts to minority businesses but also in the awarding of grants, particularly when the "target" is minority groups, in affirmative action admissions to colleges. As Benjamin Lee observes, "Issues that divided the nation in the 1960s such as race, gender, and class, have become internalized in the academy as faultlines for debates over research, teaching, and faculty hiring" (568). And Ferraro goes so far as to say that academics are especially guilty of using "the classificatory chain [in which immigrant literature is contained] as a means of registering the presence of certain voices while at the same time" diluting them (and, incidentally, ignoring others) (1).

Again, while South Asian America is often assimilated into Asian-America, it is important to insist that South Asian Americans be differently encoded, or often simply disarticulated within the accesses of high culture even on the global level, and even in "cultural studies." Thus, while "Ancient Indian Erotic Art" or "Buddhism" is deemed worthy of study, Pakistanis, Indians, or Bangladeshis as citizens—let alone as eroticized beings with alternative notions of desire's forms, or effective interlocutors with Christianity—are less frequently so considered (with a few exceptions, of course). Gilroy has argued that "the project of cultural studies is a more or less attractive candidate for institutionalization according to the ethnic garb in which it appears. The question of whose cultures are being studied is therefore an important one, as is the issue of where the instruments which will make that study possible are going to come from" (*The Black Atlantic* 5). Films such as Hanif Kureishi's *My Beautiful Laundrette* and *Sammy and Rosie Get Laid,* or Mira Nair's *Mississippi Masala,* and many other cultural products of the South Asian diaspora in the United States and elsewhere, represent the desire and sensibility of the other as found nowhere else, and that is why it is important to study them alongside what usually appears in discussions, not to mention in syllabi addressing themselves to "Asian-American" cultural products.

What is not desirable is tokenized inclusion within the category of "Asian-America," because tokenism serves only to preserve the hierarchy that I am suggesting is the problem in the first place. Solidarity with other minorities of course is a good, and separatism an evil, as far as the health of the nation-state goes. We must, however, remain open to the internally constitutive differences among the various Asian-American groups, particularly because the interests of minorities within minorities are often subsumed, presumably for the good of the greater group, or that of the nation state. An insistence on difference is not about "undermining the priority of Western liberal values [or] the Western humanistic tradition," contrary to what the Roger Kimballs of the multiculturalism debates would predictably intone (see Kimball 5, quoted in Lee 571). The real struggle is to find a way to respect differences that doesn't merely provoke further tension between ethnic constituencies, and that doesn't ossify the individual either as an isolated monad or as a member of an alienated and alien ghetto. Unfortunately, the latter is the shape of difference we most often see.

The ghettoization of South Asian Americans within "Asian-America" and within America cuts two ways. It not only gives the majority (whether Euro-American or "Asian-American"—within the context of interethnic politics) a way of containing what is construed by majoritarian perspectives as a potentially disruptive presence. It also correspondingly induces a sense of "belonging," if only within that "ghetto." Yet this sense of belonging also deflects attention away from the hegemonic subordination of that group and its members within the greater narrative of the nation state. So the near euphoria of belonging begins to seem a kind of false consciousness. Everybody needs to feel a sense of belonging, which is intimately tied to a more general sense of well-being, self-respect, and having one's needs met. But if this manna is purchased at the cost of a delusion about one's actual place in society, it turns to dust.

A cultural studies approach to the condition of South Asian Americans that (conceptually) keeps open the "gap" between them and "Asian-Americans" and between them and "America" need not therefore be a radical separatist or absolute relativist approach. If such an approach recognizes their interstitiality as at least a metaphoric diaspora, and recognizes also that it would be wrong to romanticize the condition of diaspora, it can contribute to what the Chicago Cultural Studies Group has termed a "critical" multiculturalism, in a way that is also cognizant of the increasing globalization and internationalization of the nation-space. The concept of the nation, of course, has recently received much attention.[9] But an exploration of the insertion of South Asian American presences within the construct of the national time-space usefully reopens, from a neglected point of view, the question of the nation's construction. The condition of diaspora, particularly, read as a performative of in-betweenness within the nation-space of the Western host, offers a resistance to being annexed, supplemented, to the grand and not so grand national narratives of the West against the Rest.

The exploration of diaspora in literature, perhaps more than anywhere else, supplies an intertextuality with identitarian conceptual structures so central to the struggles for agency and self-determination of marginal individuals and groups. It is also a counterweight to the facile notion of "hybridity" that infuses what Guillermo Gómez-Peña describes as an American "sport." This is the sport in which the central play is the question "Where are you from?" In a "culture of emergency" such as exists in the United States, Gómez-Peña argues, the real hybridity of the United States is effectively misrecognized by this question. This misrecognition intimates a psychic motivation. For we know that diversity talk is frequently a mask for a domestication of difference, a decorative flourish in the rhetoric of "e pluribus unum." And my argument throughout has been that the better alternative is not to erase or homogenize but to respect difference, encouraging in the service of a truly plural civil society a real openness to negotiation and a real welcoming of conversation among opposing constituencies. The interstitiality of South Asian Americans is a case that can also serve more modestly as an occasion to rethink the articulation of Asian-America itself.

AN EXAMPLE: MEENA ALEXANDER'S *FAULT LINES*

While divisiveness on the basis of ethnicity (or indeed on any basis) is an evil to be avoided if a truly harmonious society is an actual alternative, I see no compelling reason to think that the minority writer must aspire to that popular imperative represented by Daniel Aaron's privileging of "dehyphenation" through a "transcenden[ce of] a mere parochial allegiance" (215, quoted in Ferraro 3). What I have been calling the lack of "fit" of South Asian Americans within larger constituencies ("America" as well as "Asian-America") is a gap that can be productively "minded"—to use that unfashionable word—and mined, at the very least insofar as it requires a rethinking of nation, "home," and belonging. These are, after all, key terms in contemporary cultural studies.

As an instance of someone who declines the "transcendence" into dehyphenation, preferring a deliberately and self-consciously unassimilated diaspora, as well as registering the ache of dispersal, I now take up Meena Alexander's memoir, *Fault Lines*. The book is by no means a paragon of brinkmanship. But it does mine productively the seam between Asian-America and South Asian America, offering a resistance to the co-optation of that latter admittedly modest presence and explicitly thematizing multiplicity and polyvocality as agency, as distinct from any essentialized positionality. She speaks of being "cracked by multiple migrations" and being riven by multiple "fault lines," "multiple births" (3, 15, 5, 182, 201). It is the unwieldy slippage between abjected body images—"female, Indian, Other" (114)—that Alexander must work through. And it is the polygenesis—the quality of undergoing "multiple births"—that frustrates a complacent analysis of her location as an Asian-American, for it refuses a single incarnation that can be domesticated and assimilated.[10] Being born again and again, particularly through the continual (and even violent and painful) destruction of prior selves, is a powerful emblem for the diasporic, and I have elsewhere suggested that other South Asian writers have been drawn to it as confident and hopeful moths to candle flames (Dayal 65–88).

Alexander's voice also presents an academic alternative to the kind of almost establishmentarian academic voice Nancy Miller describes as the juncture of the personal essay and academic criticism in *Getting Personal*. Alexander's cannot be a subaltern voice, even though she insists on its Third World origins and social anchors. It may be unfair to suggest that Alexander's work luxuriates in the blandishments of diaspora. It does present a perspective from which to re-envision the necessity of conceptualizing civil society as a zone where cultural difference is welcomed as energizing "talk"—the conversation of different groups continually negotiating the shape and revealing the difficulties—of what is too glibly trumpeted as America's "multicultural" society. Her memoir echoes Lee's point that in the academy racial, gender, and class divisions are internalized as "fault lines" in matters of scholarship, pedagogy, and even hiring (568), fault lines that are rarely subject to rigorous examination. Should such a memoir be immune to charges of inadequately theorized exploration and aestheticization?

As an exemplar of a certain South Asian American sensibility, Alexander is interpellated as a woman of Christian South Indian background who is also privileged in terms of her education and academic location; nor is her skin color or class unimportant, even in the Indian context. Alexander's specific cultural inscription need not distract us from her membership within the group and its location in the contemporary story of America. But by the same token the specificity of her privilege in the American academy should not be occluded by her marginality as a diasporic. Nor should we discount the specific connections between the ersatz-subaltern position she sometimes so blithely seems to want to occupy in the United States, and the access to social resources she enjoys by virtue of belonging to a privileged Indian (and "exotic?") background.

Class, and the privilege that derives from class and education, is deeply inscribed in the memoir, and it is not to be occluded but rather highlighted in the interest of a more critical and self-reflexive representational politics. Her accent is in some cases a boon and in other cases almost an embarrassment. Against the backdrop of the highly visible academic profile of Asian-Americans in general (though not as a rule of South Asian Americans in general, barring the Homi Bhabhas and the Gayatri Spivaks), her accent is construed by American friends as a ticket to a good academic position. She projects an understandable discomfiture about this because it raises awkward questions about unearned relative privilege as well as about her political, institutional, and cultural alignments.

The crucial way in which Alexander's voice presents itself as an interesting alternative in the sense described above obtains when she emphasizes the body. But while the body is a central trope of Euro-American feminist discourse, the medium of the body does not unproblematically ally Alexander with her white or "Asian-American" sisters and feminist brothers; in some ways it is what differentiates her from them. She cannot quite be a part of what can only be called the white, or mainstream middle-class feminist establishment (a category in which I would include even some well-situated African-American and Asian-American feminists). Yet, her emphasis on her Third World diasporic body could not impeccably credentialize her or even facilitate a nominal solidarity, if she wished cre-dentialization or solidarity, with the recently enfranchised voices of what in a language of "authenticity" one might with some trepidation describe as *echt*-subalterns, such as we meet in the work of a Mahasweta Devi or a Rigoberta Menchú.

I have been emphasizing that her body is at once a ground of being, an ontic determinant, and a "sticking point"; she writes that her "dark fe-male body . . . is here, now, and cannot be shed. No more than any other human being can shed her or his body and still live" (202). And, although she takes great comfort from the community she shares with the many women whose lives cross the fault lines of her own, intersubjective col-laboration among women does not quite compensate for the deprivations and slights attaching to the difference of the racially marked body in the culture at large. One sharp reminder that sisterhood among women does not necessarily transcend the politics of racialized female bodies occurred when at the Fourth International Interdisciplinary Congress of Women held at Hunter College in June 1990, the names of the three women of color (Audre Lorde, Kamala Das, and Claribel Alegria), whom Alexander had invited, were left off the program. Her guest Lorde reminds her that "'they cannot bear us, Meena . . . those women of color who talk out" (74). Yet Alexander comes perilously close to a romance of the body in which all theoretical issues tremble before the existential criterion of the experiential body, where being an "Asian American" is like confronting a "bodily gate" that must be "unlocked" as an access to the writing of her life story. Self-representation tends here to be refracted and contracted into a naive embodied materialism.

What redeems this narrow conception is precisely that Alexander dis-covers and thematizes the gap between how she conceives of her own body and how her body is constructed or made grotesque, through the power of description, by Western observers, and furthermore she discovers that her body enunciates her being as always hybridized. The perplexities of her Indian/Sudanese/British accent in English, her voice coming out of that dark South Asian body, render non-self-identical her own cultural identity. That identity's abyss I am situating (is that the word?) conceptu-

ally in the "gap" that is covered over by the duplicitous inclusivity of the
sign of "Asian-America."

But one cannot discount the situations in which her vulnerability as a
South Asian American woman in America is evident, such as when a white
male biker in Minneapolis shouted "black bitch!" at her (169). Whatever
abscess of misogyny and racist disgust and male self-disgust might be in
evidence here is not investigated by Alexander. She was so shaken that she
couldn't speak of this incident to her white American husband because
she did not know if he would understand "what it mean[s] to be Unwhite
in America" (169). Instead, she confided in an Indian friend. Alexander
registers not only her humiliation and irreducible exclusion as a foreigner
in the eyes of segments of white America (regardless of her gender). She
also delineates her abjection on account of her dark body with regard to
Asian-America, because of her particular history, her accent, and so on,
and with regard to white mainstream America, including white feminist
America—intersubjective sisterhood with them offers little, judging at
least by this memoir, to offset that overdetermined abjection.

Being unwhite in America means different things for differently situated
people, and again it is the difference that must not be occluded, particularly with reference to her diasporic status. In America, if not in Britain,
being unwhite means something different from being black. And the nice
evasion tucked into the word "unwhite" needs to be unpacked, although
Alexander does not do it. Quite apart from the problem of the invisibility
of "unwhite" minorities as such, there is also the effective erasure of their
cultural differences. South Asians cannot easily "transcend" their ethnicity as social barrier even when they wish to do so, compared with white
immigrants—they are all too visible in this sense, although to some degree, of course, all minorities share this difficulty. Ronald Takaki, an emi-
nent member of one of the more powerful Asian-American groups in the
country, says that although his family has been in this country for more
than a hundred years, he often does not look "American" enough to white
Americans (*A Different Mirror* 1). So South Asian Americans are more
"visible," in one sense (they stick out as even less assimilated, less "American," as a group than Japanese or Chinese Americans), and less visible in
another sense, partly because there are fewer of them, and they are more
recent immigrants as a rule. It seems fair to say, at any rate, that Asian-
America does not always recognize the presence, on an equal footing, of
South Asian Americans.

It is all the more strange then that there is precious little acknowledgment of interethnic tensions in Alexander's book—a puzzling elision in a
book entitled *Fault Lines*. One explanation may be that her memoir,

which is by definition an intimate discourse, sees the politics of representation on an interpersonal level, rather than on a social or political level. On the other hand, perhaps (to give her the benefit of doubt) she is more interested in the question of what kinds of collaboration are possible among the various minorities. But her elision may also have something to do with the fact that she has been successful and fortunate (to the extent that her fortune has to do less with individual effort and more with what might be called the accidentals of her ontic self—her race, her class, and so on) within the academy and it might therefore seem ungracious and ungrateful to point to interethnic tensions, even when she could not help noticing them. When she does address the plurality of ethnicities that weave the skein of American society, she finesses the more invidious features of interethnic relations, and writes brightly, "There are so many strands all running together in a bright snarl of life. . . . My job is to evoke it all, altogether. For that is what America with its hotshot present tense compels me to" (198).

The risk of Alexander's blithe indifference to the nuances of interethnic tensions is that such issues as ethnic difference and, more generally, subject construction, are aestheticized, as though they posed a problem of merely textual recuperation. But in some cases, as in the case of truly subaltern groups, the struggle may well be experienced as more than an aesthetic struggle—many members of minority constituencies, including immigrants or diasporics, do not have the kind of academic access, cultural mobility, and privilege enjoyed by Alexander herself, by virtue of her class and educational opportunities. So there are unexplored fault lines that divide her from a large segment of her own "ethnic group."

To be fair, it is not as if being "unwhite"—or dark—is for Alexander only an American affliction. Even at home in India, when Meena was a young girl, her grandmother invoked the caste, class, and ethnic anxieties and prejudices against dark skin. How would she find a husband, her grandmother chastised her, if she ran around in the sun, for she was "a child without beauty, a plump dark-skinned thing" (50, 49). Were it not for the things money could buy—dresses, soap, brushes, good haircuts, there would be "no way at all of telling me apart from any servant child, or the child of any Sudra. . . . Looking the way I did, I would bring nothing but shame to the family" (43). And then again there is the undeniable fact of her being female, which is a "curse" and a painful "horror" (45, 111), both in her culture of birth and in her adopted South Asian American setting: "Sitting here in New York City . . . I recall my childhood fears about what it might mean to be born into a female body" (42). Her class, her gender, her dark skin, her race, her ethnicity, as well as her "good"

English, are factors complicating a reductive conceptualization of the cultural space occupied by her body.

Against the risk of disembodiment and deracination, Alexander seems to feel that the specificity of the diasporic postcolonial subject must be reclaimed at the level of emotional life, and at the level of the everyday body in cultural space. Thus her dissatisfaction with her master's thesis at Nottingham: though she was writing about "intentionality" and "[le] corps vecu," there was "no color there, no female flesh, no postcolonial burden" (141). But such reclamation is possible only as mediated through language, although there again she risks what I have called above an aestheticization of difference, since difference is not universally experienced, even among migrants, as primarily a problem of language. Still, Alexander's obsession with language as the home of being re-cognizes in a strong sense Werner Sollors's thematization of invention—not as indicating "originality and innovation" so much as stressing "the importance of language in the social construction of reality" (*Invention* x).

Alexander understands the epistemological point that the textualization of the world entails a practical acknowledgment that "the literal is always *discrepant*, a sharp otherness to what the imagination conjures up as it blends time, emotions, heartbeats" (31; emphasis added). But she adds to this understanding a recognition ontologically compelled by a specifically postcolonial diasporic sensibility. She writes of the

> violence in the very language, American English, that we have to face, even as we work to make it ours, decolonize it so that it will express the truth of bodies beaten and banned. After all, for such as we are the territories are not free. The world is not open. That endless space, the emptiness of the American sublime is worse than a lie. It does ceaseless damage to the imagination. (199)

This violence could of course be experienced only by those who do not identify themselves unproblematically with "America"—so Alexander's "we" in the passage quoted is clearly aligned with a diasporic sensibility, with a sensibility whose first home is not "American English."

And writing, Alexander finds, restores an intimate connection with color, with the postcolonial burden, and the female body: "Didn't Baldwin say . . . that being a Negro was the gate he had to unlock before he could write about anything else? I think being an Asian-American must be like that. Through that bodily gate the alphabets pour in. This is our life in letters" (200). But Alexander's situation is not identical with that of the "Negro" (why does Alexander choose that old-fashioned word here?), just as it is not identical with that of other, "preferred" Asian-Americans such as Japanese- or Chinese-Americans. Nevertheless, like that other expatriate Baldwin, Alexander feels the urgency to "write myself into being," to overcome her invisibility. But this writing inscribes the body even as it seems to require the destruction of its ontological integrity: "What should I write with? Milk, blood, feces, spittle, stumps of bone, torn flesh? Is this mutilation? . . . Sometimes I think I write to evade the names they have given me" (73). She does not tell us who "they" are. But perhaps the anomie she thematizes here has something to do with the face-lessness of those who have the power of description.

Writing has a "forked power," then, because it is a way to achieve "in-timacy" with her own body and being, and simultaneously a "canonical" and colonial burden—because she writes after all in the English lan-guage, steeped equally in a literary and a colonial history—a burden that alienates her "from what I was born to" (125, 129; 116, 119, 126, 199). Is "what [she] was born to" a kind of pre-Symbolic homeland?—here, as at so many crucial moments, the reader may well wonder whether she examines adequately the logical implications of her most enigmatic turns of phrase, the stylistic intricacies of which are crafted with so much evi-dent self-consciousness. At any rate, if Alexander talks about the body to emphasize the materiality of lived experience, there is no attempt at positing or projecting what Paul Smith calls a "cerned" subject (106–7). Alexander's approximation of body to city charts a multiply fissured space where self is always only "provisional" (177). This allows for the flower-ing of the enigmatic and the unpredictable—and for an emergent desire not circumscribed within the ready pedagogical which would foreclose precisely the avenues of that other desire's expression and fulfillment. Al-exander's memoir is as much about the erotics as about the ethics and the politics of diasporic agency.

Alexander's insistence on the body does not stem from an anxiety to authenticate agency by appeal to an ineffable interiority; solace can come from "exit[ing] from the self" (176). The "solution" to the problem of the South Asian American's invisibility is not in an insistence on a program-matic identity politics where the goal is merely to hew to a reified eth-nicity: "Ethnicity for such as I am comes into being as a pressure, a vio-lence from within" (202). This enigmatic, unpredictable seismology of self is preserved as possibility, as emergent from a perpetually other (not "ter-ritorialized") autochthony which is never self-identical: "We have an eth-nicity that breeds in the perpetual present, [but one] that will never be wholly spelt out" (202). Nor is a solution to be had from an emphasis on mere individual empowerment, atomized agency. As Alexander herself writes, "The bigger hunk of what needs to be told . . . where the body is, comes with rage, with the overt acknowledgment of the nature of injus-

tice. The struggle for social justice . . . is for each of us. Like ethnicity, like
the labor of poetry, it is larger than any single person. It transcends indi-
vidualism" (203). In theory, at least, Alexander then provides an obvious
answer to a pair of questions that seem to trouble Elspeth Probyn: "Is it
possible for the autobiographical voice not to be self-centred, and does
attention to one's self have to produce a hierarchy of selves?" (118).
Alexander provides an instance of how the answer to the first can be an
unequivocal yes, and to the second, no.

However, the South Asian diasporic must also invent something to
celebrate, for if South Asian Americans don't speak of their own dignity
and enjoyment, who will? In using "enjoyment" here, I invoke the full,
psychoanalytically enshrined (in the work, for instance, of Jacques Lacan
and Slavoj Zizek) sense of the ambit of desire, as well as the Rawlsian
sense of the ability of a person to enjoy "the culture of [one's] society
and to take part in its affairs, and in this way to provide . . . a secure sense
of [one's] own worth" (Rawls 101). This is the burden, perhaps, of the
enigma Alexander has taken to heart as a programmatic parable—the
katha of the stone-eating girl: "She had taught herself whatever skills she
had, learnt to use them in her own way, and to set herself up as her own
authority so that in her unmitigated gluttony . . . she became a female icon,
creator of a stern discipline, perfector of an art" (Alexander 85).

The dyspeptic discipline of the stone-eating girl suggests the complicated structure of (a feminine) desire. Yet this strange tale also suggests the
straining, on Alexander's part, to canalize writing toward a not-yet-fully
cognized pleasure. I invoke here the psychoanalytic sense of the term
"canalize," with its suggestion of channeling, characterized by the uncon-
scious narrowing, restricting, and blocking of certain thoughts and feelings. The word that Alexander chooses in the quoted passage is "gluttony"; but the image of the stone-eating girl is an image of deprivation.
"Gluttony" would be appropriate in this context only as a bitterly ironic
code for "starved." The desire of the stone-eating girl is ambiguous and
enigmatic—but it is very much a central problematic. The enigma of the
stone-eating girl's affect preserves something of the enigma of Alexander's
own, for at the heart of autobiography is a kernel of affect. And yet it is
imaginatively linked to the bittersweet desire that is translated in that
translation we call diaspora. To return to the rhetorical question she posed
in reference to her son: "What did my first-born wish for himself? Some
nothingness, some transitory zone where dreams roamed, a border country without passport or language?" (172–73).

By the same token, if there is a general flaw in this memoir, I suggest
it is in its failure to even approximate a developed notion of what enjoyment, as desire fulfillment and full participation in society, might mean for

such a person as referenced by Alexander's reconstructed autobiographical self-image. Thus in the symbolic pairing of Meena the woman and the stone-eating girl as a mirrored (dis)figuration of Meena, it is never clear whether the stone-eating girl is closer to Meena Alexander than others she presents as exempla for herself: the emancipated actress Snehaprabha, or the femme fatale in red high-heels who functions in the memoir as a kind of alter ego too, not to mention Susikali the tomboy and Sosamma the unconventional relative with whom Alexander seems to feel a bond. These are all figures in a kind of pre-Symbolic (but emphatically not a feminine intersubjective) chora, at best, to invoke Julia Kristeva's category: Alexander's exempla are all located in that realm that the memoir outlines but does not exhaustively probe (Kristeva 265). The distortions of her own figure by the tain of the mirror—which she has so minutely and densely silvered—are not explored. It is a lapse that contravenes the basic principle that James Olney, avowedly following Heraclitus and many others since, suggests animates the autobiographical impulse: "Man explores the universe continually for laws and forms not of his own making, but what, in the end, he always finds is his own face" (4).

Indeed one might go so far as to say that Alexander seems almost to seek refuge in an unanalyzed cultural past—a perpetual, dear, rooted place recollected and idealized in the imagination—and to desire the forcing (through the interstices of the memoir's "present") of the past toward an "anterior future" that could redeem the fractured time and space of the present. Thus the obsessive return, sans scrutiny, to her idyllic childhood in the generous shade of her grandfather Ilya, when she could be a relatively uncomplicated kernel of what she might not have had to become. And thus, similarly, the return at the end of the memoir to her mother, to ask her to tell the *katha,* or ritualized tale, of her mother's marriage, steeped in the douce fixative of tradition. The ritual of traditional marriage is something none of the "sophisticated" Alexander daughters, including Meena, felt they could well allow themselves to want wholeheartedly, so they entertain hopeless "fantasies" of a wedding with all the traditional trimmings (217). While this meeting with her mother suggests a possible recuperation of the (abjected) dark body and the pleasures of intersubjectivity, at least among women, through the function of mothering itself, the option seems closed to Meena—at one point, betraying all feminist sophistication, she even wishes "for a moment what I have never wished before: that I might have been born male" (222).[11] Even the "pleasure" of nostalgia is denied to Meena: she is really cut off from the enabling structures and traditions of both the West where she lives and the East where she lived. She seems alienated from her own desire.

Relatedly, Alexander seems to underestimate or underappreciate the value of the theoretical attitude, of the interminable analysis of the machinery and the politics of representation. It is not only at the level of the concrete, the bodily, that cultural articulation takes place. Belonging/not belonging—that seam is where Alexander situates her autobiographical self. This irresolution of belonging, rather than "resolution" and subsequent accommodation through assimilation and erasure of problematic difference, must remain an open question, although for many of the reasons I have discussed, diasporic South Asian communities, like others not composed primarily of intellectuals, can be oblivious, indifferent, or hostile to theory.[12] Their reluctance may spring, for instance, from the very desire for exnomination that Anannya Bhattacharjee thematizes (21). This makes the academic role of postcolonial theory that much more vital, though of course it is not clear that it has much impact outside the academy. In this respect postcolonial cultural theory, and the work of theoretically aware writers, share the condition of feminism at least in regard to Nancy Miller's brave notion that if the rallying cry of seventies feminism was that "the personal is the political," then eighties feminism promoted the credo that "the personal is also the theoretical" (21). It is in this connection that I return to my earlier question: Should such a memoir be immune to charges of inadequately theorized exploration and aestheticization? It is a pity that so much that is personal does not receive the light of theoretically informed examination in this memoir.

For Alexander self-determination takes a very literal form. However, she goes to the symbolic extent of rejecting her father's "protection" by changing her name: "As long as I lived under his protection, I was Mary Elizabeth in my passport. Then I added an alias: Meena. I felt I had changed my name to what I already was, some truer self, stripped free of the colonial burden. . . . It is also the home name my parents had chosen for me at birth" (74). Alexander seems to want to distance herself from her father's closet Royalist sympathies—"the British sense of order, or stilling the 'native' chaos in the colonies struck a chord with my father" (60, 154). For the postcolonial diasporic, there is always the question of whether the impulse toward assimilation is linked to the ambivalent desire to become like those who have historically inculcated the fable of their own superiority to the darker races that they colonized—this tendency has of course been thematized by Frantz Fanon, Albert Memmi, and more recently Homi Bhabha. But even as she renames herself to reject "Mary Elizabeth" and with it the "protection" of her father as well as the traces of missionary Christian activity (handmaiden to the colonial enterprise), she re-embraces a Hindu name, Meena, in a country where she was a member of a minority, as a Christian.[13]

As postcolonial migrant, she constantly seeks a less degrading self-translation, a less compromised complicity. But it is a kind of complicity nonetheless. And, since the issue of complicity has to do with cultural location, diaspora becomes in Alexander's memoir a point of departure for the exploration of a range of complicitous alignments, and as such it invites a contrast with the alignments of other Asian-American groups. On the one hand, then, there is a kind of leftist leaning: witness, for instance, the energetic feminism that she embraces, most vividly in her expressed solidarity with a figure such as Audre Lorde. On the other, there are all those trappings of undisguised pride in the almost aristocratic superiority of her background and all the privilege and complicity with a social elite that betokened. She seems to recognize that she is a member of a diasporic minority within a minority, but she avoids a close examination of whether her own comfortable niche in the American academy (she now teaches at Hunter College in New York City) requires a form of complicity. That is to say, her politics seem either ambiguous or ambivalent. Her thematization of self-determination remains somewhat undernourished because it lacks the fiber, the conviction, of a more self-reflexive politics, a fuller conception of the goal of civil society where she is incidentally interpellated as diasporic. If the personal really is the theoretical, then a much greater resonance with contemporary cultural critique is conspicuous in its absence from her pages. While it points everywhere to much larger social themes alive to the politics of contemporary multicultural America, Alexander's memoir seems unable, because of its very fault lines, to sustain a surface tension because of the paucity of substance that might have given it a critical mass. It sags under the weight of its own inwardness, its centripetal inertia toward a center of selfhood that she has been at such pains to evacuate.

Perhaps this is too harsh. It is possible that her reticence to address the tendentious debates about multiculturalism is not just an academic discretion. But it is equally likely that it is a silence born of the impulse to deflect attention from the contradiction between the privilege she has enjoyed as a member of a respected South Indian Christian family of a certain class and her occasionally voguish self-portrayal as a disenfranchised minority within a (U.S.) minority. This has an inevitable impact on the *topoi* to which she can attach the multifarious fragments of the identity she permits herself to acknowledge, recognize, in this memoir. Indeed, what is being memorialized here is the absent center of this fragmentary identity, a center whose decentering is both celebrated in a kind of crypto-deconstructive flourish of antiessentialism and polyvocality, and lamented in a kind of faux-poetic identification with the downtrodden and dispossessed of transnational spaces and places. If her aim in writing this memoir was to regain a sense of the fissured self, it is also true that its very silences, in some measure beyond the author's design, disenable full self-recognition. The contradictions at the heart of the decentered self of this memoir cannot be "discerned"—to adapt Paul Smith's pun—on the one hand, because of the fault lines traversed by this diasporic in the external world and, on the other hand, because she flinches from her own repressions and misrecognitions.

The problematic of self-determination is also keyed to place. Place, or space, is not to be conceived only in geographical terms, but also in terms of the imaginary, that unnamable that Donatella Mazzoleni locates "behind" the physical city-space (285). Listing the many cities and towns she has lived in ("Allahabad, Tiruvella, Kozencheri, Pune, Delhi, Hyderabad . . . Khartoum . . . Nottingham . . . Manhattan"), Alexander wonders how meaning can be forged out of spatial dispersion, another name for diaspora: "How should I spell out these fragments of a broken geography?" (2). She thinks she could "lift these scraps of place and much as a dressmaker, cut them into shape" (30). Such a diasporic hermeneutics, such politicized vigilance, is necessary not only for the worlding of a livable space but also for the brinkmanship required of the nomadic migrant described in Sujata Bhatt's poem, from which the epigraph to this essay comes—the migrant who relinquishes any home. Alexander also speaks of the "Other who I am . . . she has no home, no fixed address, no shelter . . . she is a nowhere creature" (30).

There may be something naively sanguine about this vision of a nomadic cultural positionality. But one of the undesirable alternatives to such a vigilance is the kind of oneiric limbo into which the migrant often lapses without it. Another South Asian diasporic, Bharati Mukherjee, well describes this trap in her vignette of the prototypical migrant lives of the Vadheras, an immigrant couple in *Jasmine*. The husband dreams of his past eminence as a professor in India while he spins elaborate fictions in the present to compensate for his failure to achieve even his watered-down American dream. His wife is caught between her obsession with viewing videotapes of Indian films (a virtual recapture of a lost reality) and a near-total withdrawal from everyday social life—she too lives in a kind of immigrant American nightmare, unable to live in the India she has left behind or in the country in which she is exiled by her marriage. In both cases the migrant is undone by an inability to grasp the symbolic power of self-definition and by a systemic exclusion of the migrant from real participation from the public sphere where, I have been arguing, civil society is negotiable.

In contrast to this limbo of the migrant's deracination, the eponymous character Jasmine, in Mukherjee's novel, and here Alexander's autobiographical self, are presented as active poets—creators—of their own habitations and self-images. Both authors understand the power of the imaginary. Alexander writes that "in my dreams, I am haunted by thoughts of a homeland I will never find. So I have tuned my lines to a different aesthetic, one that I build up out of all the stuff around me, improvising as I go along. I am surrounded by jetsam. It is what I am, the marks of my being." (27). Alexander's diaspora is an alternative to assimilation. She construes it as becoming like a hermit crab, carrying one's borrowed homes on one's back and changing them frequently, unpredictably (193).

The persistence of the homeland as a mythology preserves the diasporic's fantasy of return, a retrograde narrative Alexander is counseled by none other than Talal Asad to "demystify" (177–78). Rooting identities in a past and in a place they know they have for all practical purposes left for good is the dream not of the diasporic, but of the sojourner. And Alexander, despite her own obsessive imaginary return to sites of her past, ultimately grasps this: "The old notions of exile, that high estate, are gone; smashed underfoot in the transit lounges, the supermarkets, the video parlors of the world. . . . History is maquillage. No homeland here" (193).

CONCLUSION

In a crucial sense, diaspora is precisely a measure for the "gap" created by Alexander's positionality as South Asian America. The point is to contrast this positionality to the modality of assimilation, which for immigrant groups is offered as a carrot as much as it is a stick, and this is nowhere more true than in the case of the South Asian diaspora in the United States. There is no doubt that assimilation for diasporic constituencies means inclusion in the story of their new country. But the blandishments of assimilation should not obscure the costs. The expressed desire for assimilation, where it is not simply evidence of a disadvantaged group's unacknowledged insularity and desire for exnomination, ends up being indistinguishable from a wish for invisibility, a self-induced disenfranchisement and evacuation of agency, or a kind of ossification of self-image that disables a full apprehension of one's interpellation within the narratives of nation and of one's ability to transform them. Members of a model minority may achieve exnomination in the safe zone of the model minority but they may also be effectively depoliticized in the process. Those migrants who do not attempt to participate in inscribing their own histories into the ongoing narrative of the host nation risk being reduced to ciphers. That reduction ultimately pulverizes them into a single, unifying alphabet, a smooth singular history in which there are no counterpoints to the anthems of the reigning order.

Even in the short term, the assimilationist tendency can in some cases militate against success and raise the level of tolerance of unjust treatment. Social resistance, in the form of political or critical participation, is often seen as antithetical to assimilationist or communitarian ideas: divisively particularist, opportunistic, appropriative of the hard-won achievements of the more "significant" minorities such as the African-American or Japanese-American minorities. Even within the rarefied atmosphere of academe, several critics, such as Anthony Appiah and Arif Dirlik (to name two recent examples), have accused postcolonial diasporic critics of such opportunism. But tensions as well as possibilities for coalitions among ethnic groups, alignments of minority individuals and members of majority groups, negotiation between "Americans" and those who are not quite—these are precisely what need to be talked about more openly, and diaspora studies offer a productive discursive site. Alexander's autobiography betrays what is perhaps a characteristic trait of the work of well-placed, middle-class academics—the discreet papering over of competition among minority groups in academe but also in society at large. But the imbalances of marginality cannot remain a dirty secret, and should be aired frankly. The lack of fit, the gap, between South Asian America and "Asian-America" or "America" should be acknowledged (since it is there even though one might have wished otherwise in some Utopia), as well as mined for its heuristic possibilities within cultural studies, not in a spirit of bloody-minded selfishness but in a spirit of honest, politically engaged participation in cultural Realpolitik.

Although there may be some uniting struggles among members of diverse minorities, where there is already an asymmetry of representation, there cannot be true cooperation, let alone true reciprocity. Thus one of the underemphasized initiatives of what is called "multiculturalism" is the redress of such imbalance. Rawls touches on the notion of reciprocity as "implicit in the notion of a well-ordered society" (14). Calls for true reciprocity are often met with the response that what is by definition needed then is a putting aside of difference—it is suggested then that an emphasis on difference, such as mine, is potentially disruptive, illiberal, or just misguided. But we cannot ignore the fact that it is easier for a minority in the majority to eschew competition in favor of cooperation than it is for the minority in the minority. I hope this doesn't seem a small-minded complaint. But in any case the large, substantive struggle isn't ultimately between unequal minorities. If it were, the struggles could hardly be anything but mutually degrading, and the multiculturalist slogans espoused by them would conveniently play to the advantage of the less admirable purposes of the majority. In fact the struggle is about a more universal principle of social justice, as well as about a communal sense of self-worth that arises within and out of difference and not despite it, a communal sense that is not an enforced ghettoization of some groups, but a really reciprocal arrangement.

In purely literary terms, too, it is a matter less of competition among minorities or between minoritarian and majoritarian cultural production than it is a matter of recognizing and theorizing the crucial place of difference occupied (although this participle is certainly to be put under erasure) by "ethnic" literature in the very constitution of "America." Sollors's work in *Beyond Ethnicity* is one important instance of such theorizing, although many critics have pointed out the shortcomings of his approach.[14]

I take the case of South Asian America then not as promising a "marriage," as in Richard Rodriguez' proposal, but as a refiguration of the "hyphen" as preserving the "hymen" Jacques Derrida has deconstructed— and reconstructed. This particular diaspora offers an opportunity that could easily dissolve into an unquestioning acquiescence to the path of least resistance, assimilation. There are many voices in the multicultural-ism debates calling for assimilation in the genuine, naive, or calculating belief that difference threatens something they think they recognize as "the American way of life"—tellingly in the singular. This opportunity to occupy the border, or what Drucilla Cornell in a feminist context has called a "limit," "can and should be read as an opening to a new meaning, including the dreams of [an] imaginary which can never be completely fore-closed" (6). Such an opening is under threat of foreclosure for South Asian Americans, just when their success as a minority seems within their grasp, when social justice and equality appear in the shape of the seductive call to, and promise of, undifferentiated and exnominated assimilation into Asian-America and into America. Everything depends, of course, on distinguishing between a puerile, rebellious separatism and the self-reflexive and fully theorized border politics I am arguing for as an ideal. It is unquestioning assimilation that impoverishes multiculturalism and the grab bag of "diversity." A border politics can nourish the internal differences of the narrative of nation in the United States as a site from which to open that narrative to an understanding of its larger and inevitable transnational context. The American nation-state has precious little meaning except as considered within that context.

NOTES

1. Note that elsewhere in this volume, the hyphen is not used in the term "Asian American," in accordance with *The Chicago Manual of Style,* 14th ed. (Chicago: University of Chicago Press, 1993). For the purposes of this essay it will be retained.

2. This talking cure may seem uncontroversial as a model for civil society, but it is precisely the positionality of the citizen "as a talker"—in Kingwell's terminology— rather than as "a rational chooser" (along the lines of Enlightenment theories of society) that minorities such as South Asian Americans find hard to occupy. The implications of such "talking," for civil society, is not that there is some a priori, transcendental utopic space around which civil society may be expected to form itself, or toward which telos to proceed. Rather it is implied that a discursive space within which negotiation can continually occur is itself a token of the success of society. And it is just because assimilation to an already existing imaginary called "America" fails to capture the sort of openness entailed by such negotiation, my suggestion is that one might look toward diaspora groups (and here I take up the instance of South Asian Americans) for one particularly promising contemporary revitalization of this principled exchange at the heart of civil society.

3. Here I am indebted to a reviewer at Temple University Press for suggesting I rethink the linkages between diaspora and particular readings of nationality.

4. In a discussion of university multicultural political rhetoric, Alice Roy discusses the pairing of *inclusion* and *inclusivity* as companion terms with *diversity*. She writes, "*Include* remains a transitive verb. It entails an includer and, so to speak, an includee, and, because of the property of negation in human language, an 'excludee' as well. Our policies and pedagogies may acknowledge diversity, yet in effect exclude those diverse others who cannot negotiate the financial minefield created by unemployment, budget reductions, and increased fees, or who in other ways do not fit traditional notions of appropriate members of the academic community. . . . The language, and the act of selecting language, can beguile both producers and consumers of that language into believing that inclusivity and diversity have been successfully incorporated in official communications to faculty, students, and the community. But it may be that by not challenging the conditions that militate against our well-intentioned efforts, we are reinforcing them" (193).

5. Gayatri Spivak is perhaps the most prominent case in point. See Spivak, *The Post-Colonial Critic*, 77. See also the more general criticism of Arif Dirlik, in his "The Postcolonial Aura," 328–56.

6. Dotbusters were a group of white males who verbally and physically attacked Indian Americans in Jersey City with the aim of running them out of the area.

7. As Mazumdar also notes, "In Britain, Canada and South Africa, the overt color bar and institutionalized racism to which South Asians are subject has served to politicize segments of many South Asian communities. The black consciousness movement and the black women's movement have drawn together individuals from the Afro-Caribbean and Asian communities in Britain. . . . In the United States, in contrast . . . it is still too early to tell whether segments of the South Asians in the United States will become sufficiently politicized to form similar alliances with blacks and other people of color" (36).

8. I have personally been informed, on at least two occasions, that South Asian Americans were not among the "preferred" (that was the actual bureaucratic term) minorities. This is remarkable in a job market mediated through such repu-

table organs (not to attach to them the Althusserian squib of "apparatuses") as accredited academic institutions advertising in the *Modern Language Association Job Listing* and the *Chronicle of Higher Education.*

9. The list of recent works on the topic of "nation" is too long to even begin to represent here. But among the more prominent texts one might include Aijaz Ahmad, *In Theory: Nations, Classes, Literatures;* Benedict Anderson, *Imagined Communities;* Homi Bhabha, ed., *Nation and Narration;* Ernest Gellner, *Nations and Nationalism;* Paul Gilroy, *There Ain't No Black in the Union Jack;* Eric J. Hobsbawm, *Nations and Nationalism Since 1788;* Peter Jackson and Jan Penrose, eds., *Constructions of Race, Place, and Nation;* Tom Nairn, *The Break Up of Britain;* and George Mosse, *Nationalism and Sexuality.*

10. Another outspoken cultivator of the ethnic margin, Richard Rodriguez, observes that autobiography is "the genre of the discontinuous life" (*The Invention of Ethnicity* 8). But here and elsewhere Rodriguez advocates a considerably more assimilationist view than I am arguing is necessary for a critical South Asian American discourse. In his vision, the presence of Hispanic-Americans should lead us to expect "marriage" as well as "bastard themes." This vision borders on the overly sanguine, although I find compelling and true his belief that plurality is something that "America" needs and must see as contributing to its long-term health as a nation. And "the nation" as a unitary figment is the limit of Rodriguez' conception.

11. Again, I am grateful to the anonymous reviewers at Temple University Press for pointing to the possible "recuperation of the body in the transcendental function of mothering," but I hope it is clear from my reading that this possibility is foreclosed, as an unproblematic option, for Meena herself. So there is really no medium here for the "intersubjective community" that the reviewer suggests may be an alternative open to Meena.

12. See Prasenjit Duara, 779–804.

13. In the discussion of the implications of Meena's name change, I have greatly benefited from the suggestions of Lavina Shankar and Rajini Srikanth.

14. See Curtis C. Smith, and also Wald, for instance.

WORKS CITED

Aaron, Daniel. "The Hyphenate Writer and American Letters." *Smith Alumnae Quarterly* (July 1964): 215.

Aijaz, Ahmad. *In Theory: Nations, Classes, Literatures.* London: Verso, 1992.

Alexander, Meena. *Fault Lines.* New York: Feminist Press, 1992.

Anderson, Benedict. *Imagined Communities: Reflections on the Origin and Spread of Nationalism.* London: Verso, 1983.

Appiah, Kwame Anthony. "The Conservation of 'Race.'" *Black American Literature Forum* 23.1 (Spring 1989): 37–60.

Bhabha, Homi, ed. *Nation and Narration.* London: Routledge, 1990.

Bhatt, Sujata. "The One Who Goes Away." *The New Statesman and Society* (April 21, 1995): 41.

Bhattacharjee, Anannya. "The Habit of Ex-Nomination: Nation, Woman, and the Indian Immigrant Bourgeoisie." *Public Culture* 5.1 (Fall 1992): 19–44.

Blundell, Valda, John Shepherd, and Ian Taylor, eds. *Relocating Cultural Studies: Developments in Theory and Research.* New York: Routledge, 1993.

Buell, Frederick. *National Culture and the New Global System.* Baltimore: Johns Hopkins University Press, 1994.

Carter, Erica, James Donald, and Judith Squires. *Space and Place: Theories of Identity and Location.* London: Lawrence & Wishart, 1993.

Chicago Cultural Studies Group. "Critical Multiculturalism." *Critical Inquiry* 18 (Spring 1992): 530–55.

Cornell, Drucilla. *Transformations: Recollective Imagination and Sexual Difference.* New York and London: Routledge, 1993.

Dayal, Samir. "Creating, Preserving, Destroying: Violence in Bharati Mukherjee's *Jasmine*." In *Bharati Mukherjee: Critical Perspectives,* edited by Emmanuel S. Nelson. New York: Garland, 1993, 65–88.

Derrida, Jacques. *Dissemination.* Translated by Barbara Johnson. Chicago: University of Chicago Press, 1981.

Dirlik, Arif. "The Postcolonial Aura: Third World Criticism in the Age of Global Capitalism." *Critical Inquiry* 20 (Winter 1994): 328–56.

Duara, Prasenjit. "Bifurcating Linear History: Nation and Histories in China and India." *Positions: East Asia Cultures Critique* 1.3 (Winter 1993): 779–804.

Ferraro, Thomas J. *Ethnic Passages: Literary Immigrants in Twentieth-Century America.* Chicago: University of Chicago Press, 1993.

Fiedler, Leslie. *Waiting for the End.* New York: Stein and Day, 1964.

Furth, Isabella. "Bee-e-een! Nation, Transformation and the Hyphen of Ethnicity in Kingston's Tripmaster Monkey." *Modern Fiction Studies* 40.1 (Spring 1994): 33–49.

Gellner, Ernest. *Nations and Nationalism.* Oxford: Basil Blackwell, 1983.

Gilroy, Paul. *The Black Atlantic: Modernity and Double Consciousness.* Cambridge: Harvard University Press, 1993.

———. *There Ain't No Black in the Union Jack: The Cultural Politics of Race and Nation.* Chicago: University of Chicago Press, 1991. Originally published 1987.

Gómez-Peña, Guillermo. "La Plaza." PBS Broadcast, July 12, 1995.

Gordon, Susan. *Recent American Immigrants: Asian Indians.* New York: Franklin Watts, 1990.

Griffiths, Philip Jones. "The Desi Chain: The Rewriting of American Identity." *Newsweek,* July 10, 1995, 34.

Hess, Gary R. "The Forgotten Asian-Americans: The East Indian Community in the United States." In *The Asian-American,* edited by Norris Hundley, Jr., 157–77.

Hobsbawm, Eric J. *Nations and Nationalism Since 1780: Programme, Myth, Reality.* London: Cambridge University Press, 1990.

Hundley, Norris, Jr., ed. *The Asian-American: The Historical Experience.* Oxford: Clio Books, 1976.

Jackson, Peter, and Jan Penrose, eds. *Constructions of Race, Place, and Nation.* London: University College London Press, 1993.

Jensen, Joan M. *Passage from India: Asian Indian Immigrants in North America.* New Haven: Yale University Press, 1988.

Katz, William Loren. *A History of Multicultural America: Minorities Today.* Austin, Tex.: Raintree Steck-Vaughn Press, 1993.

Kimball, Roger. "Tenured Radicals: A Postscript." *New Criterion.* January 1991: 4–13.

Kingwell, Mark. *A Civil Tongue: Justice, Dialogue, and the Politics of Pluralism.* University Park, Penn.: Pennsylvania State University Press, 1995.

Kuo, Wen H. "Coping with Racial Discrimination: The Case of Asian-Americans." *Ethnic and Racial Issues* 18.1 (Jan. 1995): 109–27.

Kristeva, Julia. *Desire in Language: A Semiotic Approach to Literature and Art.* Translated by Thomas Gora, Alice Jardine, and Leon S. Roudiez. Edited by Leon S. Roudiez. New York: Columbia University Press, 1980.

Lee, Benjamin. "Critical Internationalism." *Public Culture* 7 (1995): 559–92.

Malkki, Liisa. "Citizens of Humanity: Internationalism and the Imagined Community of Nations." *Diaspora* 3.1 (1994): 41–68.

Mazumdar, Sucheta. "Race and Racism: South Asians in the United States." In *Frontiers of Asian American Studies,* edited by Gail Nomura et al., 25–38.

Mazzoleni, Donatella. "The City and the Imaginary." Translated by John Koumantarakis. In *Space and Place,* edited by Erica Carter et al., 285–301.

Miller, Nancy K. *Getting Personal: Feminist Occasions and Other Autobiographical Acts.* New York and London: Routledge, 1991.

Mosse, George. *Nationalism and Sexuality: Middle-Class Morality and Sexual Norms in Modern Europe.* Madison: University of Wisconsin Press, 1985.

Mukherjee, Bharati. *Jasmine.* New York: Grove Weidenfeld, 1989.

Nairn, Tom. *The Break Up of Britain.* London: New Left Books, 1977.

Nomura, Gail, Russell Endo, Stephen H. Sumida, and Russell C. Leong, eds. *Frontiers of Asian American Studies: Writing, Research, and Commentary.* Pullman, Wash.: Washington State University Press, 1989.

Olney, James. *Metaphors of Self: The Meaning of Autobiography.* Princeton, N.J.: Princeton University Press, 1972.

Probyn, Elspeth. "True Voices and Real People: The 'Problem' of the Autobiographical in Cultural Studies." In *Relocating Cultural Studies,* edited by Valda Blundell et al.

Rawls, John. *A Theory of Justice.* Cambridge: Harvard University Press, 1971.

Rodriguez, Richard. "An American Writer." In *The Invention of Ethnicity,* edited by Werner Sollors, 3–13.

Roy, Alice. "The Grammar and Rhetoric of Inclusion." *College English* 57.2 (Feb. 1995): 182–95.

Saran, Parmatma, and Edwin Eames, eds. *The New Ethnics: Asian Indians in the United States.* New York: Praeger, 1980.

Sharpe, Jenny. "Is the United States Postcolonial? Transnationalism, Immigration, and Race." *Diaspora* 4.2 (1995): 181–99.

Singh, Anita Inder. "Is Ethnicity Enough?" Review of John Hutchinson, *Modern*

Nationalism, and John Hutchinson and Anthony D. Smith, eds. *Nationalism. Times Literary Supplement,* Mar. 17, 1995: 12.

Smith, Curtis C. "Werner Sollors's *Beyond Ethnicity* and Afro-American Literature." *MELUS* 14 (Summer 1987): 65–72.

Smith, Paul. *Discerning the Subject.* Minneapolis: University of Minnesota Press, 1988.

Sollors, Werner. *Beyond Ethnicity: Consent and Descent in American Culture.* New York: Oxford University Press, 1986.

———, ed. *The Invention of Ethnicity.* New York: Oxford University Press, 1989.

Spivak, Gayatri C. *The Post-Colonial Critic.* Edited by Sarah Harasym. New York: Routledge, 1990.

Takaki, Ronald T. *A Different Mirror: A History of Multicultural America.* Boston: Little, Brown, 1993.

———. *Strangers from a Different Shore: A History of Asian Americans.* Boston: Little, Brown, 1989.

Varma, Baidya Nath. "Indians as New Ethnics: A Theoretical Note." In *The New Ethnics,* edited by Parmatma Saran and Edwin Eames, 29–41.

Wald, Alan. "Theorizing Cultural Difference: A Critique of the 'Ethnicity School.'" *MELUS* 14 (Summer 1987): 21–34.

Contributors

DEEPIKA BAHRI teaches postcolonial literature amd theory at Emory University. She is coeditor of *Between the Lines: South Asians and Postcoloniality* (1996) and has published articles in *Ariel: A Review of International English Literature, Postmodern Culture,* and *College English.*

SAMIR DAYAL is Assistant Professor of English at Bentley College in Massachusetts. He is editing a critical anthology entitled *Postcolonial Diasporas: Displacement, Hybridity, Transnationalism,* and is working on a book about Salman Rushdie's major fiction. His recent work has appeared, or is forthcoming, in journals including *Genders, College English, Cultural Critique, Colby Quarterly,* and *Journal of the Midwest Modern Languate Association,* and *MELUS,* as well as in several edited collections.

ANU GUPTA was born and raised in New York City and continues to build bridges between South Asian and Asian American communities. She was given the American Medical Association's Leadership Award for her activism with ethnic groups. Her fiction has been published in *Living in America* and *Making More Waves.* She is a physician at Yale-New Haven Hospital in Connecticut.

RUTH HSIAO teaches courses in Asian American literature, the Chinese Diaspora, and non-Western women writers at Tufts University in Massachusetts, and is among the first scholars to have taught Asian American literature as a college course in the Northeast in the 1980s. Her publications include an article on teaching Asian American literature in *Radical Teacher.*

NAZLI KIBRIA is currently Assistant Professor of Sociology and the Director of the Women's Studies Program at Boston University. Her previous publications include *Family Tightrope: The Changing Lives of Vietnamese Americans* (Princeton University Press, 1993) and articles in *Amerasia Journal.*

VIJAY PRASHAD is Assistant Professor of International Studies at Trinity College, in Hartford, Connecticut. He has written the forthcoming book *Untouchable Freedom: A Social History of Delhi's Balmikis.* He is a member of the Forum of Indian Leftists (FOIL) and serves on the editorial collective of the Canadian journal *Left History.*

SANDIP ROY is the editor of *Trikone,* the journal of South Asian American gays and lesbians. His recent publications include a short story in the *APA Journal* and articles and short fiction in South Asian edited collections.

LAVINA DHINGRA Shankar is Assistant Professor of English at Bates College in Maine, where she teaches postcolonial and Asian American literature and theory, modern British literature, and Women's Studies. Her previous publications include articles in edited volumes including *Teaching What You're Not: Identity Politics in Higher Education, Multiculturalism and Representation,* and journals such as *Critical Mass: A Journal of Asian American Cultural Criticism* and *Studies in Popular Culture.*

RAJIV SHANKAR is an economist by training and a historian by avocation. His family has contributed significantly to the development, performance, and teaching of classical music and dance of South Asia, and has been instrumental in cultural exchanges between India and the West since the 1930s.

SUMANTRA TITO SINHA serves on the boards of directors of the Asian American Legal Defense and Education Fund, and the Nav Nirmaan Foundation, and he is also a founding board member of South Asian Youth Action! (SAYA!). He is a graduate of the City University of New York School of Law in Queens.

MIN SONG is a doctoral candidate in English at Tufts University, where he is currently finishing his dissertation on Sui Sin Far and Henry James. He has taught courses focusing on Asian American issues at Tufts University and at Smith College.

RAJINI SRIKANTH is co-editor of *Contours of the Heart: South Asians Map North America,* an anthology of fiction by first- and second-generation South Asian Americans/Canadians. This book received the 1997 Before Columbus Foundation American Book Award. Srikanth's interdisciplinary research centers on issues in Asian American studies. She teaches at Wellesley College and Tufts University and is co-editing a forthcoming book called *Geographies of Encounters: Asians in the Americas.*

Asian American History and Culture

edited by Sucheng Chan, David Palumbo-Liu, and Michael Omi

1991

Sucheng Chan, ed., *Entry Denied: Exclusion and the Chinese Community in America, 1882–1943*
(1994-pb)

Gary Y. Okihiro, *Cane Fires: The Anti-Japanese Movement in Hawaii, 1865–1945*
(1992-pb)

1992

Yen Le Espiritu, *Asian American Panethnicity: Bridging Institutions and Identities*
(1993-pb)

Karen Isaksen Leonard, *Making Ethnic Choices: California's Punjabi Mexican Americans*
(1994-pb)

Shirley Geok-lin Lim and Amy Ling, eds., *Reading the Literatures of Asian America*
(1992-pb)

Renqiu Yu, *To Save China, To Save Ourselves: The Chinese Hand Laundry Alliance of New York*
(1995-pb)

1993

Velina Hasu Houston, ed., *The Politics of Life: Four Plays by Asian American Women*
(1993-pb)

William Wei, *The Asian American Movement*
(1993-pb)

1994

Timothy P. Fong, *The First Suburban Chinatown: The Remaking of Monterey Park, California*
(1994-pb)

Sucheng Chan, ed., *Hmong Means Free: Life in Laos and America*
(1994-pb)

Chris Friday, *Organizing Asian American Labor: The Pacific Coast Canned-Salmon Industry, 1870–1942*
(1995-pb)

Paul Ong, Edna Bonacich, and Lucie Cheng, eds., *The New Asian Immigration in Los Angeles and Global Restructuring*
(1994-pb)

1995

Carlos Bulosan, *The Cry and the Dedication,* edited and with an introduction by E. San Juan, Jr.
(1995-pb)

Yen Le Espiritu, *Filipino American Lives*
(1995-pb)

Vicente L. Rafael, ed., *Discrepant Histories: Translocal Essays on Filipino Cultures*
(1995-pb)

E. San Juan, Jr., ed., *On Becoming Filipino: Selected Writings of Carlos Bulosan*
(1995-pb)

1996

Deepika Bahri and Mary Vasudeva, eds., *Between the Lines: South Asians and Postcoloniality*

E. San Juan, Jr., *The Philippine Temptation: Dialectics of Philippines-U.S. Literary Relations*

1997

Velina Hasu Houston, ed., *But Still, Like Air, I'll Rise: New Asian American Plays*

Josephine Lee, *Performing Asian America: Race and Ethnicity on the Contemporary Stage*

Jere Takahashi, *Nisei/Sansei: Shifting Japanese American Identities and Politics*

1998

Lavina Dhingra Shankar and Rajini Srikanth, eds., *A Part, Yet Apart: South Asians in Asian America*

K. Scott Worn and Sucheng Chan, eds., *Claiming America: Constructing Chinese American Identities during the Exclusion Era*